The Boys from up the Hill

Geron Swann and Andrew Ward

DEDICATION

In memory of Peter Houseman
1945-77

The Boys from up the Hill

An Oral History of Oxford United

Geron Swann and Andrew Ward

Crowberry

First Published in Great Britain by Crowberry, PO Box 623, Oxford, OX2 6DA, England.

Cover picture: Players wave to fans after winning the Third Division Championship in May 1968. *Left to right:* Arthur Turner (manager), Ken Skeen, Ron Atkinson (captain), Jim Barron, Colin Clarke and Colin Harrington. *News Team/Oxford Mail (Jim Griffiths)*

ISBN 0 9507568 2 2

Cover Design by Ian Nixon. Design and Typesetting by Claire Palmer and Ian Nixon.
Arcadia Designs Ltd. 46 Nelson Street, Oxford OX2 6BE.

Printed in Great Britain by Hillman Printers, Frome, Somerset.

Contents

AUTHORS' ACKNOWLEDGEMENTS

In June 1992 BBC Radio Oxford commissioned us to produce a documentary – "Oxford United: Village Club to Wembley Winners". When we set off for our first interview the omens were not good – a violent thunderstorm hit Oxfordshire that night and water ran down the streets of Middle Barton – but we returned with great enthusiasm. Colin Harrington had excited us as much with his anecdotes and analysis as he had with his pace and unpredictability on the football field. The project was off and running, just like Harrington down the slope at the Manor Ground in the sixties.

Our documentary, first broadcast on 2 January 1993, led to an 18-part radio series – "United Memories" – which was broadcast during Oxford United's centenary season (1993-94). We are particularly grateful to a number of BBC Radio Oxford staff at that time: John Bright, David Campbell, Adam Hollingworth, Helen Eyres, Andrew Peach, Peter Baker, John Clayton, Richard Riley, Bill Rennells, Hedley Feast and Conrad Keating.

In addition, we were involved in the club's centenary exhibition – "The Boys from up the Hill" – which ran at the Museum of Oxford from 19 March 1994 to 14 May 1994. The museum staff, particularly Pat O'Neill, were very helpful, and special thanks must go to the exhibition designer, Ian Nixon, who has provided support and encouragement throughout our project. Fittingly, he was an original member of an Oxford band called Arthur Turner's Lovechild, named in honour of one of United's most famous managers.

Others who went out of their way to help were Anthony Binnington, Chris Brewer, Mick Brown (Oxford United), Jocelyn Goddard (Westgate Library Oral History Archive), Mike and Holly Hardy, Nick Harris, Mickey Iannotta (Fox FM), Alan Jenkins and Colin May.

Our task was made easier by Andy and Roger Howland's invaluable reference book, *Oxford United: A Complete Record, 1893-1989.* Their statistical detail and historical groundwork allowed us to collect folklore tales of the club, showing what Oxford United has meant to people. We have, therefore, omitted some of the dryer stories of the club's history, including the elaborate story of the search for a new ground.

Our greatest debt is to the interviewees, who were very generous with their time. It was a privilege to interview them, and we are grateful for their co-operation. Their passion for the club enticed us further and further into the project. We all have our own important memories of Oxford United but this particular collection belongs to 53 people: Ron Atkinson, Vic Barney, Jim Barron, Les Bateman, Cyril Beavon, Chris Bishop, Percy Blake, Sandy Brewer, Mick Brown (club secretary), Mick Brown (former manager), Jeremy Charles, Colin Clarke, Sam Cook, Percy Cooper, Vic Couling, Bobby Craig, Winifred Crawford, Geoff Denial, Alf Douglas, Fred Ellis, Kaye Ellis, Maurice Evans, Chris Fallows, Jack Fallows, Ken Fish, Peter Foley, Mike Ford, Edmund Gibbs, Pat Giles, Ian Greaves, Colin Harrington, Nick Harris, Brian Horton, Jim Hunt, Alf Jefferies, Harold Kimber, Alison Kinnear, Eric Kowalski, Mark Lawrenson, Mac, Barbara Manger, Peter Marsh, Vic Morris, Peter Rhoades-Brown, Reg Ricketts, John Shuker, Denis Smith, Jimmy Smith (Headington United player), Jim Smith (former manager), Tim Sparrowhawk, Gerry Summers, Harry Thompson and Arthur Turner.

Most of the interviews were conducted between June 1992 and July 1994. The only exceptions were Percy Cooper and Vic Couling (the early 1980s), Mike Ford, Mac and Denis Smith (May 1996), and Alf Jefferies, who was interviewed in April 1995 for our radio documentary on Oxford City called "White House to Wembley". The quotes from Jeremy Charles and Cyril Beavon are from their talks at the centenary exhibition.

1 *"The boys from up the hill"*

VILLAGE AMATEURS, 1893-1948

Headington United, formed in the Britannia Inn on 27 October 1893, played in the Oxford City Junior League and Oxfordshire District League before joining the Oxfordshire Senior League in 1921-22. They moved permanently to the Manor Ground in 1925. United's first major trophies were the Oxfordshire Charity Cup (1930-31) and the Senior League championship (1938-39). They joined the Spartan League in 1947. The next season saw two key wins against Oxford City: 1-0 in the Oxfordshire Senior Cup Final in front of 7,796 people at Iffley Road; and 1-0 in the Hospital Cup Final, watched by 6,500 at the White House Ground.

THE VILLAGE LIFE, 1919-39

Percy Cooper: It was the life, the village life. You were brought up with football. I was, especially, because my family was all involved. I used to do all the footballs up when I was seven, eight or nine. They were the old leather-balls then, of course, the old lacers, about three times as heavy as they are today. We had to grease them, dubbin them, all with our hands, and lace them up with leather tongs.

Barbara Manger [daughter of Stewie Jacobs, club secretary/treasurer]: It was my father's life. All my life and my mother's life was centred around the football and the cricket, mainly the football. He used to spend all his evening writing minutes and agendas. All by hand of course. He didn't have a typewriter. In those days we didn't have a telephone. It meant going out to make sure that everyone could play or attend a meeting. And the finance. He was very pleased to get it as financially viable as he could. They just hadn't got any money. Everything had to be accounted for, right down to the last halfpenny.

Percy Cooper: My elder brother, George Cooper, was a good footballer. He was captain in the early days, when they were only in junior football. My other brother, Cyril, played for them. My sisters were all involved, little or much, by washing and getting our clothes ready. We had an old washer and laundry place out there in the croft, and our Mum used to do all the washing. Got the line across in the old yard and that was it. There were no washing-machines or drying-machines, just an old copper, stoking the old copper up and boiling it. When my Mum died, Harry Smith's wife, the chairman's wife, used to do it. All voluntary. It was all part and parcel of the club. If anything wanted doing for the club it was done, no arguments.

Barbara Manger: I can remember seeing the strip on the line in our garden in Headington. It wasn't your fancy nylon, it was cotton-knit which used to stretch. The shirts used to be so long when dripping on the line. Long shorts, of course, and thick woollen socks that used to get matted. The goalie used to wear a thick green polo-neck sweater and an ordinary working man's cap. We had to make sure that Mr Jacobs, in old Headington, had blown up the balls, which he used to bring up in a net-bag on the handlebars of a very upright old bicycle. I remember the old-fashioned football-boots that my father used to have. They were such hard leather, with big hard leather studs, which you knocked in with nails. They were as hard as wood.

Reg Ricketts: We wore yellow-and-blue downward stripes and then it went to yellow and black. We bought everything ourselves. In one or two cases we helped each other buy a pair of boots. There was real Headington spirit in those days.

Barbara Manger: It was about the only thing going on on a Saturday afternoon. Alright, there was a cinema down in New High Street, but apart from that there was nothing. For entertainment, people used to go and watch the football.

On the Pitch

Reg Ricketts: I must have been about 15, I suppose. It was Eastertime. I was on the touch-line with my boots on, watching the senior side and Harry Creed, the centre-half, got tight and he couldn't turn out. They were short of a player so they called me over and I had to play centre-half. They had a big fellow, Don Allison, who played centre-forward for Oxford City. He finished up an amateur international. I had him to mark. Anyway, I must have made a pretty good job of it because they took me as first reserve on the Monday to Chipping Norton to play in a final of the Chipping Norton Hospital Cup. I had a medal without even playing.

Alf Douglas: The first game I played was against Brackley and Frank Margetts played his first game then and he scored the equalising goal. Frank Margetts was a big chap, taller than me, and this particular match he came up to me and said, "I like to run on to the ball, Alf." I said, "Alright, do you want me to push it through to you?" "Yes, that's what I want." It was five minutes to go and we were losing 1-0 and I took the ball off a Brackley player, past three men and put it just where he wanted it. He took a first-time shot and it went straight in the corner of the net to make it 1-1. They always used to talk about that goal. We were a well-known couple in Headington. We got pally and in the end we played cricket and all for Headington for 25 years. I got well-known in the world, no matter where I went – Bicester, Banbury, Henley. People I hadn't seen for years would come and shake hands and all the rest of it.

Reg Ricketts: I remember one game especially. It was in the County Junior Shield semi-final. We was drawn against Goring. Well, Ray Milner and one other went over to see Goring and they came back and said, "Cor, it's in our pockets. All they can do is knock and rush. They slung it up the field and ran after it. It's in our pockets." They were so sure of themselves. Of course we went to the White House Ground and lost 6-1. They were like greyhounds. They hit long balls up the pitch, they were after it and bang. That was very amusing.

Alf Douglas: At Banbury Stones one day I met a ball from Billy Jones and

I never let it touch the ground. I caught it knee high, practically 20 yards out, and it hit the net like a rocket. Another one, against Banbury Harriers up here, I picked it up on the halfway-line, went straight through three players, around the goalie and put it in the net. I took about 75 penalties – and I missed three. I know where I missed one – at Bletchington. They didn't mark the ground out with whitening and on the penalty spot they'd chipped a little hole. I hit the flippin' post with that penalty, only for that reason. I used to drive them home. It didn't matter which foot I took it with, you see, which was a big asset. I always went up to the ball middle way so the goalie didn't know which foot I was using. That was the key to the whole business.

Reg Ricketts: One of the sides from Banbury had a very strong amateur boxer playing on the left wing. I was playing right-half and he kept bumping me and bumping me, and in the finish I bumped him. Of course he turned on me with his fists up. Before you could say "Jack Robinson", Perce Cooper was under the rope and between us. Old Perce used to use his fists a bit in those days.

The Paddock, 1922-25

Alf Douglas: They used to play up the paddock of the hospital. I worked there for 15 years and I was there at the time and I used to get the old scythe out after I'd finished work and cut round the sides of the field because the grass got long there. We changed in the chicken-house unless we came already changed, which was the order of the day then. It was more-or-less a hen's roost, buckets of water for washing, but you weren't ever dirty because there was too much grass on the pitch.

Reg Ricketts: Before we went on the Manor we played on what we called "the old rifle range". That was behind the Manor House in the old paddock. At the end of Osler Road, just as you went round the bend, there was a gate in the wall labelled "Rifle Range". That was the entrance to the paddock. Of course it's all nurses' quarters now for the John Radcliffe Hospital.

The Manor Ground

Winifred Crawford: That ground belonged to Mattock's, the rose-growers. I got a job at Mattock's when I was sixteen. I used to have to go up to the nursery at the ground, first thing in the morning, with a basket, on an iron bike, and get some rose-buds for them to make bouquets at the shop, in

Market Street. It was a fruit-shop as well.

Reg Ricketts: My father was one of the originals who bought the Manor Sports Ground for the youth of Headington. The new owners were called Headington Sports Ground Ltd. They bought the ground for £400 and it was opened up for cricket, football, bowls and tennis. We had to change the football-pitch three-parts of the way through the season, longways, to allow a square to develop for the cricket. We played crossways for two-thirds of the season.

Alf Douglas: My Dad looked after the pavilion. He used to get the baths ready and the boiling water. He fitted it up with oil-lamps so that when you came up at night you could play cards. The pavilion was just an extra large shed with a sloping roof, ten or 12 yards long, five yards wide. It was more or less pushed down at the finish. The ground had a big hedge all round it and wire ropes and iron posts. Before we played, we used to turn Dring's horses off the ground, and clear up the muck they'd left behind.

Reg Ricketts: The horses used to graze there. They did their work during the day and then were turned out there at night. I can see them now – two browns and a white. The bowls green had been a dump where horses and carts used to dump all their rubbish. When I was a child that was a good playground for us. There was always somewhere to hide and dodge about. Rubbish and soil and weeds. From Beech Road up to Cuckoo Lane was a three-strand barbed-wire fence. That was all. There were allotments the other side. The houses got built later.

Barbara Manger: Along the Cuckoo Lane end it was just a hedge. When we were little and fed up with watching football we'd play in the hedge. The other thing that made it seem more rural was that Mrs Blackburn had the field where Horwood Close is now, and you could hear the farmyard noises of chickens and animals. She was always a bit menacing, grey hair scraped back into a bun, and I don't think she ever gave the ball back when it went over there.

Reg Ricketts: Up against Cuckoo Lane, in the far left corner, we had three or four sheets of galvanised iron for a urinal. Because the ground was uneven the pavilion was raised on pillars and we used to put the nets and wheelbarrows and all the equipment underneath it, so you can tell how high it was. They approached William Morris [Lord Nuffield] and I think he either paid for the pavilion outright or he gave them a large sum of money to build it. It was between Beech Road and the Cuckoo Lane end, an oblong building, all wood, its main entrance half way along. At the far end we made one dressing-room, at the other we made another dressing-room – home and away. An old fella, Mr Douglas, used to boil the water in a copper outside. Of course, you only had about a bucketful. He emptied the copper between the two dressing-rooms. You had a few pegs to hang your clothes on and long wooden trestle-stools to sit on. Sometimes when you went away you never had anything like that. You'd come home in your mud. That was in the Senior League days.

Barbara Manger: The pavilion was used by the cricket club as well as the football club. It was just a wooden building on brick piers. When we were children we used to play under it. You could stoop down and crawl underneath. It had a side door and one central door, with a few wooden steps going up. The cricket stuff was stored underneath in the winter, and in the summer the football goal-posts and nets.

Percy Blake: When I used to watch Headington United, when I was six, seven and eight, we'd have our own little game with a tennis-ball at the London Road end. There was nothing there. It was open to the London Road, all the way down.

Travelling Away

Barbara Manger: When they went away it was always a bit of an event. It was a lot to organise because it wasn't just a question of players getting into their own cars. They either had to go by bike, or, if it was a long way, by coach. A lot of people in those days couldn't afford bikes, and it was a question of walking. They were all quite poor people. It was a working man's team. They all worked locally, and in the summer they played cricket together.

Harold Kimber: We had to find our own transport to the local matches. We went on push-bikes to Cowley, Pressed Steel and Osberton Radiators. Morris Motors played in Crescent Road. They had a good side. We had Dring's coach for Banbury and Thame.

Alf Douglas: Dring had a couple of taxis and I drove one. I had to drive about six players and he sent the others with his son. We had that for quite a time. We went to Banbury several times. There was a lot of Banbury teams in those days – Banbury Stones, Banbury GWR, Banbury Harriers.

Harold Kimber: We used to change in a public house at Bicester. Heyford RAF had good facilities. They gave us sausage, beans and chips after the game. They had a good side during the war.

Reg Ricketts: Very often when we used to go out with Dring's in their coach to an away match, say Witney Town or Chipping Norton, I'd have to go out again on Sunday morning and collect up the bags. Two or three of the players were too tight to carry them home the night before!

The Early Players

Percy Cooper: If you're talking about the old Headington team, Brady Webb was one of our star men for years. Why he didn't turn professional, we'll never know.

Reg Ricketts: Brady Webb was a smashing ball-player. He should have gone further. He was a local Quarry man. He used to get so nervous he couldn't lace his own boots up before a semi-final or final! I always had to lace his boots up for him. In those days most of the finals were played on the White House Ground. "Curly" Horwood used to play outside-right. A jovial type. When we saw one another in the distance you'd shout out, "Wriggle." He was the originator of that. Right up till he died if he saw me anywhere he'd shout, "Wriggle!" A question of dribbling the ball and going in and out of players. He always called it "wriggle". It was "dribble" really but he always said, "wriggle". All these Quarry men had nicknames – "Mighty" Webb, "Shonner" Wharton, "Tubby" Washington.

Barbara Manger: They were all the old Headington names – the Washingtons, the Kimbers, the Jacobs. It's the names I remember more than anything. "Baggy" Lones. Charlie Machin. Billy Jones. Frank Margetts. "Baggy" Lones I remember because it was a funny name, and I suppose he wore baggy trousers, and I remember Charlie Machin because he was bald. Billy Jones was a good player. He lived opposite the church in Old Headington. During the war they really scratched around for players. Some of them would turn out when they came home on leave. It was quite an occasion if someone like Henry Blake or Jimmy Smith turned up.

Jimmy Smith: I started playing for Headington in 1938 when I was still at the High School, and of course I could only play during the holidays because I was only 14. The team was selected by committee. There was a chap called Tom Webb, the trainer, who later came over from the amateur side to the professional side, which was quite a step. He was one of the main selectors. Then there was Percy Cooper and Vic Couling, and the captain used to sit on the selection committee. We didn't have a manager. But it was certainly an ambitious club. They were playing in the Oxfordshire Senior League and they won most of the trophies they entered for.

Raising Money

Harold Kimber: We had two teams – one in the Senior League and one in the Intermediate League – and I played for the Senior League team. We had several hundred people to watch us. No admission fee. One of our supporters went round with a little box while the game was going on. And we had raffles and dances. There was a dance hall, where the Gateway supermarket is now in the Old High Street, and it had a spring floor. The club had functions in there in the thirties and forties.

Percy Cooper: When we first used to take money, we used to have a tiny thing like a sentry-box and a bloke standing there taking the money, or we used to go round the ground with tickets on a roll and collect it from them, threepence or fourpence, whatever, all brought home and counted. We had an old coal fire then and we used to dry out the £1 notes and ten-bob notes.

Barbara Manger: My father used to have these rolls of tickets. I remember there were some pink ones and blue ones. There was some sort of excise fee you had to pay [entertainment tax]. I used to unwind these rolls of tickets, and stick stamps on each ticket, and then roll them up again ready for him to take up to the match. It was just one job before an early lunch on Saturday.

Vic Morris: On match-days there was only one entrance. That was in Manor Road [now Osler Road]. They'd tear the ticket off and give it to you as you went in. No turnstiles. The wife used to go and I used to take our first kiddie in a pushchair or pram. To see the game clearly we had to get up by the wire. Headington had a band at that time. They used to play before the match. Then we enjoyed the match after that. There was refreshments on the ground. It was all soft drinks and sweets. The kiosk used to be in that top corner, where the recent scoreboard was. And they had one at the bottom end of the ground. They had a small wooden stand (backing on to what is now the bowling green) which they bought from Cowley FC when they became defunct [1946]. You used to pay to go into the ground and pay a bit more to go into this stand. There was no other cover on the ground. None at all. Then that stand blew down in a gale one year, and they re-erected it at the Osler Road end. Of course, after it had been moved twice it became rather dilapidated, but it lasted a few more years. That was still in existence after they turned professional and went in the Southern League, that old wooden one at the top.

The Rivalry with Oxford City

Harold Kimber: Oxford City were the top team. They used to go to London to play in the Isthmian League and several thousand watched them. In 1934 they played Gillingham in the Cup and had over 7,000 watching them at the City. Several local Headington players went to City because they had a better chance of making the grade there. Oxford City nearly produced a League side from this area. Freddie Arnold's brother, Johnny, went to Fulham and played for England at cricket and football. Frank Hartley went to Tottenham. After the war, Cliff Holton went to the Arsenal, Rex Adams to Blackpool, Alf Jefferies to Brentford, Percy James to Luton, Dave Meeson to Reading, Alec Blakeman to Brentford, Tom Berry to Hull, Eddie Wilcox to West Brom and Dennis Gordon to West Brom.

Alf Jefferies: I often wonder what would have happened if we'd all stayed at Oxford City. The first year after the war we had a wonderful season. We attracted crowds of 5,000 to 6,000, and we only lost the Isthmian League by two points. Oxford City nearly turned professional, just before Headington United. Meetings were held in the town hall, and they were going to buy some ground along the Botley Road (which was later bought by the Co-op) or play at the dog stadium. That fell through. They'd got to change the ground, you see, because under the White House lease no professional football could be played.

Jack Fallows: I used to go and see Oxford City, and it was quite good football. But I heard about Headington United, and what they proposed and their aspirations and I went up in 1946. I think there was a rope around the ground and an old cricket hut. We used to watch them and I thought they had more enthusiasm than down in the city.

Sandy Brewer: There seemed to be a lot of anti-Headington feeling in the town in the early days. A lot of people seemed to have been brought up as Oxford City supporters, and Headington was more-or-less the village team to them in the early days. I remember one City supporter telling me that wild horses would never get him to the Manor Ground but I did eventually see him there.

Vic Morris: In the amateur days Oxford City were Isthmian League and Headington got into the Spartan League [in 1947]. The Isthmian League was a little bit above the Spartan League, but when it came to local Cup ties, it came to a point where Headington were beating City more than City were beating Headington.

Jimmy Smith: I think the one that stands out more than anything is the Oxfordshire Senior Cup Final [1948] when we played Oxford City on the Iffley Road running ground and won 1-0. It was the big challenge of Oxford City versus Headington, or "The Boys from up the Hill", as we were known then. At that time I was living in Hill Top Road. We had the whole of the team to lunch and then went from Hill Top Road to Iffley Road, and it really was a great day for us. There was Tony Harper, Ernie Lee, Henry Blake, Ray Mansell, and the captain was Jack Ramsden. Jack Ramsden scored the goal, with a shot from just outside the penalty area. I missed a penalty in the last five minutes. A chap called Aubrey Oakey, who was well-known in local football, was in goal for Oxford City. I shot the ball just outside the left-hand post. Still, we won 1-0. After the match we went round the town in the coach and displayed the Cup. It was very emotional then. I think the standard was improving all the time, and it was evident then that there was a good following for good football in Oxford. With us beating Oxford City, that helped considerably when we were thinking of moving into a higher grade of football.

Vic Morris: That same year [1948], Oxford City and Headington got to the Final of what was then called the Oxford Hospitals Cup. That was on the White House ground. We won that one 1-0. I was in the stand behind our goal, and Gerry Woodward, our goalkeeper, played most of the game with concussion, wandering about as if he didn't know where he was, but he still stopped the ball. We won that Cup that day and then paraded it round all the different pubs in Headington the same night. A huge thing. It was so big that when anybody took a drink out of it, it came down the side.

2 *"We were turning professional"*

PROFESSIONALISM AND THE SOUTHERN LEAGUE, 1948-50

One of the most important years in United's history was 1949, when the club turned professional and were elected to the Southern League. There were many heroes at that time: people like Vic Couling who fought for professionalism; player-manager Harry Thompson, the club's first employee; the players who kept the team in the Southern League; and, perhaps above all, the volunteers who worked behind the scenes.

A STEP FORWARD

Edmund Gibbs: Vic Couling was the one who moved the resolution for professionalism. It lost in 1948 but he came back. Vic was a very obstinate chap, a bit like a terrier; he would never leave go. He was the main mover. They owed him a great deal. They would have gone professional eventually, I'm sure, but it was Vic who shoved it hard and got it through in 1949.

Percy Cooper: I remember Mr Stewart Jacobs. He was secretary of the Oxfordshire Football Association. Him and I were the only two who walked out of the meeting because we didn't want it. When it was passed that we were turning professional, Stewie and I walked out. We were dead against it. We were dedicated to Headington and just couldn't see it going off.

Alf Jefferies: My father and Stewie Jacobs worked together, and Stewie Jacobs was quite annoyed when I signed professional for Brentford. He didn't have a lot of time for professional football. He once said to my father, "I can't understand your lad wanting to become a professional, I can't see why he doesn't remain an amateur." My answer to him was this: "You were good with your hands as a bricklayer and you're now a general foreman. You've used your skills to earn your living. My skills as a goalkeeper are in my hands, too, and I've been offered the chance to earn a living with my skills. What is the difference?"

Percy Cooper: George Mattock, who used to be a goalkeeper, and Bertie Knight, who used to be an inside-forward for Headington, were the two people who voted for professionalism in the first instance. I think it was because of Banbury. They had started being semi-pros, you see. I suppose they were more progressive than I was, a bit younger than I was.

Edmund Gibbs: And it was Vic Couling, with the people he had met at the Southern League, who was the main mover in getting us *into* the Southern League. We applied for Division Two of the Southern League, but when we got to the meeting the division collapsed. Most of the clubs withdrew and only three were left, and we couldn't have a new division with only three in it.

Jimmy Smith: Instead the Southern League increased its size by two more teams, and Headington was one that got in. My brother, Peter, was secretary, and he and Vic Couling went to the annual meeting, and they had to give the submission to the management committee. Then there was a vote on it. They scraped in by one vote.

Vic Couling: Our application went through for membership of the Southern League and at the time I was promoting professional boxing in Oxford at the Oxford Town Hall. We had meetings once a month, all the promoters, about sixty or seventy of us, at Jack Solomon's gym, in Great Windmill Street, London, and it was there that I met a Mr Jack Jones, who was promoting at Hereford. He was chairman of Hereford Football Club at the time, and when he found out that we were making an application to become members of the Southern League, he was rather interested. Over lunch he said that he would get his colleagues to give us their support. So it came to the meeting and we got in by one vote.

Llanelli had nine and we had ten. It was only afterwards, when Mrs Couling and myself went to Jack Jones' hotel in Hereford, that he and Len Weston, who was the cider man, told us that Hereford had voted for us and not for Llanelli as they were first going to. So it meant that the Hereford vote had got us into the Southern League. Had it gone the other way, Llanelli would have been elected and not us.

Sam Cook: I remember the day, very clearly, when they were elected into the Southern League. That was 1949. That was obviously the beginning of professionalism. It was more important than going in the Football League. That was the push-off for professionalism.

Jimmy Smith: My brother was a fairly quiet person, and he came home, and I looked at him, and he looked at me, and I said, "We're in, aren't we?" and he said, "Yeah, yeah, let's go and have a drink." And he told me then how close it had been. Then they realised what the repercussions were likely to be, because the ground had to be upgraded, we had to get players, and there was little money around. I think a lot of them put their own money in in those days, without any fuss.

Issuing Shares

Les Bateman: My first association with Headington United was back in Spartan League days when I was on the supporters' club committee. That's when we used to play Hemel Hempstead, Berkhamsted and Henley and places like that. They had to get shareholders and I was one of the first to be a shareholder back in 1949. Mr Gibbs was at the meeting. It was to get some money for the club so that they could form a limited company.

Edmund Gibbs: I went along to the meeting at St Margaret's School and there must have been a couple of hundred people there. The original seven were sitting at the top and they introduced me as the new club auditor. Vic Couling said, towards the end of the meeting, "We have £800 out of the old club" – and that's all they had got – "and anyone can buy up to £21 worth of shares." The shares were issued in £7 shares and the maximum any one person could hold was three. The idea was that it should be some form of co-operative and should be owned by the people of Headington so no one person should control it, exactly the opposite to what happened in the later years when Maxwell came along and Rosser. Vic Couling said, "Would you form a queue and hand over the money to Mr Gibbs." Luckily I had a receipt book on me and some sheets of foolscap and a clipboard. I always carried clipboards from the old army days. And so there I was, noting all these names and addresses. I suppose the average purchase was £14 and many of them bought just one £7 share because £7 in those days was quite a bit. Anyhow, at the end of the meeting we all went on to the Quarry Gate and in my bag I had 1,400 pound notes. It said something for the climate of those days that there was I, standing at the bar with Arthur Harris and the rest of them, a crowd of people drinking with us, and my briefcase was sitting on the floor with £1,400 in it.

Voluntary Work on the Ground, 1949

Vic Morris: Headington were elected into the Southern League, and they weren't ready for that sort of football. The whole ground wasn't ready, the dressing-rooms and terracing. There wasn't anything there at all. As soon as they were elected to the Southern League they had to do all sorts of things to get the ground ready for when the season started. They got plans to build new dressing-rooms in the top left-hand corner, at the Cuckoo Lane End. Permission was rushed through quickly, and it was all done with voluntary labour. While they were building the dressing-rooms and the little stand above it, other people were making concrete slabs. The following day, when the slabs were set, we built them into terraces, all along the London Road end and up the Beech Road side. Sometimes thirty, forty men, up there, mixing concrete, putting them into these moulds. Next day lifting them out and building them up. And I was one of them.

Harry Thompson: One director, Percy Cooper, was a builder's foreman. He arranged all the building operations on the ground, and it was all voluntary labour in those days. Percy knew what was wanted, and he used to find the men to do the job. There was Tom Leys, he was an electrician. Everybody helped. Well, they had to. There was so much to do in those early days.

Edmund Gibbs: Many of the people involved – the Coppocks and the Lawrences and the Coopers and the Kimbers – were all Quarry people. All the same names kept cropping up.

Percy Cooper: We were all involved. We did it ourselves. When they put the drains in from the new dressing-rooms, which were down on the corner of the ground then, I asked for volunteers and I should think we had about 300 people up there with ruddy spades and shovels to dig us out. They'd have dug the whole Manor Ground in no time, they were that keen. Over Osler Road, all those concrete steps were made with voluntary labour. It was all dug out by hand, then the terracing put up. Frank Lawrence, the coal-business people, had his lorry in there. They used to load the lorry up and cart the soil away. It was all voluntary. We could never have paid for it. There were four or five blokes in there, shovelling as fast as they could go, with their shirts off. And if some of them wanted to pack up, there was always a gang there waiting to mick in. It was unbelievable, the amount of help to do all that. I used to be at my wit's end to keep them from the digging the ground up, they were so keen.

Reg Ricketts: Perce Cooper and I played in junior football. To be honest, he wasn't built for football, a big-boned lad, but I can't say enough about what he done for the village. He was general foreman for Knowles, the builder, and he had a good knowledge of building. He was a born leader. Anyone would do anything for Perce. He'd swear and give you a mouthful one moment, if you made a mistake, and he was the best of pals a minute after. That's the type of man. He spoke his mind. Everybody liked him and he worked really hard for that club and for the village. I was carrying buckets of concrete up a ladder to Perce when we built the first dressing-rooms. And one very amusing incident. It was turned eleven at night, we'd just finished the main bath and a dividing wall. I'd been cutting tiles and Perce had been fixing these tiles. We'd just finished and I went to get out of the cold bath and caught my toe on the tiles. The air was blue for five minutes. That was 12 o'clock by the time we finished that wall.

Vic Morris: They were all people that loved the club, people who'd grown up with it and were determined for it to be a success. It was as simple as that, really. There was no question of anybody wanting any payment. The only thing we had was free pints of shandy or something. It was summertime, hot nights, and people worked for hours and hours, until it was dark. Then Saturdays and Sundays. No lights to work with. You used to take a shovel or whatever you could take. My Dad used to take his own tools up. He was a master bricklayer, and he spent ages up there, on the dressing-room stand, which was across the top of the ground. There were carpenters, all these sort of people, taking their own stuff up there... after a day's work. And I was tired when I finished at Pressed Steel, I can tell you! In those days everybody was just so keen to get the club off the ground as a professional club.

Jimmy Smith: When we went training, there was always somebody on the ground doing something, repairing this or mowing that, or making this. Fantastic. Wonderful.

Vic Morris: We were working up there one Sunday morning, with a whole lot of concrete blocks which were set in the moulds, and the first thing we had to do was lift them out, two people, one at each end. They were built up on other blocks, and I went to lift one out and I felt a pain shoot through my back. It wasn't too bad at first, but it got worse as the days went on. Evidently the disc had been moved. I went on holiday the week after I'd done it, and it was real agony. After I came back from holiday the club took me up to an osteopath, a chap named Jackson in Banbury Road, and I had treatment. He eased it, but it troubled me for about 20 years, one way or another. It's one of the prices you pay for enjoying your club!

Harry Thompson, Manager 1949-59

Sandy Brewer: I think Harry Thompson was very important. He had to get a team together from nothing in about a month, if I remember rightly. He did extremely well. Really, he held the team together, playing first at wing-half and then at centre-half. And a good captain too. Very cool, calm and collected.

Harry Thompson: I was playing with Northampton at the time, and I think Headington advertised for a player-manager. Initially I didn't know where Headington was. I thought it was somewhere in Yorkshire. It was one hell of a struggle because we hadn't any players. I had quite a few connections in Yorkshire. I had a little fellow in Scotland who sent me players down. It was a question of getting together a team as soon as I possibly could. It was as desperate as that. Jim Howe, who was the works manager, personnel manager, at Pressed Steel, said, "If I can help you in any way, just let me know." I forget what the maximum wage was in the Football League in those days: £8 or £10, something like that. Well, what I could do, I could find them a job at Pressed Steel, pay them a part-time wage and they'd be better off than playing in full-time football.

Jimmy Smith: I think a great deal of the credit must go to Harry Thompson, our first manager. He got hold of players who were good ball-players, people who would knit together as a team. He had means and ways of getting things over in a quiet, unassuming way, which I think was a great asset.

Bobby Craig: Harry Thompson talked common sense. If you'd played badly he told you. He never went into tactics. He just came along and talked you through the week. He'd put you right, but the main thing was that he was just instilling a bit of pride in you that you were playing for Headington.

Jimmy Smith: He was fair. If you played badly he would drop you, and he would tell you. Although I was not a professional player, I was treated just the same as anybody else. He treated everybody the same. There were no stars, and I think that was a great asset. He might have had some stars in the back of his mind, but he never showed it.

The Southern League, 1949-50

Jimmy Smith: I've always said that the biggest step that Headington made was going from Spartan League football into Southern League professional football. Although it was called the Southern League it was also football in South Wales, football in the West Country, football in Kent. It covered an enormous area. It was an enormous step forward.

Vic Morris: The first match in the Southern League was away to Hastings and we took about ten coaches away with us. We got beat 5-2, and the team didn't really look good enough. Hastings made Headington look very second-rate. It was a very hot summer's day. We were 5-0 down at one time, but had the little consolation of getting two goals back late in the game, which gave us a bit of a boost.

Jimmy Smith: There was more finesse attached to Southern League football. There wasn't quite so much body contact. The first match I played, we got our first Southern League point. We drew at Worcester, 1-1, and I scored the goal. We were absolutely thrilled because we'd got this very first point in the Southern League, and Worcester City in those days had a pretty good side.

Vic Morris: When the season started, they still hadn't finished the dressing-rooms, and they had to use the wooden hut, which wasn't very good for the top-of-the-League sides like Colchester and Gillingham. They had to use the little wooden hut for about a month, I think, before we eventually got the other one ready.

Sandy Brewer: I certainly remember the first game I saw there. It was an FA Cup qualifying round. They played Huntley and Palmer's Biscuitworks team from Reading. I think the result was 9-4 in favour of Headington.

Sam Cook: Some of the places you went to were fantastic. Merthyr Tydfil. Have you ever been to Merthyr Tydfil on a Wednesday afternoon when it's hammering down with rain? That's the place to go. Wouldn't recommend it for a holiday, but for football, ankle-deep in mud... I think they lost 8-2 that day. Merthyr were established in that League then. They were a very good side. I think we had a lot of local amateurs in our side.

Jimmy Smith: It was a totally different environment. You think of Llanelli and Barry and Gravesend and Gillingham. There were places that were completely foreign to us. If you had a couple of loads of buses, with our supporters on, that made a whale of a difference. It was a great fillip. And in those days there weren't many M roads around, were there? I can remember the first time I went to Wales. We left Oxford at half past seven in the morning to play the match at three o'clock, so you can imagine what time we got home at night. And a busload of supporters went as well.

Sandy Brewer: It was a rather scratch team that first season, got together in a hurry by Harry Thompson. Not very successful. Quite a struggle. In fact I remember Harry Thompson seemed to be carrying them on his own back at one time, playing centre-half, managing them. He did it very well.

Jimmy Smith: I remember we played Gravesend and Northfleet. We won 6-5, and there were 5,500 people on Manor Road ground standing in the rain for the whole match. They were six deep around the ground. Amazing. They'd never had an opportunity to see football of this calibre.

Vic Morris: That first year in the Southern League, we had to win the last match, at Weymouth, to stop applying for re-election. You didn't know what might happen with other teams applying to come in.

Jimmy Smith: I think the one match I remember more than anything was the last match of the season at Weymouth. We won 3-2. Cliff Nugent scored two goals and Cyril Toulouse scored the other goal that day.

Vic Morris: That was another great day. We all went. More went to that one than went to Hastings. You'd have thought, coming back, at the various stopping places, that they'd won the FA Cup or something. Stopping at Salisbury and places like that on the way back, all the coaches were pulling in to the main town-centre square. Great celebrations.

Jimmy Smith: We went by train. I think we must have been met at Oxford station by half of Headington on our return. The chairman of the time, Vic Couling, and several of the directors met us at the station when we came back, and it was such a thrill. The first year, 1949-50, was also a happy year because I finished top goalscorer that season with 14 goals.

Peter Smith

Edmund Gibbs: Peter Smith was fixtures secretary. He was a very able fellow in his younger days, very able. He was the one who arranged all the fixtures and manipulated it so that we always played at home on Good Friday and this sort of thing. By the way, there was enormous University opposition to playing on Good Friday: "We should all go to church on Good Friday; you shouldn't play football." But he was the one who first got floodlights at the ground and who first introduced this thing about under-pitch heating. At that time people laughed, but Peter would say, "Well, even bad publicity is good publicity." Peter Smith was an enormous worker for the club.

Jimmy Smith: I think everybody suddenly realised what the implications were of going from just a local Headington football club to a Southern League professional club. There was so much work to do. I think a lot of their jobs suffered, to be quite honest with you. Certainly my brother's job suffered. I always said to him, "You spend more time at football than you do at work."

Edmund Gibbs: One year Peter Smith stood for the chairmanship against Vic Couling and the board was split clearly down the middle. So they put me in the chair and I said, "Look, you're going to put me in a hell of a spot. If it's a dead heat, it's going to finish up with me deciding who is going to be chairman." And that's precisely what happened. I voted for Couling and the status quo.

Professionals and Amateurs

Sandy Brewer: Vic Barney always used to say that he would foul somebody before they fouled him, and I think he kept his promise on that, because it always seemed that if there was any trouble in a game he was in it. I don't know whether he's still around. I better not say any more in case he comes along here and thinks he'll get the first blow in with me! He came from Grimsby, I think, and had been at Reading and Bristol City.

Vic Barney: I was always rough and ready. You have to look after yourself in football. I was an old-fashioned inside-forward who made goals and scored his share. I'm only guessing now but I think I was the first full-time professional at Headington. All the rest did their training at night because they had jobs. I trained on my own for about two hours each morning, five mornings a week. In the afternoons I used to clean windows. I had a friend with a window-cleaning business in Headington and he said, "I could do with some help, Vic." I had two years of being the skipper at Headington and I enjoyed it very much.

Jimmy Smith: I still think Peter Buchanan was one of the best players to play for Headington in my time, which was 1938 to 1955. He was towards the end of his career. He had played for Celtic, and he went off and played for Guildford after us.

Sandy Brewer: I remember Peter Buchanan very well because I'd seen him back in the 1930s, playing for Chelsea, and I saw him playing for Brentford, too, in the 1940s. He wasn't here for very long but he certainly played in one thrilling game against Gravesend, which they won 6-5. He seemed to be the mainspring of the Headington attack. He was dazzling on his day. He had been a Scottish international.

Jimmy Smith: Peter Buchanan could hold the forward-line together. He was a great ball-player. I was playing on the left wing and he was playing on the right wing and he used to say to me, "Don't watch where I'm going, don't watch the ball, all I want you to do is to run to the edge of the 18-yard line." I used to do that and I would say that 99 times out of 100 the ball turned up. He had that sort of skill. A great passer of the ball, and a great dribbler. He used to weave around all over the place, and the ball still turned up in the right spot.

Sandy Brewer: We had Cliff Nugent in the early days. I remember Nugent very well, because I'd seen him play for Oxford City. He came to the Manor and played at outside-left, and eventually transferred to Cardiff City. A good little player, Nugent. Very good ball control. Very accurate centres.

Jimmy Smith: Cliff Nugent went for £2,500. That was a lot of money in those days. He had an opportunity to go to a Second Division club and why should we stand in his way? It would help the club financially, obviously, but also it would help the club to be better known in the professional world.

Sam Cook: After a season or so I became boot-boy with them and used to travel around the country with them, in the old coach, to Southern League grounds. I think the club atmosphere was closer-knit in those days and they were a very nice set of lads. We used to have some real fun. We trained with them and that sort of thing. I cleaned the boots, made sure they were studded and that, and went to games at the weekend. I remember their boots. There was a bloke named Fred Tappin who used to have half an inch of grease on his. Cyril Toulouse had size twelves, I think, boots like punts. Of course, they were real boots in those days, not these carpet slippers they play in now. Real boots. You used to see them hanging up outside Capes, down St Ebbes, with leather about half an inch thick.

Harry Thompson: Professor Harold Thompson helped me tremendously in those early days. He had some fine amateur players – Jimmy Potts was one – and he allowed these players to play for us. They called themselves Pegasus, and they were a really tip-top amateur football club, probably the best in the country, but they only lasted a few years.

Bobby Craig: We had one lad who was an amateur. That was Jimmy Smith. Jimmy was good at everything. Cricket. Football. Whatever he took up. He played for the county a lot of times.

Harry Thompson: Jimmy Smith was an excellent winger. He was strong on the ball. He had two very good feet. He could bang them in from anywhere. Yes, Jimmy was an excellent winger. But later on I found out that he was an excellent centre-back. He was marvellous. Good in the air. Strong in the tackle. A marvellous player, Jimmy, and he was an amateur.

Sandy Brewer: He scored one of the best goals I've ever seen at the Manor. He was playing left-half and he hit one from what appeared to be just over the halfway-line. It sailed into the far top corner. He really could hit a ball, Jim Smith.

Bobby Craig: You could put him at full-back, centre-half, centre-forward, outside-left, outside-right, and he gave you 100 per cent plus. The first year I came we had 14 professionals and Jimmy Smith, and three of the professionals were goalkeepers. Jimmy just filled in and never grumbled. I would call him "Mr Headington United" really. We were all professionals, but Jimmy used to run his own car wherever we went. We used to say to Jimmy, "Have you had your expenses yet?" And that's all he got. He used to say, "No, my brother won't give me them. There's not enough money in the kitty yet." Things like this. It just proved what a hotch-potch it was to start with, but I've never had so many laughs in my life.

3 *"I took to Headington straightaway"*

SOUTHERN LEAGUE RESPECTABILITY, 1950-59

Harry Thompson persuaded some fine players to move to Headington, and, in 1952-53, his team won the Southern League Championship and the Southern League Cup. The following season United achieved national fame by reaching the fourth round of the FA Cup as a non-League club. The home tie with First Division Bolton Wanderers, the previous year's Cup-finalists, attracted widespread publicity. Bolton included famous internationals like Willie Moir, Nat Lofthouse and Malcolm Barrass. A record crowd of 16,670 watched the game. The late-1950s saw a rapid turnover of players, but the team maintained a respectable position in the Southern League.

UNDER FLOODLIGHTS

Harry Thompson: I think we were the first club in the country to play a match under floodlights [18 December 1950]. We had an electrician on the board of directors and we had a builder on the board. The electrician said, "I can supply all the electrical equipment." And the builder said, "I can supply all the scaffold-poles to go around the ground." We said, "Alright, let's go ahead." The builder got all the scaffold-poles, put them all round the ground, 10 or 12 yards apart. The electrician rigged them all up with electricity and pans with bulbs in, and of course they were open pans, with the bulbs exposed to the elements. We hadn't been playing long when it started to rain, and the cold rain started to beat in on these hot bulbs. You can imagine what was happening. One by one they went "pop". I thought, "Bloody hell, we're going to be in darkness before very long," but fortunately the rain stopped and we didn't have many bulbs go.

Les Bateman: I took on the job of groundsman in 1950. The first floodlights were scaffold-poles which came from the Slade Army Camp. One Sunday afternoon I helped the electrician put cotton-reels in the scaffold-poles to bind the wire that went all the way round. After a time they didn't seem to work so they got some firm – Revo – to put some more pylons up. They put five along each side of the ground. At night I had to go round and switch them all on. On these pylons, they'd left a space to let the heat out, but it meant that the fine rain dripped in and went on the bulbs. They were popping off and they were £2 a time. The electrician said he'd do something about that and he got tape to put along the top where the rain was coming in. We had a big ladder on wheels that we took round. Before a match, the electrician would say, "Les, I've got to put two bulbs in there," so I had to help him pull it round.

Bobby Craig: To get us in at night-time, when we were training, he had to go round and switch the lights off, and as he went round all the team followed him round, still playing football until it was completely dark. We had to come in then because we couldn't see.

Sandy Brewer: We had a very popular team come to the Manor to play under lights. That was Wolves. They were one of the leading First Division teams of the day, and I think they won about 3-1. But it was interesting to see some star players in a friendly like that.

FA Cup, 1951-52

Vic Barney: I enjoyed the local rivalry. I remember playing Oxford City in an FA Cup match up at the Manor. We had a young centre-forward called Sammy Chung who was a fine prospect. He later went to Reading, Norwich and Watford, and finished up as manager of Wolves. But Oxford City were beating us, 2-1, with about ten minutes to go. It was a turn-up for the books. The way Oxford City played that day they should have won the game but John Crichton saved the day for us. I don't know whether he meant it but he floated one over and it went in the net. We went down to the White House Ground midweek and beat them quite easily in the replay. Then we played Wycombe in the FA Cup at the Manor and we beat them 3-2. A good game. A hard game. But Wycombe lodged a protest and we were chucked out of the FA Cup for playing a player without permission. I'd been injured on the previous Saturday – I'd hurt my back – and I'd had treatment every day to get me fit to play Wycombe. The trainer then was a very nice man called Tom Webb and I remember they were talking about playing Colin McDonald against Wycombe. Colin McDonald was a Burnley player, a very good goalkeeper, and he was doing his National Service nearby. I was lying on the table listening to what they were saying. I remember saying that they shouldn't play him. Even though they had permission to play him in the League games, they hadn't got permission to play him in Cup games, and once he was Cup-tied his own club would lose him for that season's FA Cup competition. But they went ahead and played him. Colin was an exceptional goalkeeper. He later played for England in the World Cup Finals [1958].

Southern League Champions, 1952-53

Bobby Craig: I was on the transfer list at Sunderland. Harry Thompson came up with the full-back, Frank Ramshaw, and they started talking to me, and they said, "Do you want to come non-League?" I never gave it a thought. Good wages. I thought I'd signed for Headingley, in Yorkshire. I said to my Mum, "I'll probably just travel down on Fridays, stop there and come back on the Saturday." Then I got a ticket for Oxford, and I thought, "Oh, my God, where's this at?" I came down and immediately fell in love with it. Lovely and clean. I took to Headington straightaway, and met probably the best group of lads I've ever met. We had a damn good team and very young. Of course we all clicked. The second year we won the Southern League. Then we won the Southern League Cup and it just went on from there.

Jimmy Smith: We had a team that was quite well-balanced. Frank Ramshaw was the captain. He was a great motivator and set a good example. He was a 90-minute player. Bobby Craig played centre-half, and Johnny Crichton was a great ball-player. The goalkeeper, Ansell, was a player who controlled the six-yard box.

Bobby Craig: Our goalkeeper was a great goalkeeper, but he had broken his leg while at Northampton. Jack didn't play as well on hard grounds as he did on soft grounds. On soft grounds he threw himself about. I never used to bother heading the ball when it was coming across. He used to shout, "My ball, Bob," and he used to come out and he had hands like shovels. If the centre-forward was there he just hit him as well. He used to punch Ronnie Rooke [Bedford Town] as regular as clockwork. A lot of goalkeepers used to get thumped into the back of the net, but not big Jack Ansell. He was probably 6 ft 3 in, and his command of the whole area was absolutely fantastic. He was the Boss. I remember playing at Llanelli, and they hammered us for about 88 minutes. They murdered us. Our centre-forward kicked the ball off our goal-line. I'm the centre-half and he was behind me. That's what I call defence in depth. We broke away once and scored. Beat them 1-0.

Harry Thompson: You have to have this happy blend of strikers and ball-players and tacklers. The first thing you've got to have is good strong men to get you the ball, because without getting the ball you might as well go home. We had one with us – Ernie Hudson. I got him from up Scotland. A terrific man. He'd get you the ball and push it away to someone else who could do all the fiddling about with it.

Bobby Craig: In the forward-line we had Harry Yates. He was top goalscorer everywhere he went and people used to call him "Dobbin". Well, that was a misnomer because I was fast and in a 100-yard sprint he was just behind me. He had a good football brain but he had a very ungainly stride. People used to be amazed. He used to knock in 30 or 40 goals a season. He'd start the move off in our half, and when the ball came across he was the one who nodded it in the net. People used to laugh and make jokes about him, but he was good. We had little Taffy Maskell at outside-left. He was a young Welsh lad, a favourite with the crowd. All left-foot, but he used to crack them across, and if the centre-forward missed them, Harry Yates got them. Harry used to head them in with his shoulders and bounce them in off his knee-cap, but they went in that net. It was uncanny. I think Benny Duncan was one of the best footballers we had in our team. A beautiful ball-player. Crichton was a great passer of the ball. He couldn't tackle, but there was no need to because we had big Ernie Hudson at right-half. Frank Ramshaw was a good professional. If he had to frighten a player he did, and if he couldn't frighten him he played him by football. He could play either way, and that's the mark of a good footballer.

Sandy Brewer: I remember the first time they topped the Southern League. I think the game was played at six o'clock in the evening after the FA Cup Final, and they needed to win to make sure of the Southern League title. Ronnie Steel, a very useful winger, a straightforward player, shot one in, just inside the far upright. That settled everyone's nerves. They went on to win 2-0.

The FA Cup, 1953-54

Jimmy Smith: I was at Millwall for the second round and we were winning 3-1 with ten minutes to go and we drew 3-3 and were disappointed. But then we brought them to Headington and beat them 1-0. I didn't go to Stockport for the third round but I spoke to all the chaps when they came back to Oxford, and it was a very, very heavy ground and a pretty hard match.

Sandy Brewer: They went to Stockport and drew, and won the replay. A centre-forward called Ken Smith scored the goal. He later went to Sunderland and scored three in a First Division game.

Bobby Craig: And then we got the big 'un. Lofthouse. Bolton Wanderers.

Harry Thompson: Bolton Wanderers were a very good team. Nat Lofthouse was playing in those days, and we had a job to cram the crowd in the Manor. We had two builders on the board of directors, and they supplied us with extra gear for terracing and so forth.

Jimmy Smith: It was really absolutely super, wasn't it? There was a lot of publicity, a big following. We used to have what we called "training egg sessions". We used to train and then we'd have raw eggs afterwards to build us up. They used to crack the eggs, put them in the bowl with a little drop of sherry. Sherry and eggs. Only on training nights, Tuesdays and Thursdays. Not during the match!

Harry Thompson: I think we said, "Right, let's give the boys some sherry and egg. Build them up. Get them fit for Saturday." I think we were "the sherry-and-egg team". It was just a gimmick. You've got to do these things, to keep in the public eye.

Jimmy Smith: I worked at the Nuffield Orthopaedic Centre in those days and it didn't matter where I went during the day, they were all talking about football. If you went in the local pub, they were talking about football. If you went into the local shop, they were talking about football.

Even in church there were fans who were talking about the Bolton match. It was real history for Oxford football, wasn't it?

Bobby Craig: Temporary stands. SGB must have made a fortune. All the stands were covered with this corrugated sheeting. Underneath it was just wind whistling through it. My parents came down from Leadgate. I think it was the first time my Mum had ever seen me play football. My Mum and Dad had travelling rugs wrapped round them. I couldn't get them a ticket in the main stand. There were 17,000 there that day.

Winifred Crawford: It was bitterly cold. It was ever so cold. Anyway, we had a nice hot tea with a drop of whisky in to keep us warm.

Sandy Brewer: I can remember that the crowd overflowed on to the pitch a bit, even before the game, there were so many packed into the ground. A few Bolton supporters made their way on and were ushered off again. There was a small wooden stand at the top end of the ground which was a relic of their amateur days. I don't know whether we expected Headington to win but we were a bit optimistic if we did.

Les Bateman: We had snow all over the ground, and it was like concrete underneath. The referee came to me and said, "I don't think I like all that snow on there." I said, "I don't think there's much I can do about it because I'm a one-man band," so I brushed the lines all the way round.

Bobby Craig: It was icy. There was just no give-and-take. Lofthouse, although he was an English international, hurled himself about. He didn't wrap himself in cotton-wool. He had the goalkeeper in the back of the net. I was black and blue. In fact, I've still got one or two bruises! He put himself about like a youngster trying to make his name. It makes you feel good in one way that he didn't belittle you. When he walked off, he said, "Well played, kid." He was the old-fashioned type. He didn't try and go round you. He used to knock you down and stand on you. I used to do the same to him! All forgiven when you walk off the park. I think they beat us 4-2. Whereas we hit the goal-post a couple of times theirs slotted into goal. Mistakes were inevitable on that ground. How it was played, I don't know. Probably these days you wouldn't play on that pitch. I don't think there was a good goal among the whole lot. It was bouncing, somebody miskicked it, it bounced, hit someone on his knees or his ankles. They were going in all ways. Benny Duncan hit the post a couple of times. Even that long ago, I cannot bring back any beautiful memories and tell you lies and say, "We should have won." I don't think we should have done, and we didn't. But a few days like that in your life makes it.

Southern League Supporters

Bobby Craig: I think I played at the best time. I would go out on a dirty, snowy day, look around, and there'd be thousands watching me. I used to think, "Christ, I'm getting paid. What have *you* come for?" This was Headington. I've just got fantastic memories of it. And I never kissed a bloke in my life. If anyone had come up to me when I'd scored a goal, I'd have bloody clobbered him.

Sam Cook: Always a good atmosphere and no trouble. Just the one copper who walked round the ground before kick-off and that was it. All local supporters then, of course. Very few from away.

Jack Fallows: A lot of supporters in the old days, they were characters. One old boy up there used to have about six or seven handbells in his pocket. "Come on, 'Eddy," he used to say, and ring these bells.

Bobby Craig: We had a big American cheerleader who used to run round the ground. He had a bottle of whisky and a damn big cigar. People just came and joined in.

Sandy Brewer: I remember the big American. I think he was from one of the local camps. Everyone used to cheer him. He was quite a popular figure. Then there was a little man who used to run after him; for some reason the crowd didn't like him. I don't quite know why. He was a small, thin chap. The crowd booed instead of cheering. The American was more of a cheerleader. He'd go around, put his hands up to the crowd and they'd all give him a cheer. A big strong man in a pullover.

Bobby Craig: I don't think they were orientated for professional football when we first came. We were playing good football on the ground, because we had people like Crichton and Steel and Yates, and the spectators were very subdued. Then you'd kick the ball up in the air and they thought it was magic. I used to be left-back to start with, and Johnny Crichton played left-half. Johnny would come back and say, "It's a bit quiet, Bob. Kick it up in the air. The Lord's on our side."

Vic Morris: At Pressed Steel we talked about football all the time, especially on a Monday after the match. Nearly everybody at the Pressed Steel seemed to be a Headington supporter. We used to discuss the team, who they'd dropped and who they shouldn't have dropped, all that sort of thing. Pressed Steel was full of managers. Everybody knew more about it than the manager!

Bobby Craig: When I was at Headington I was in the building trade and I often went to work on a bus. From Wednesday, all you were getting bombarded with was: "What's the team?" "What are we going to do?" "Are we going to win?" On the bus I talked football five days a week to people I had never met. People would come up and say, "Hello, Bobby, how are you getting on?" All this sort of thing. And I hadn't seen them before in my life, but they talked to you as though they were great friends. They were so friendly, so nice.

Jimmy Smith: Everybody had the opinion that they were part of something. There wasn't a "them and us" situation. When it started off, it was just one happy family – the players, officials, even the tea-ladies. Everybody had their part to play, and everybody appreciated that, and put hours and hours into the ground, for absolutely nothing. They never got paid.

Bobby Craig: If there was snow on the pitch, 200 people would turn up on Saturday morning to clear the pitch. There was a jungle drum or something, and people used to come down with their shovels. "Where are you going?" "Just going to clear the Manor."

Sandy Brewer: I do remember once being in a jam-packed crowd. Stanley Matthews played in a friendly game, and we were packed in like sardines in the entrance to the ground off London Road.

Jimmy Smith: Sir Stanley Matthews came and played in my benefit match. I went and met him at Oxford station, and we spoke about football. At the end of the match he gave me the boots that he'd worn. I also had a football that was autographed by him. He was a super chap. It was very good of him to come all that way and play in that match for me. That was the second highest gate, wasn't it? There were 11,200 people at the Manor that night. It was Oxford United and a Representative XI. 1955.

The Players

Vic Morris: One of the main characters then was Tony Harper. Mad as a hatter, but a great footballer. He kept everybody alive at the club. I used to go up there some training nights, and Tony Harper was jumping and running about. It was only a wooden floor in the dressing-rooms. In the centre area they had a table-tennis table, and I remember him jumping up and putting his foot right through the wooden floor. A fiery chap. Eventually he went to Brentford for a fee.

Jack Fallows: Tony Harper later came back from Brentford, and he was vigorous. Well, he was boisterous. If he went in on the tackle, three blokes went over the touch-line. The old-fashioned sliding-tackle. Tony was one of the toughest players I've seen.

Geoff Denial: He was an energetic, forceful player who could put himself about. He was a "no frills" type of player, perhaps a little bit lacking in skill but making up for it in endeavour and enthusiasm. He was a good attacking wing-half. He was an ex-League player as well. He was a bit of a character. He used to smoke like a train. His fingers were dark brown and you couldn't stop him from smoking on the coach to away matches. But he was a good player. He had one lung. How the hell he played football, smoking as many fags as he did and having one lung, God only knows.

Sandy Brewer: There was an outside-right called Smillie. He had a spell one season where it seemed every time he got near the opposing goal he scored, and from outside-right that was tremendous. I can't remember how many goals he got, but he must have got about 20 very quickly. Then he seemed to dry up. Of the centre-forwards, there was Rowston, who was extremely good with his head. I remember him very well. Unfortunately, he was not quite as good with his feet, or he wouldn't have been playing at the Manor. There was a chap called Mitchell. He was quite useful. Turner was very good. He came from Charlton, I believe.

Geoff Denial: Headington United seemed to have a policy to kick out maybe 15 or 20 players and retain five or six, and have an influx of new players every year. When I went there, I think there was only five or six people from the previous year, people like Tony Harper and Frank Ramshaw. We trained Tuesday and Thursday evenings, and the spirit was good. It got very nervous towards the end of the season because people had moved to the area on a one-year contract. I think about two or three weeks before the end of the season they would announce the retained list. If they only retained six, it was very disturbing, especially for guys with families. There's no sentiment in football unfortunately. At the end of my first season [1956-57] a lot of players went, good players who I didn't think ought to go. There was a guy called Bobby Odell, who came from the Isle of Wight. He was a centre-half. I think they'd signed him from Reading the previous year. I thought he was a good player. The first five or six years there was a big turnover of players.

The Pitch With A Slope

Edmund Gibbs: The Manor Ground was owned by Headington Sports Ground Ltd which was given to the people of Headington and run by AH Franklin & Son, solicitors, on behalf of all sport. We had a licence to play football during the football season. But cricket and football clashed at the beginning of the football season, so the first games had to be arranged away. Luckily for us, Horace Bradley of Weeks and Co, the confectioners and bakers, was on the board and he gave the United Cricket Club a ground further out in Headington. It took us about 10 years to buy the ground from Headington Sports Ground Ltd. All our capital was going into building on somebody else's ground which we held on a 14-year licence. So it was very important to get the freehold. Eventually Headington Sports Ground Ltd agreed to sell to us but it was the supporters' club that coughed up the money. Part of the bargain was that they would be allowed a chunk of land on which they could build their own club, which they did. We also bought a number of houses down Osler Road. One of them allowed us to build an entrance from Osler Road.

Les Bateman: When I started, in 1950, the playing surface was very bad. When it rained the water used to run down the Manor Road entrance and straight across the field. In the middle of the field there was a big basin that collected water. When they built the Technical College I had all the soil carted up from there and dumped by the fence where Mr Fenton used to live. I kept pushing a barrow-load to the middle of the field, until I gradually built up the middle. From Cuckoo Lane to London Road the drop is actually seven feet. It goes two feet till it gets to the centre-spot and then it slopes a bit more, but when it gets to the 18-yard line it drops quickly to the London Road goal.

Geoff Denial: The pitch was always good at the start of the season, and we trained on the pitch. There were no training grounds in those days. It was a big advantage to kick up the hill first half and go down the hill second half. Clubs playing us knew that if we played that way second half they were going to get bombed. The bottom goal seemed to be a terrible area to get out of, especially if the goalmouth was heavy. Although it wasn't a big slope, it felt like a big slope. There was talk that they were going to level it out, but they never did.

Harry Thompson: We thought it would be nice to get the ground level, and have a nice level ground to play on. We started the machinery in motion, got the bulldozer out, and started pushing ground from the top to the bottom. We found out that you've about six or eight inches of ordinary soil and then you're into sand. We thought, "Nothing we can do about it, we'll just have to leave things as they are and push the soil back." The sand makes it one of the finest pitches in the country for draining.

Sandy Brewer: I remember a game when I was with a couple of friends and it was so foggy and we were seeing so little of the game that we wandered over to the pub on the corner, just opposite, had a drink and wandered back to see the end of the game, and we still didn't see any more. The fog used to drift in off the ground above the Manor in those days.

On The Road

Geoff Denial: The first team were in the Southern League, the second team played in the Metropolitan League, and the third team played in the Hellenic League. You could find yourself playing in the first team on the Saturday and then the third team on the Wednesday evening, just to make up the numbers. The "A" team, as I recall, used to play at the Barracks. We had very few spectators and it was a bit soul-destroying to have to play there because they played on the wide-open spaces of the barracks, but if you played in the "A" team at Thame or Witney then there was always a bit of a needle and it was a better atmosphere because they had a few spectators. Fortunately I didn't play too many games in the "A" team.

Percy Blake: We used to play Tottenham "A" in the Metropolitan League. I remember we went up one night and we were short of a player, Vic Barney couldn't play. Harry Thompson said we couldn't go up with ten men. I said, "Let's pick up Brian Lewis from Green Road and see if he'll come." Well, Brian was in. He was only a youngster. He used to play cricket for Headington United but he never played football very much. And Harry persuaded him to turn out. I always remember he played against George Ludford. He saw the programme and said, "Crikey, you would put me up against a player like that." Poor old Brian didn't know whether he was coming or going.

Reg Ricketts: Harry Thompson was paying for transport out of his own pocket to get lads in from Bletchington and Aylesbury and places like that to give them trials. Players flocked round him like workers flocked round Perce Cooper. We had some very amusing trips to away matches. Harry used to sit on the back seat playing a ukalele, singing and getting the whole coach going. They were really a team of pals.

Harry Thompson: Dartford were in the League in those days. There was this special pub, and the landlord had three or four beautiful daughters. Wherever we were playing in the south of England, we would aim to get back to Dartford to this pub for a meal. The players used to take over the running of the pub. They used to go behind the bar and serve. The landlord never used to worry at all. We never got away from there before midnight. One night we left Dartford, and the coach driver still had his paper hat on, because he'd been joining in the merriment.

Vic Barney: On the way back we nearly always stopped somewhere special. We stopped at a pub in the Mile End Road in London and the landlord had fought for the British heavyweight boxing Championship – Eddie Phillips. They had the old "joanna" there and we'd have a nice night out.

Geoff Denial: Travelling was a lot different to what it is now. When we travelled to London, down the A40, it was a three and a half hour trip to Dartford, whereas perhaps you can do it in an hour and a quarter now. There was always a card school on the coach, and you could either lose your week's wages or win your week's wages. The majority would sit and read, or chat, and then you'd get half a dozen at the back of the coach playing cards. I don't recall us ever staying overnight when we were in the Southern League. We always left early on the Saturday morning and got back maybe nine o'clock Saturday night. Your Saturday was football, from early morning to late at night. Then we'd go across to the Britannia pub, have a couple of beers and make our way home.

Harry Thompson: They were all jokers and characters. There was always something happening. One day they all turned up wearing bow-ties. Another time, we played down south somewhere, probably Hastings, and we stopped at the pub to have a meal and a drink on the way back. We used to have a check-up, and see that we'd got everybody and then say, "Right, let's go. Everybody's in." So we were on our way back and we'd been going for quite a while, and somebody says, "Hey, so-and-so's missing." I said, "They can't be. We had a check-up." "Well, he's missing. He's not on the coach." Wry smiles here and there. "Stop the coach." We stopped the coach and we were one missing. As I say, we'd had a count-up before we set out. They were all giggling away there. I said, "Come on now. What's been happening?" Do you know what they'd done? They'd lifted the back seat out, slipped him under the back seat. Those were the things they used to do, and those were the things that helped to build up team spirit.

Vic Barney: I lived at Shipton-under-Wychwood and if I got back to Oxford at a certain time of night I was stuck there because the last train had gone. There was a little old chap with a heart of gold who worked as a porter at Oxford station. He used to say to me, "Are you going to be late tonight, Vic?" "Yes," I said. "Don't worry," he said, "I'll have the fire going in the waiting-room and a couple of coats, and you can sleep in the waiting-room." I'd get back from an away game about 12 o'clock at night and go in the waiting-room – a couple of coats and the old fire – and in the morning he used to go round the corner to the railway canteen and bring me a cup of tea and toast, and we'd talk about the game. That's how people were in those days.

4 *"Even the directors called him 'boss'"*

ARTHUR TURNER, MANAGER, 1959-69

Arthur Turner, manager from 1959 to 1969, piloted the club's rise from Southern League to the Second Division of the Football League. Before joining United, Turner had played for Stoke City, Birmingham and Southport, and had managed Crewe Alexandra and Birmingham City. Turner later became general manager (1969 to 1972).

AN EXPERIENCED MANAGER

Arthur Turner: I played for Harry Storer for about three seasons at Birmingham and I learned a lot from him, discipline-wise. He was a tough manager. He called a spade a spade, and whatever he said you took notice of. After a period at Crewe, the directors, nine of them, thought it was time to have a change, so they politely put me on my bicycle. That really sickened me. I thought, "Managing's not for me." I went in with Bob McGrory at Stoke City and they made me assistant manager, which was absolutely fantastic because I loved Stoke. I stayed there for two or three years and then I got a phone call from Birmingham City. I went over to

Stafford, met them, and was appointed manager. I think I'm right in saying they were fourth from bottom of the Second Division. When we won the last match of the season, 5-0 at Doncaster, we were Champions, which I think was a fantastic achievement. I didn't buy any players. I used a great deal of discipline and exercised authority. The following season we finished in the top half of the First Division and went to the semi-final of the Cup. The following season we went to the Final of the Cup when Manchester City beat us. Then the following season we didn't get off to a very good start and they started stirring the pudding. I came in for a great deal of criticism and I was still the same fellow! Eventually I threw my resignation on the table.

The Headington Job

Arthur Turner: I thought I'd open a business in Newcastle-under-Lyme, which is my home town. I was on the verge of doing that when I got a phone call from a newspaper man named John Ross. He said, "Arthur, I was down at Headington last night, at a match, and they're looking for a manager, and I mentioned you." I said, "Well, you're wasting your time because I'm not interested." He said, "I had a good chat with them, and I really gave you a good recommendation. The chairman's going to ring you up." The chairman of Oxford came on the phone. It was Mr Ron Coppock, and he sounded charming. He said they'd been looking for a manager and I'd been strongly recommended, would I go down and see them. "No," I said. "I'm not interested, Mr Coppock. I've just had enough. I'm fed up with it." He arranged a meeting with the directors, and then he came on the phone again. He said, "Well, Mr Turner" – he didn't call me Arthur – "I've arranged for the board to meet, and we'd like you to come down and have a chat." I said, "Well, you've been very courteous to me. The nicest thing I can do is to come down and see you." I watched them play at Corby, and when I saw the team, I thought "Oh dear." I went and they interviewed me and they offered me a good contract, and I can assure you, without any doubt at all, the contract that they gave me at Oxford United was a better contract than I'd got with Birmingham City, who were a First Division club. Now you'd find that hard to believe, wouldn't you? But that was the truth.

Les Bateman: The chairman came to me and said, "Mr Turner's coming here tomorrow," and that happened to be New Year's Day. He says, "Ring me up when he comes." And I see him coming in. He walked round the

Manor Ground and I took him into what was the tea-room, office and board-room, all in one. I went and made him a cup of tea and then went to ring the chairman.

Arthur Turner: I didn't even know where the club was, to be truthful. I got the phone call, and when he said, "Headington United," I thought "Where's Headington?" Anyway, I found out where it was and I made my way down by train. I walked up from Oxford station up to the football ground. When I saw it in the daylight, the ground, the pitch, honestly, it had more docks on it than it had grass. It had a big slope on it, and the bottom end there they had about four or five rows of terracing and a little bit of embankment. The stand that the supporters' club had built, which was a credit to them, was at the side of that and there was a little embankment there. The dressing-rooms were that little place in the top corner, and the top end was just a bit of embankment. There was no terracing or anything like that. I said, "What about the strips? Where's the strips?" "Oh, the lady's got them, she's washing the shirts for Saturday." There was one set of shirts for the first team, and the throw-outs for the Reserves.

Management Style

Arthur Turner: I had 30 or 40 lads on the pitch, three or four nights a week, digging the docks out before we sowed the grass seeds. It really was awful. I met the supporters' club secretary, Jim Knapp, who was a great fellow, and his committee and said, "Look, we've got to get this organised. I've got to get a drying-room, and a place where we have some kit." The supporters' club had a place under the stand, at the end of the stand, that they used as an office. They moved into another section, and we had it turned into a drying-room and a room for the kit. We had cupboards put in there. I phoned a chap in London and I think I ordered around about six or eight sets of strip. I had a new skip [to carry the kit] and made us look like a football team when we were going away. I said, "Wherever we go, while I'm the manager of this club, when we go on the field we go on looking like a football team. We're going on smart, so the people can say, 'Look at this lot, don't they look good.'" I always believed in appearance. The supporters' club gave me the money and I had kit galore.

Les Bateman: Arthur Turner says to me, "What is your job here?" I said, "Groundsman." He said, "What? You seem to be a jack of all trades," because I had to clean the board-room, wash the beer glasses, sweep the ground and all these jobs. And he says, "You're going to have a staff of apprentices. I'll get some. You can't go on like this." He got Graham Atkinson and two or three other lads and I showed them where the brooms were to sweep the terracing. I had such a laugh and Arthur Turner comes out and says, "Les, that Graham doesn't seem to be getting on very well." I said to Graham, "What's wrong?" and he says "I didn't think I'd got to do all this work, I'll ask for my cards." And of course I told Arthur. Next day Arthur comes out and says, "Tell Graham I want to see him." And Graham went in and started talking and Arthur said, "I understand you want your cards, do you want them straightaway or do you want time to go home and pack?" And Graham came out with his head hanging low. I said, "What's up then, Graham?" And Graham said, "I've changed my mind."

Edmund Gibbs: Arthur Turner had only been with us two or three months and Leeds approached. We were paying him £700 a year. Leeds suddenly came one night and offered Arthur £1,000 to go to Leeds. Arthur was going but Ron Coppock called a meeting in his house and got hold of Arthur Turner and just upped that figure to hold him. We couldn't afford it then but we just had to.

Ron Atkinson: He could have had the Leeds job, ironically enough, just before Don Revie took over. It just shows how things change in football. What Arthur Turner did, he organised Headington on the basis of a League club. If I could say I've taken anything from him, it was that he always tried to get people with character into his side. Most of the players he signed, I would say, had good character. He never used to pay us any money, but he always produced sides that had good character and fighting spirit. Managers were a bit different in those days. We would see Arthur after a match one Saturday and it could be a week before we saw him again, the following Saturday. The trainer always took the training sessions, or the coaching sessions, but the manager would let you know if he thought you were out of order.

Colin Harrington: We rarely saw him through the week. At ten o'clock on a Friday he'd pin up the team-sheet, and, depending on what sort of team changes he'd made, he'd run off and disappear.

Geoff Denial: Arthur Turner was an ex-League manager who had a lot of contacts within the game, and I think he had a very progressive attitude. I think the directors at that time employed him to get the club into the League, which he did, through his contacts with other managers and people who could help the club. His first year was the year that Cyril Beavon came, and Maurice Kyle, and Ron and Graham Atkinson, and Owen Medlock. Arthur Turner did a brilliant job when he brought those players. It was because he had contacts in the Midlands. He brought those five players and that started the influx of good players. He built a team around those players.

John Shuker: His style was to give you as little as possible and get as much as he could out of you, which is possibly a good way as a manager! But Arthur did a great job at Oxford. Nobody can get away from that. He's probably had more success than any manager at Oxford. As a manager he'd talk to players when he felt like it, but he got the best out of the players. We all knew where we stood with him, and that's what you need as a manager.

Jim Barron: Anybody who knows Arthur will appreciate this story. He came to sign me at Stamford Bridge and at the time I'd bought a house in Essex. He said, "No problem, we've got club houses, and frankly there's a club house in the same street as me." I thought, "That can't be bad, the same street as the manager." Unfortunately, when I came to Oxford, Arthur's house in Windmill Road was right at the bottom end by the hospital, and mine was a little terraced house right at the top end by the traffic lights. He conned me a little bit with the size of the house, Arthur, but he was okay.

Arthur Turner: I never made any rash promises to them, but I filled them in on what it was like. I would pay them the best money that I could. When they got into the Football League I paid them Football League money. When I went there, I said to the directors, "We've got a lot of boys here who are a good type of player, your Kyles, your Ronnies, your Beavons, your Pat Quartermains. They're good servants to this club. I want to be in a position to pay them a benefit." They looked at me and said, "We can't afford benefits." I said, "You don't have to pay benefits. You give me permission that I can pay certain players a benefit, and leave the rest to me." And they agreed. That's why Cyril Beavon and Maurice Kyle and Ron Atkinson and one or two more of them all had a benefit while I was manager at Oxford. The club didn't pay them. I arranged friendly games for them, got some money in that respect, put it in a benefit fund. That's how we mounted up the benefit fund so we could pay them. I'm not saying they got £1,500 or anything like that, but if I remember rightly they got around £400 or £500 apiece, which I think they deserved and I think they earned.

Geoff Denial: My opinion of Arthur Turner was that although I played for maybe five years under him, I felt that he did me an injustice at the end of my career at Oxford by promising me certain things that didn't materialise, and unfortunately I left with a little bit of distaste. As far as being a manager of men, he was a good manager. I think his technicalities and thinking was a little bit lax, but nevertheless he was a good manager. His man-management was excellent.

Colin Harrington: Although Arthur Turner had a certain charisma, it didn't exist within the dressing-room. I can remember, in certain matches, Arthur used to come in and rant and rave, but that didn't change the way of the game. The leadership was not there with Arthur.

Ron Atkinson: Very often at half-time, if things weren't going well, he'd pick on four players. It used to be the goalkeeper, whoever was in goal, Pat Quartermain, myself and Bud Houghton. I think he worked on the premise that he would get a reaction from us. If he insulted my ability, whilst I wouldn't be very happy and probably up in arms, I'd try to prove him wrong in the second half, just to prove a point. I used that as a tactic sometimes with Bryan Robson at Manchester. I knew that if you insulted Robbo's ability, he would want to prove you wrong. I suppose that's something I picked up from Arthur Turner.

Colin Clarke: Arthur was the old breed, and so dour. He would slaughter players with his bluntness. I can remember one match with John Shuker. John believed that he was playing on the left wing, so he promptly donned the number-11 shirt, and Arthur, as he was prone to do, came in 20 minutes or a quarter of an hour before the kick-off. He's looked around the dressing-room and he's seen John Shuker in the number-11 shirt, and he says, "What you doing with that shirt on? You're not playing. Get the bloody thing off. Johnny Love's playing." John was absolutely dumbfounded, because he was expecting to play. But that was Arthur. He was so blunt. I know it sounds a bit cruel but it was a really funny incident at the time. John can remember that, but he laughs when he tells the story.

Colin Harrington: I mean, to give you an idea of what sort of power he had, even the directors called him "Boss". You used to get on the team coach at Oxford and they used to refer to Arthur Turner as "Boss". Players, as a matter of course, always called the manager "Boss" but the directors called Arthur "Boss". Arthur ate, slept and drank football and that was it. You couldn't speak to Arthur on anything other than football. He had difficulty in actually communicating with the players and this is where Ken Fish came in really. Ken kept a good sense of discipline and he was able to communicate with players in language they could understand. Arthur was a strict disciplinarian, a martinet really. Honestly, if you'd been at some of the half-time team-talks you couldn't believe it. Some of the words! You used to have to put up with this as a player. You used to get called all the names under the sun but when you're getting thrashed 3-1 you don't want to be told you're playing rubbish. You already know that. This is why some of the older players would say, "We've heard that one before, Boss, let's have the reason why we're playing badly."

Jim Barron: I wouldn't say Arthur was the best coach in the world. We did a lot of team planning in the cafe across the road. Every day we used to go there and work out free-kicks and how we should play, and in that respect I suppose I learned as much there on the coaching side as I did anywhere else.

Ron Atkinson: We were short of a centre-forward because Bud Houghton was injured, and I always remember getting hold of Arthur Turner at an away game at Bradford City and asking if we could switch the system, and play what is considered now to be a normal system, but was a little bit revolutionary then. We didn't play with a centre-forward. We left two men up the field and we went into a four- or five-man midfield, with everybody given the licence to attack. I actually gave the team-talk on the back of the team coach at Bradford, how we were going to play. We went to Bradford, who were then a very good side, and beat them 4-1.

John Shuker: I was playing at centre-forward and we decided – the lads themselves, and Ronnie, who was the captain then – that I should drop back and play just in front of the defenders. I kicked the ball off when we played at Bradford and straightaway dropped back in front of the back four. Arthur Turner couldn't understand what was happening and he was shouting at me to get up because I had a number-nine on my back. Arthur wasn't very happy with me doing that. When we played at home the following week, he said, "Look, you're a centre-forward, number nine." We went out on the park and big Ron says to me, "Hey, Shukes, same again, at the back." Well, who was going to argue with big Ron? I wasn't. So I did exactly what they said, and we kept winning. But Arthur wasn't very happy with me.

Colin Clarke: Arthur was one of the old brigade, and there was a change in tactics. The 1966 World Cup had been won with a 4-3-3 system, and Arthur didn't have any truck with these systems. Anyway, we had to adjust because other teams were adjusting. We more or less did it ourselves. Ron would get the lads together and we'd decide. The previous week we'd played the 4-3-3 system, but not really with Arthur's blessing. So Arthur came in, and it's 15 minutes before the kick-off, and Ron says to him, "What system are we playing then, Boss?" Arthur says, "The system we've been using. You know the system." Ron says, "Exactly what system is it, Boss?" "The same one that we used last week." "The same one?" "Aye, that'll do." Ron says, "One or two of the lads are not really sure. What was the system we used last week?" "Well, it was four, four, four, er, four-four-three." "Four-four-three?" "Aye, like last week, four-four-three." So Ron says to him, "That's 12, Boss." "Well, take one of the midfield players off then." We were all in hysterics. We all knew that he wasn't sure what system we were playing. So that went down a bundle. Everybody was in hysterics. Everybody's shoulders were shaking in the background, while Arthur was getting really stroppy.

5 *"We changed the name to Oxford United"*

INTO THE FOOTBALL LEAGUE AND UP FOR THE CUP, 1959-64

Arthur Turner not only signed good players but also structured the club along full-time professional lines. After the change of name from Headington United to Oxford United in 1960, United won successive Southern League Championships in 1960-61 and 1961-62 and canvassed strongly to take the place of defunct Accrington Stanley in the Football League. On Saturday 2 June 1962, they were elected. Two years later they created a sensation by becoming the first Fourth Division team to reach the FA Cup sixth round.

FULL-TIME PROFESSIONALISM, 1959

Arthur Turner: I'd only been there about three or four weeks and a player came in and I said he could have his cards. He said, "Mr Turner, I feel sorry for you." I said, "You feel sorry for me?" and he said, "I do, you coming into this club as the manager; you know, the players here don't call it a football club, they call it a Christmas club." I had to live in a hotel for about three months, travel weekends to Birmingham to see my wife, and I started to get it all sorted out. Headington then were all part-timers living all over the country. The first thing they did when they saw me on a Saturday was hand in their expense-sheets. All due respect to anybody who's been in the game professionally but the fact was that there were players who were absolutely no use at all. They hadn't got the quality to get the club out of trouble. I'd only been there about three or four weeks and I offered about 12 of them their freedom. I used to ring up some of the Southern League clubs – I knew many of the managers – and say, "Are you looking for any players?" I let certain players go and I paid half of their wages. The club that they went to paid half the wages and I paid the other half to make up for the contract that they'd got with me. You'd got to get rid of them if you were going to make any more signings. The directors were very ambitious. They had ideas about the Football League. I spoke to the chairman and he understood the position, so I said to the board, "Look, gentlemen, if you want to fulfil what you want to do, there's only one course of action, and that's to go full-time." "Full-time? How can we afford full-time?" Well, they had an outstanding supporters' club who contributed a weekly amount of money to help run the club. I spoke to the committee on this score and they backed it. The board said, "Yes, alright." They would go full-time.

Vic Couling: Arthur introduced us into full professionalism, even before we entered the Football League. We employed full-time players and a full-time coach. He engaged eight scouts throughout the country, searching for players, and a full-time secretary in the office.

Arthur Turner: The following season in the Southern League [1959-60], when it became the Premier League, we finished runners-up, which was quite an achievement. I'd probably got about 10 or 11 full-timers and the rest part-time. The following season we were Champions. The following season we were Champions again, and at the end of that season we were admitted to the Football League, which, not being boastful about it, was a fantastic achievement.

Geoff Denial: I think that perhaps the last three years of our Southern League days were the best, where we had quite a few players who were there from one year to another, like the Atkinson brothers, Bud Houghton, Tony Jones, Maurice Kyle, Owen Medlock, Cyril Beavon. The majority of the players were full-time players then. I wasn't because I thought it was in my interests to stay part-time and work. The financial gains were better for me. When we were part-time, I think the majority of players who came worked at the factory. They worked long hours at the factory and then trained in the evening. When they went full-time, a lot of the players also got part-time jobs to fill the time, because they only trained in the mornings. Bud Houghton and Ron Atkinson were window-cleaners. Maurice Kyle was a qualified electrician. Tony Jones did a bit of lorry-driving. I remember Ron working for Cooper's in Paradise Street.

Arthur Turner: The directors backed the idea of going full-time, paying good wages for better players, finding them accommodation in Oxford and buying properties, with the help of the supporters' club, who contributed so much. If I was interested in a player, and I wanted to purchase him, it was the supporters' club that came across with a lot of the money. As an example, there was a boy named Maurice Kyle who played with Wolves. Stan Cullis sold him to me for £5,000, which was a lot of money for us in those days, but what a signing he turned out to be. The supporters' club also contributed a weekly sum of money, which helped to pay the players' wages. They were the backbone. Oxford United, in my opinion, couldn't have got where they were without the supporters' club, because it was probably one of the best in the country. That's why we were able to go full-time.

Edmund Gibbs: The supporters' club ran a lottery, but all the time you had to keep ahead of the law. We had so many schemes. Every time we thought the police were going to pounce on us we switched to something else. A number would be drawn out of a drum and it generated a fantastic amount of money. The supporters' club paid for the Beech Road Stand entirely.

The Change of Name, 1960

Vic Couling: After 1952 I put our first application in for membership of the Football League, and then every year we asked members to make an application for admission to the Football League, so our name came up every year with the Wigans, the Bedfords and the Yeovils and all those, and we felt rather proud of the fact that we were associated with them. Peter Smith and myself, and Harry Thompson, used to go up every year to the meetings at the Cafe Royal in Regent Street. It was always interesting that the journalists asked, "Where's Headington?" because they'd never heard of Headington, and when they knew it was close to Oxford, they said, "Why don't you change your name to Oxford?" That gave us a lot of thought, for several seasons.

Edmund Gibbs: We had enormous troubles in the first ten years when we wanted to change the name. We had trouble on both sides. Oxford City were violently against it, and the Oxfordshire Football Association and the people of Headington of course. We compromised for one year and it was called Headington and Oxford United – a terrible name.

Harry Thompson: You mention Headington to anybody outside the city, and they'll say, "Where the hell's that?" unless they've been on the route between London and Oxford. As soon as they changed the name to Oxford United, it was a different matter. Everybody knows where Oxford is. Then they were on their way.

A Football League Club, June 1962

Arthur Turner: If I'd kept a clock, or a book, on the amount of miles I did to get the votes to get Oxford United into the Football League, people would never believe it. I went all over the country. I travelled to the north of England, I travelled to the south. I met club chairmen, I met club managers, after the votes, after the votes, and how well I remember when we went to London to the Annual General Meeting, which I'll never forget, and there was about five directors that went with me, including Mr Coppock, and they were all, "Think we shall make it?" I said, "We shall make it if everybody honours what they said and votes for us." I can assure you of this, and I'm not being big-headed when I say this, the number of chairmen that told me, "We're not going to vote for Oxford United, Arthur, we're going to vote for you." That is God's truth. They said, "We're voting for you, Arthur, because of your reputation."

Vic Couling: We would go round to other clubs and Arthur was always welcome at them. He introduced us into the board-rooms. If Arthur hadn't been with us we would never have got beyond the car-parks.

John Shuker: I was on my summer break in Manchester. Accrington had dropped out of the League and in the summer Oxford were voted in. They had to be voted in. They'd just won the Southern League and they had the highest attendance of a non-League club.

Nick Harris: It was a Saturday. We used to go to school on Saturday mornings, which I always used to hate, and I remember coming back on the bus on the Saturday lunch-time and listening to the news. There was a curt announcement on Radio Whatever-it-was-then, that Oxford United had been elected into the League in the place of Accrington Stanley, who'd bowed out the previous season. It was an incredibly exciting time.

John Shuker: Oxford had always been a town associated with the university and amateur sport. Once Oxford United got into the League they got known nationally, and it was a good thing for Oxford. A lot more people wanted to watch the games because they were in the Football League. Because of that, football in Oxfordshire grew.

The Directors

Edmund Gibbs: The board-meetings were originally at the British Workmen's Club in Old High Street and, when that was occupied for some reason or other, we met in a room at the back of the Britannia. The village policeman would come along and tap on the window and come and sit in with us and have a pint of beer. He was checking that beer wasn't being sold after hours and there he was sitting with us having a pint. He was very much a local bobby. Meetings would start about seven o'clock but they got so involved in the team and the rest of it. You can imagine the sort of things that went on there, the arguments about who should be centre-half and who should be left out and who must be in. Because individual directors used to get individual things about particular players: "That young Knight is the finest right winger we've ever seen." And the rest would say, "He's bloody rubbish." These arguments would go on and we'd rarely finish before one o'clock in the morning.

John Shuker: When they first went into the League, there was nobody on the board who were millionaires. They were all local business-people, people like Mr Coppock, Mr Jones, Mr Kersley, Mr Leys. They were all just local people who took the plunge to go into the Football League and it was a big decision for those people, and they played a big part in the rise of Oxford United.

Edmund Gibbs: Ron Coppock was a great chap. He worked at Axtell and Perry, before they eventually went in with Symm and Co. There was something about Ron. He knew where he wanted to go. He was the one who was instrumental in getting Arthur Turner. Coppock would fight anybody on behalf of Turner and Turner was the same with Coppock. They became very close personally.

Arthur Turner: I got on like a house on fire with Ron Coppock. Ron Coppock was a very likeable chap, and a very understanding chap. Never at any time did I see Ron Coppock losing his shirt when he sat in the chair. He'd listen. He'd talk. And the directors went along with him. In my book he was a smashing chairman. He wasn't the wealthiest I ever worked with, but at least he could handle the board. Some of those directors knew nothing. They didn't know whether the ball was round or square. But as far as I was concerned, they were fine. They were great with me, because they never interfered.

Geoff Denial: Ron Coppock lived in the Quarry. The directors in those days were people who lived around the football ground. I remember Fred Jones quite vividly. He was the old fishmonger down Windmill Road. There were some lovely occasions when he'd bring fish as a gift to players.

Edmund Gibbs: Freddie Jones was a great mate of mine. Old Fred used to run an advert in the programme: "Monday Thame, Tuesday Bicester, Wednesday Oxford, Thursday Witney, Friday somewhere else and Saturday Football." He had a great sense of humour. Some of us went away with the team and when you got up to your room you'd find there was no bed in it because Fred Jones had been in there with someone else and stuck it on the landing. This sort of thing went on.

Ron Atkinson: We'd be in the bath after the match, and Freddie Jones would come in with a great big salmon or a live lobster and throw it in the bath. You did see people shift a bit quick.

Edmund Gibbs: I remember going away once. I think we were playing Dover, a lovely ground right on the cliff top. We stopped at this hotel and old Fred had brought a crab with him. He put it in what he thought was Ronnie Atkinson's bed and, unfortunately, he picked a honeymoon couple's room and shoved this crab in their bed. An enormous uproar occurred. We were nearly slung out, team and all.

The Fourth Division, 1962-63

Sam Cook: I can remember their first game – Barrow away. They lost 3-2 and Graham Atkinson scored the first goal in the League, if I remember correctly.

Sandy Brewer: The first home game was against my home-town team, Lincoln, because I wasn't sure which team I was supporting when I went to the match. Lincoln scored first – an outside-left called Scanlon, a survivor of the Manchester United air crash – but I knew immediately Oxford scored I was an Oxford supporter. They went on to win 2-1. I was delighted that they'd got those points. Two points in those days, of course.

John Shuker: I remember playing at Workington one year, the first time we went there. We had a look on the field before the game, as you normally do, and the terracing was old railway sleepers. As we went to kick off, just next door to the ground was a bingo-hall, and there was more noise coming from the bingo-hall than there was from the crowd, because they had the microphones in there and they were shouting the numbers.

Colin Harrington: Now I think back, there were a lot of hard-core supporters who would actually follow you to the end of the earth, going up to Barrow and Workington, down to Torquay and Exeter, across to Grimsby and Hartlepools. There weren't motorways then. You're talking about a six-hour journey to Barrow and Workington.

John Shuker: I think it was Rochdale we played one day. They had an old railway-carriage as a dressing-room, behind the stands. But some of the grounds were really good. Lincoln City and Bury. Their playing fields were among the best in the League. We had some good trips. The first time we went to Chester, we played the game and after the game we were all stood in the dressing-room, taking off our kit, wondering where the showers or the bath was, and we couldn't find them anywhere. There was no other door, so we asked one of their stewards: "Could you tell us where the showers are?" "Oh," he said, "I'm sorry. Hasn't the chap been in yet?" We said, "No." So he came in and he lifted a piece of the wall out. It was a wooden wall and a door halfway up which we had to climb through to get into the bath, which was next door. That was Chester at the time. I think it's changed now.

Geoff Denial: I think the first year in the Fourth Division was a feeler really. Everybody was so chuffed at being able to play in the League that we had the episodes of going away and having a good time. I don't think our away record that year was very good!

Ron Atkinson: There wasn't a lot of difference in the ordinary working day, because we had been a full-time outfit in non-League anyway. Obviously we were playing different clubs and there was an awful lot more travelling involved. Because we'd dominated non-League soccer for three years, both home and away, we automatically assumed we could go on all-out attack in away games. Mind you, to be fair, you used to do that a bit more in those days anyway. The first big realisation was that away games weren't going to be as easy as they had been in the past. I think the first year or so was more-or-less like a learning process, but I think the second year we came to terms with it. That was the year of the Cup run, which probably was as exciting a time, certainly in my time, as Oxford have known, comparable to later years when they went to the Final of the Milk Cup and rose from the Third to the First Division.

FA Cup, 1963-64

Colin Harrington: I just about made the first team by the end of the first season and I was about to establish myself. I was in at the beginning of the Cup run, and we really struggled. People only remember the Blackburn game and the Preston game. They forget we struggled against places like Kettering. We really made a hash of it but came good in the match that really mattered.

Nick Harris: I vaguely remember the early rounds. I think we played Kettering. There were some pretty dire games. We played somebody in a very foggy game which was won. The games I remember very well are the Brentford games in the fourth round. We drew 2-2 at home, and then going away to Brentford was incredible. I remember Lime Walk that day. I think there were 50 coaches in Lime Walk. Incredible away support for United. And, this dates it, they were building the M4 at the time. Terrible congestion in London. In fact, I don't think many of the United fans got in the ground until half-time. I remember queuing outside the ground and Brentford scoring. There was a great "Awwww dear", then getting in there at half-time and United playing brilliantly in the second half, and Billy Calder scored both the goals. It was just amazing. I'd never been part of something as exciting as that. That away game at Brentford, I think, was probably the highlight, even more than when they beat Blackburn, although that was an incredible day as well.

Jack Fallows: I think football is a working-class game because I remember when we played Blackburn Rovers, and they were interviewing people. They were interviewing the wrong people. They were interviewing the undergraduates, who had nothing to do with United. They didn't know the first names of the players. Of course, when the Blackburn Rovers supporters came, they said, "Where's all the university girls?" I said, "What university girls? There's no university girls come up here to watch blithering Oxford United."

Ron Atkinson: Blackburn had a galaxy of international stars, people like Ronnie Clayton, the England captain, Bryan Douglas, big Mike England, Fred Pickering, and Keith Newton, and they were top of the First Division at the time. They'd just beaten West Ham 8-1, a West Ham side including Hurst, Moore, Peters and so forth, and they came to the Manor Ground. Early on in the game I always remember winning a challenge against Fred Pickering, who was then the hottest centre-forward in the game, and I remember actually knocking him over and, the funny thing was, I looked at him then and he seemed frightened. It was the first time I'd ever seen it in a player. Obviously they were nervous because they were on a hiding to nothing.

Colin Harrington: I think the other thing that got to their players when they came to Oxford was the ground itself and the closeness of the crowd. The supporters were right on top of them and it was frightening. That was a new environment for Blackburn.

Jack Fallows: In my memory, the Blackburn game was one of the greatest moments of my life watching football, to see an underdog beat a top-notcher, and I remember Arthur Turner standing on the touch-line waving them on: "Come on, come on, get into the area." I think the biggest cheer I've ever heard up at the Manor, and that's with First Division football, Second and Third, was when Tony Jones put the first goal in for Oxford United.

Vic Morris: Astonishingly, we were the better team. We took the lead through Tony Jones. That was the half-time score, which was unbelievable in itself. We came out and got another one. Again Tony Jones. Two-nil. Nobody could believe it. Then Blackburn came back into the game a bit. Well into the second half they got a goal back through one of their internationals, a boy called Bryan Douglas. Of course, then, for the rest of the game it was all Blackburn Rovers. We were desperately defending. Then, just couple of minutes from the end, when it was still 2-1, somebody released the ball over to Pat Quartermain, who was at left-back, and he ran all the way up the wing, centred the ball, and Bill Calder scored the third goal.

Edmund Gibbs: I always remember when that third goal went in and made it 3-1 to Oxford. There was a fellow called Ivor Davies, who was the

Liberal candidate in the Oxford City constituency. When they scored, my friend Freddie Jones plucked his hat off his head and threw it in the air and the last we saw of this chap's hat was it sailing off. The whole ground was in uproar – great cheers – because that clinched it.

Vic Morris: The crowd went on the pitch and the referee had a job to play the last two minutes. Everybody was scared in case he was going to have to call it off. All the Oxford players, like Cyril Beavon, were trying to get them off. Eventually they did, and they played the last two minutes.

Nick Harris: I remember running on the pitch at the end, as did everybody else. Some of the players came out of the dressing-room. Cyril Beavon, I remember, and Ron Atkinson came out at a later stage. Great excitement.

Ron Atkinson: Sometimes, when you have high moments, the aftermath's not always as good, but that was brilliant. It was really the first time a lot of us had tasted what you'd call the real big time. We all went up to Minchery Farm Country Club and we had an all-night party which was fabulous and everybody was in just a great mood. It was terrific.

Nick Harris: I remember when they'd beaten Blackburn, being at school, sitting in the back of Latin, with the old transistor radio, waiting for the draw. I think it would be Monday lunch-time in those days. When it came out, Preston at home, I think we honestly believed that United were going to get to Wembley.

Sandy Brewer: I do remember queuing halfway to Marston for one Cup tie. The queue was right down London Road to Sandfield Road, right down Sandfield Road, beyond the far end of Sandfield Road. We were a long way down there. I remember that on a Sunday morning, queuing for tickets. We were mad, weren't we?

Colin Harrington: After we'd made this one huge leap to beat Blackburn, the next few matches we were awful. Before we played Preston, we were up at Halifax, and we lost 3-1. This sort of inconsistency tends to be very much part of the lower leagues. Before the Preston game we spent the morning autographing. You know, 500 autographs at a time. Of course, the papers loved this sort of thing. I think they got all the players in gowns and mortar-boards. The dressing-room was electric before the match, really electric. When I look back now, I'm quite surprised how well the older professionals conducted themselves. Nervousness only seems to creep in when you're getting older, when you're a bit more worried about your game. Being young – I was about 20 at the time – you don't have the same view of those sorts of things. People like Arthur Turner, who was the manager, were more on tenterhooks. He was overcome with nerves. Before we went out, he passed a bottle of whisky round. It was probably the biggest match at the club at the time and the bell had just gone and some of the players were walking through brick walls at the time and Arthur said, "Hold it down a bit, lads, I don't want you to forget this – we're at Newport on Monday."

John Shuker: The Preston centre-forward was Alex Dawson and our centre-half was Maurice Kyle. I think Alex scored the first goal after about ten or twelve minutes, and we said to Maurice, "Come on, Maurice, put the good hard tackles in against him." Maurice, being the gentleman that he was, refused to do it, so the word went round the team to get big Ron to have a go at him. Obviously Ron went in with a few hard tackles and it upset Dawson and we came back into the game. But Maurice was a gentleman, he wouldn't kick anybody. He wouldn't do anything that was against the rules.

Arthur Turner: Oxford United should have gone to the Final that year, in my opinion. We went to the sixth round of the Cup, and lost 2-1 to Preston, and I never thought we should have lost. I know we played all the matches at home, but I'm firmly convinced, when I looked back afterwards at who the semi-finalists would have been, that the club might easily have got to Wembley. We didn't, but to get to the sixth round was quite an achievement with the players that we had. It's nice in the history book.

Ron Atkinson: The winning goal, by Alex Dawson, in everybody's opinion except the man who mattered most, the referee, was five to ten yards offside. It was so far offside it was laughable. You never know what might have happened. If we'd got into the semi-final we'd have drawn Swansea, and we might have created a real piece of history. Whereas we were pumped up for the Blackburn game and the adrenalin was flowing, to a certain extent we didn't do ourselves justice in the sixth-round match. We didn't play as well as we should have done, but still could have won it. That Cup run lifted the whole season. I think that gave us the confidence next year to go on and clinch promotion.

6 *"I didn't sign many flops"*

ARTHUR TURNER'S SIGNINGS, 1959-69

Arthur Turner proved to be exceptionally shrewd in the transfer market. His early free-transfer signings included Graham Atkinson, Ron Atkinson, Cyril Beavon, Tony Jones, Peter Knight and Owen Medlock. Colin Harrington and John Shuker also came without a fee, and he spent modest amounts on Bud Houghton, Alan Willey and Maurice Kyle. When United got into the Football League he added players like Harry Fearnley, Colin Booth, Billy Calder and Arthur Longbottom.

BUILDING A SIDE

Arthur Turner: There was only about eight or nine I kept. All the others were on their bicycles. I kept Johnny Love, Geoff Denial and Joe Dickson. I kept Pat Quartermain. I wrote a pile of letters to clubs around the country because I had so many friends in the managerial side and, I must admit, some of them were very helpful. I got some lovely letters back from those who were willing to help me, none better than Stan Cullis, who was manager of Wolves. Stan let me have three or four really good players. When I think of some of the players that made the club successful, I think of Owen Medlock, Harry Fearnley, Cyril Beavon, Pat Quartermain. Better club men never played football than Pat Quartermain and Cyril Beavon. You'd got Ron Atkinson, Maurice Kyle centre-half, Tony Jones. And you pick up players like Alan Willey for about £1,000, Graham Atkinson for nothing, Peter Knight for nothing, Tony Jones for nothing, Ron for nothing, Colin Clarke from the Arsenal for nothing. I didn't sign anybody on somebody else's recommendation. I watched them myself, because I was the one who had to carry the can. If they were a flop it was my fault. I can honestly say, and I might be big-headed when I say this, I didn't sign many flops, because I saw them perform.

Tim Sparrowhawk: I particularly remember Ron Atkinson leading the team out, legs smothered with wintergreen. You could smell him from several yards away. He used to try and juggle the ball as he came out of the dressing-room, which used to be at the corner of the Beech Road and Cuckoo Lane end.

Ken Fish: Ron Atkinson was the oil king. If there had been sponsorship in those days he would have made a fortune for an olive-oil company. He was a fantastic motivator on the field of play. He was always going hard at it, with olive oil on his legs, just in case the sun came out too strongly in the winter.

Ron Atkinson: I used to put a load of oil on my body and then try to punch anybody who was near me in the dressing-room, just to get myself wound up aggressively. I always tried to get to the lads that when we come out of the dressing-room we explode out of the dressing-room, not to come out as if it's a chore, but to try to explode and race on to the field. I very often used to just whack the ball up in the air as we came out.

Arthur Turner: Ron Atkinson was on Villa's books. I had a friend in Birmingham, a fellow named Jack Malone, and he rang me up about any young player that he saw. He wasn't officially a scout for me but a great friend. He rang me up one day, and he said about this lad Ron Atkinson. I went to watch Ron in a Reserve game, and I thought he could play a bit, but I was firmly convinced he was in his wrong position, because he was in the forward-line. He was a big, powerful lad, a glutton for work. Anyway, I went and signed him in Birmingham, took him on full-time when he was single. When he'd signed for me, I said, "Now, you're not going to play inside-forward or centre-forward for me." He said, "Aren't I?" I said, "No. I'm going to play you at wing-half, right-half." "Wing-half!" he said. "I've never played there in my life."

Ron Atkinson: It was in the days of the maximum wage, and I was approached by Arthur Turner to join what he considered to be an ambitious non-League outfit who had great designs on going into the Football League. I've got to be perfectly honest, I don't think I'd seen a non-League game before and I actually thought Headington was somewhere near London.

Arthur Turner: After a period of time, 18 months or a couple of years, I made him captain, because he always set a good example. I think Ron on the field was like I used to be. I had enough gusto in me to get on to players, get on to their backs, and they could get on to my back. He was always my captain. At the start of the season I didn't have to say who my captain was, and whenever he put his shirt on you always felt you were a goal up.

Ron Atkinson: I think the first year, Geoff Denial, who was a pal of mine, had been captain. At the start of the second year, I think I was about 20 at the time, and Arthur Turner said he was going to make me captain, because he thought that I'd got the qualities for captain. Consequently I think I was skipper for about 11 or 12 years. One thing he always said to me, one of the arts of captaincy, was that even if you're not playing particularly well, you've still got to be brave enough and bold enough to make sure the others are at it, and that's something I've tried to imbue into anybody that's captained sides under me as a manager. I captained the side 200 times or more at the Manor Ground, and I bet I only lost the toss a maximum of 15 times. It was always the ritual: we won the toss and we kicked up the hill first. If we were a goal down at half-time and coming down the hill, we never worried. If it was all-square, or if we were leading, coming down the hill, we always fancied our chance. We always thought, "We'll just storm all over people." People speak to me about those days, and they say they used to hate coming to play against us.

Fred Ellis: Ron Atkinson was not a great man as far as skill goes but he played as much as he could, as hard as he could, as long as he could. I can remember him coming out in the second half with a headband on. Well, it wasn't really a headband, it was just a bandage around his head soaked with blood, and he still played in the second half.

Geoff Denial: I remember playing in this practice-match, as an inside-forward, and I've laid this ball off to someone and turned to take the return, and he just hit me. I couldn't get out the way. He was just like a brick wall. He was so solid. I could understand why the opposition didn't like to play against him. He had a few nicknames, like "Tank" and "Fatty" and one or two more, but he could put it about. I recall Ron, when he was captain, running out with his shorts pulled up to the sides of his legs. He looked more like a weight-lifter than a footballer.

Jim Barron: He was never the best player in the world. What he was was the best captain I ever played with in terms of motivation, passion for the game and wanting to be a winner. He had all those things wrapped up in one. He was a good leader of the team. He didn't mind who he had a go at or who he stuck up for. He would rollick you one minute and stick up for you the next if that was the situation. Overall, I think he was very, very instrumental in Oxford's success.

Ron Atkinson: Cyril Beavon was right-back. Well, he was just right-back every week. They used to have the team-list, it used to say "first team" and they just used to put Bev on for 42 games a season. He was a steady Eddie of a full-back. Brilliant feet. I always used to say I did all his running and covering for him but he'd got two great feet, and he was Yorkshire, so he could be a little bit nasty when necessary. A very, very accurate kicker of the ball.

Colin Harrington: Cyril Beavon was a fixture at the club from when I joined until right into the Second Division. Cyril was one of these "smokers for England". He always had a cigarette. You'd get on the team coach and the first thing he'd do would be to light up. He'd have a cigarette practically on the go until five minutes before kick-off time. That was until Ken Fish arrived. With Cyril, it would be cards all the way there, and cards all the way back. Nothing interrupted it. He was a terrific player.

Ron Atkinson: Pat Quartermain at left-back. Pat was a good pal of mine. I used to wind him up, because he was quite an aggressive footballer. Sometimes, if the winger was giving him a little bit of a chasing, I used to call him all sorts of names, like "You're a bit of a fairy" and this, that and the other. I bet the winger never went past him next time. Pat would put him over the gravel, then look at me, and I'd start laughing at him and say, "Well done, Pat." He was a good character.

Colin Harrington: Pat was, like me, one of the few local boys in the team. He was a very enthusiastic player, very sturdy in the tackle. When people are thrown together you find this camaraderie, and, again, he was a terrific personality, a good laugh.

Jack Fallows: I think the best centre-half I've seen up there is Maurice Kyle. When he headed the ball, he didn't just head it anywhere, he headed it to one of his players and sent them on the attack, and Maurice was always there when there was trouble in the penalty area. His anticipation was terrific. He had the height, he had the stature, he had the ability. It's a pity really that he didn't go to a higher class of football.

Ken Fish: If ever there was a gentleman in football, it was Maurice Kyle. He should never have been a professional footballer. He should have been an artist or something like that. He was a great player, plenty of skill and ability, but he would never go in and tackle a player. He was lacking the drive to go in and hit him. I said, "Why don't you stand up, don't let them knock you about." "No, I don't play football like that." How Wolves let him go, I don't know.

Arthur Turner: Maurice Kyle was probably one of my best signings. I can remember Billy Wright ringing me up about Maurice Kyle. Billy was manager of Arsenal then, but I never wanted to sell Maurice Kyle.

Colin Clarke: He was the epitome of everything that a good player should be. For a big man he was tremendously well-balanced. Lovely feet. And a beautiful nature to go along with it. Arthur always used to say of him, "Maurice, if you were a mean bugger, you'd be a hell of a player." He always referred to him as a gentle giant.

Ron Atkinson: "Noddy" Jones used to fluctuate between left-half and inside-left. He'd have a long spell at left-half, where he was a hard worker and a decent passer. But he'd got this nose for a goal, and every so often, when we had a bit of a problem with goalscoring, he'd move up into the inside-left position and always weighed in with a few goals. In fact, he did it in the Cup run, with the two goals against Blackburn.

Ken Fish: Graham Atkinson was one of the best players I've ever seen. He liked his fag. His only weakness was that he didn't like training. But he should have had more caps than Billy Wright, and Billy Wright had over a hundred.

Arthur Turner: Graham Atkinson got so much criticism, and yet Graham could go past players as if they weren't there. He had so much ability. Then he'd drop his head when he made a mistake. He'd got this little tendency to drop his head and be a bit sheepish, and the crowd murdered him at times, yet look what he did for the club.

Ron Atkinson: I've always said that if he'd have had my drive and aggression he would have played many times for England. His ability was unquestionable and he had a knack of scoring goals. Sometimes it appeared that he wasn't as totally committed to the game as maybe I was. He used to frustrate me because I could see what great talent he'd got and on the field I probably used to get on to him more than any other player. But I think that was basically because I wanted to extract his ability out of him. He always says to me, "I couldn't have been that bad, I played nearly 500 games."

Sandy Brewer: We had Bud Houghton, of course. He was a friend of Ron Atkinson. Physically he was a strong chap. He could bustle his way through. He wasn't the most skilful player but he certainly had the physique and in those days you could probably make more use of it than you can nowadays. He was very useful. Yes, he got some good goals in that first season in the League.

Ron Atkinson: He was one of our gang. Big Bud. He'd seen something on television one day. He'd seen di Stefano play for Real Madrid on television, and di Stefano had this habit of going back and taking the ball off his own players' toes. We're playing this game at Brentford and Bud starts doing this to me. He did it three times. I said, "Bud, if you come back and do that once more, I shall volley you straight in the stand." He said, "Well, I'm just trying to do what di Stefano does." I said, "Well, he scores as well, so get up the other end of the field and see if you can do that."

Colin Harrington: Bud was one of those players that Arthur must have dreamed about. He was everything – big, tremendous shot – but he was never able to come to terms with the game at Oxford. Arthur Turner used to say that if he applied himself he could play for his country, and we used to laugh because Bud was born in India.

Arthur Turner: Look at John Shuker, the service he did for Oxford, a lad that came down on trial from Manchester. He came as an outside-left and I converted him into a left-back. A better lad never put a pair of football boots on. A great fellow. A great club man. He loved the game, and he could play the game. A beautiful left foot. He never cost us a bean.

John Shuker: I was playing in Manchester, in the local league, and there was a chap up there who was friendly with Arthur Turner. He saw me play a few times and asked me to come down to play a trial match. I played two or three times in the Reserves, and at the end of that season they asked me to play as a part-time professional. It was the last year in the Southern League. At the end of the season [1961-62] I was given a free-transfer but I played in the end-of-season friendly against Bury and after that I signed back on, and I stayed for 17 years.

Football League Signings, 1962-65

Ron Atkinson: One of the biggest characters we ever had was a goalkeeper called Harry Fearnley, who was a big Yorkshireman, back to the days when they played with the big roll-neck fishermen's sweater. In those days you could sign virtually up to kick-off time, and I remember we were playing at Newport and Harry had just been signed. This big Yorkshireman came out, and we had a goal-kick, so we all ran up to the halfway-line. Harry was about 6 ft 2 in, and about 14 st. Left-footed, he kicked it about five yards outside the penalty-box. We hadn't realised that he was a hopeless kicker, so we were all running back towards our own goalmouth then. Then they had a free-kick on the edge of the box and I started lining up our defensive wall, and Harry was shouting something, and I honestly hadn't a clue what he was on about. In the end, I turned round to Cyril Beavon. I said, "Hey, Bev, you're from Yorkshire, what *is* he talking about?" He was "ee, by gum," I hadn't a clue.

Arthur Turner: I'd seen Harry Fearnley play a few times for Huddersfield Town, and I'd always thought he was a very capable 'keeper. The manager at that time was an old Sheffield United player [Eddie Boot]. I rang him up a few times about Harry Fearnley. "Oh, no, I couldn't sell Harry Fearnley," he said. Eventually he rang me. He said, "Are you still interested in Fearnley, Arthur, because he's available." I went to watch him play and I signed him. I think I gave about £2,500. Getting properties for players was proving a bit expensive, so we never got him a property. It soured Harry off a lot. He would have come down to live in Oxford, but I had to let him live in Huddersfield.

Ron Atkinson: I remember one time, at half-time, we were in the dressing-room and Arthur Turner's having some words, and all of a sudden someone rushed in the dressing-room and said, "Harry, your missus is on the phone." Apparently the chimney was on fire at home in Huddersfield.

Colin Harrington: Harry always had some fanciful story to tell. If he came down by train, he never sat next to AN Other, it was Simon Templar or

Roger Moore. He was always pulling jokes.

Ken Fish: After one match, I said to him, "How is it that you let the goal go through your legs." He said, "As I went down to get that ball, being tall, 6 ft 2 in, I bent down and just as I was going to take the ball some silly bugger in the London Road end, behind the goal, took an apple core and slung it and it hit the ball and the ball ricocheted and when I went down my legs went apart and it went through my legs."

Cyril Beavon: No-one ever knew how old Harry was. I'm from Yorkshire and I watched Harry playing for Huddersfield Town Reserves when I was still at school, and Harry reckoned he was younger than me!

Sam Cook: Harry Fearnley was one of my favourites. He'd been a League goalkeeper for some time and he'd seen everything – I think he'd done everything – and he was an entertainer. Not the greatest 'keeper, far from the greatest, but an entertainer, a crowd-pleaser. He enjoyed it, which was what it was all about.

Fred Ellis: He played football when centre-forwards bowled goalkeepers into the back of the net. I can remember some great battles between him and Pat Terry, the Reading centre-forward. They didn't get along too well! There were punches thrown, punches that nobody saw unless you were looking for them (and we always were of course). Pat Terry was a hard man, and Reading and Oxford, like Swindon and Oxford, were bitter rivals.

Colin Harrington: The signing that seemed to start the act rolling was Colin Booth. A big name. He'd been at Forest and Wolves. A really class player. I think the players themselves then started to believe in it. Colin Booth was a very unassuming player. You'd never think he'd been a quality player until he got on the field. He was a terrific passer of the ball, both feet, with terrific control. I think he scored 24 goals in his first season.

Ron Atkinson: For me, the best football player I ever played with while I was there was Colin Booth. He was inside-right ahead of me – I was right-half – and he had played in the Wolves Championship side. Technically he was a great player. His career [at Oxford] was only 18 months. He got cut short with a very bad injury, but while he was there he was brilliant in terms of passing on knowledge. I was 23, I thought I knew everything, but Boothy was very intelligent, and I learned a lot from him.

Tim Sparrowhawk: Colin Harrington was an exciting but frustrating player. Some days terrible, some days mercurial. I suppose the most recent equivalent was George Lawrence, in that mould, on the wing. Colin Harrington was famous for the unexpected. The dribble would often continue with the ball left somewhere behind. That was one of the characteristics of Flash's play. In other games he was just out of this world.

John Shuker: Sometimes he'd go down the wing and cross the ball and we weren't there because we weren't quick enough. There was a little gate at the bottom of the London Road end, on the left. I think he was running so quick some days that he used to go to the Britannia and have a pint and come back. They used to say, "Give him the ball and try to stop him before he hits the fence." He was a good lad. We had some good times together.

Ken Fish: He held the schoolboy championship of 100 yards and he could really go down the wing. There was always a wag at the bottom of the London Road end, and he used to turn round and say, "Here comes Harrington. Open the gates. Let him go."

Ron Atkinson: Colin was supposed to be the brain-box. He'd got 15 'O' levels. It was unfortunate that he never had one in "Crossing the Ball". He could have done with that. Lightning quick. He could run from one end of the pitch to the other and sometimes further, which wasn't much help when you needed him to cross it. He was certainly one of the quickest players I've ever seen.

Arthur Turner: A section of the crowd got at Colin. A lot of people used to think he was a bloody comedian. I think some of the players used to go "Oh, dearie me" when he'd miss a sitter. But I always used to think that if we got the ball out to Colin, then you're no sooner on defence than you're on attack.

Ron Atkinson: We played Fulham one night and they had George Cohen, who was the England full-back, and he absolutely buried Cohen. The England full-back didn't know whether he was coming or going at one time. Then we played Blackpool when Jimmy Armfield was also the England right-full-back and Colin absolutely destroyed him. But you would play against someone like Watford with Ken Furphy at right-back, who was about 76 at the time, and we'd say, "Go on, Colin, you'll see them off today," and he wouldn't have a kick. He was a complex character. A great lad.

Chris Fallows: He was a bit before my time, Harrington, but I remember I was up the Manor once and somebody picked up the ball in the centre-circle and they hit this pass right out to the wing and it was to no one and it went straight out for a throw. This bloke next to me said, "I think he was looking for the ghost of Colin Harrington."

Team Spirit

Colin Harrington: If you go back and look at those players – Maurice Kyle, Cyril Beavon, Pat Quartermain, Ronnie, Tony Jones, John Shuker, myself, Graham Atkinson – they all had lots of years service. Teams these days don't seem to have that sort of continuity. I think that in itself must have some effect on the team pattern. Players who know one another. You build up this respect for one another. You may not be friends, but it's more than friendship. You know players, you know their strengths and weaknesses, and you respect them for it.

Ron Atkinson: A group of lads came together, and the nucleus of seven or eight of us were around 19 or 20, and we just felt that whoever we played we could beat. If we ever went out anywhere, on an away trip or anything, we all went out as a group. There were no cliques. We all stuck together. I think that came through on the field.

Geoff Denial: We'd go out socially as well. There used to be the Northgate Tavern, which is now a music store. It was a meeting-place for us. We'd go there Saturday nights with the wives and have a good night out. We had parties and things like that. We were very closely knit.

John Shuker: We were always having laughs and jokes in those days because we knew each other so well. Quite often we'd have a few jokes, and then we'd have a go at each other. We'd nearly get to blows sometimes in the dressing-room, at half-time, then full-time we'd have a go at one another. But once we were changed and in the bar, having a drink, everything was forgotten. We were just mates again.

Colin Harrington: There was quite a racing fraternity. There was Cyril Beavon, Peter Knight, John Shuker and Ray Colfar. On Fridays you could always tell where they were going because they came with binoculars. They'd be looking at their watches, thinking, "Well, it'll take us an hour to get to Newbury. Will we miss the first race?" Or Cheltenham. They used to take bets on where Ray Colfar would have his copy of the *Sporting Life*. Would he have it in his pocket, or would he be reading it, or would he have it under one of his arms? There was another one called Ronnie

Spelman. His main concern was racing, and then, if there was time, he'd think about football.

Geoff Denial: We got up to all sorts of things, things that I daren't tell you about, especially on away matches. I remember when we were in the Fourth Division. We went to Manchester, I forget who we were playing. But two players disappeared at midnight and didn't come back until four o'clock in the morning. They were night-clubbing. And the two players in question played really well the following day. There was a hose-pipe at the Manor, to wash the old bath out (when it was under the little corner-stand there). If you were in the bath any longer than the rest of them you would get hammered with this high-spray hose-pipe. And you'd come back and find things in your shoes. It was very enjoyable in those years.

Edmund Gibbs: Everyone smoked then, including the players, and I was standing at a bar somewhere and Bud Houghton said, "Will you have one of my cigarettes?" He offered me one. The players returned to the corner and I could see them all looking at me, and I thought, "What are they up to?" And suddenly an enormous explosion. Of course, he'd put an explosive pellet in the middle and there was this cigarette all splayed up and me black all over, whilst all the players were having hysterics in the corner.

7 *"Everything seemed to happen every three years"*

RISING THROUGH THE DIVISIONS, 1964-1969

Throughout the sixties, the nucleus of Arthur Turner's team remained constant. New signings included Jim Barron, Mickey Bullock, Colin Clarke, Rodney Smithson, Ken Skeen and David Sloan. After being promoted to the Third in 1964-65, a magnificent late run brought United the Third Division Championship in 1967-68. In the Second Division, United struggled through 1968-69 until new manager Ron Saunders arrived. Bottom of the table in March, United escaped relegation by three points.

THE SAME PLAYERS

John Shuker: In those early years, everything seemed to happen every three years. We got into the League. Three years after that we won promotion and three years after that we won promotion again into the Second. With the same team. We didn't have many new players.

Cyril Beavon: I think that was our strength. We kept virtually the same team for five or six years. Obviously you must get better as time goes on.

We actually had six players from the Southern League days who got to the Second Division – myself, Ron and Graham Atkinson, Maurice Kyle, Pat Quartermain and John Shuker.

Promotion from the Fourth Division, 1964-65

Tim Sparrowhawk: I remember a game I missed. It was the only game I missed that season. I smashed a neighbour's window and missed the 1-1 draw with Southport. I remember that more than the games that I saw, because of the disappointment. The one I do remember was against Darlington, the last home game, a massive crowd, and Cyril Beavon scored a penalty near the end of the game. There was this great pitch invasion at the end – it would be frowned upon now no doubt but it was harmless stuff – and the next day I went to my aunt's and there was a picture in one of the Sunday newspapers of this Oxford crowd on the pitch, and I thought, "I was one of them."

Ron Atkinson: Cyril Beavon scored a penalty to win 1-0, and, like it happens, there was a radio message that the other team had been beaten, which meant we were up, but it hadn't actually happened, so we had to wait until the following Tuesday until we realised we were up.

Third Division Champions, 1967-68

Colin Clarke: I didn't really find my feet in that era until the promotion year, 67-68, when I believe I scored about eight goals in the midfield role. We beat Walsall 4-0 at the Manor and they were top of the League at the time. We absolutely slaughtered them, and at that point we were aware that we'd gain momentum. We weren't really in contention until Eastertime when suddenly we were flying past everyone and we won the title in the home straight, as it were. I remember Walsall had a blinding run till Christmas. So did Torquay. But we swept past them all and we beat Bury for the top spot.

Colin Harrington: In the early part of that particular season I had an exploratory operation on my knee. I had visions of not coming back. It was when operations on your knee were a bit more serious. And of course after a certain length of time of being out of the side, teams tend to play without you. You're not part of the pattern anymore. Arthur suddenly put me in the side about that time they started getting a winning combination together. We went to places like Colchester and won. We got a result over at Swindon; Don Rogers had one of his quietest games against John Lloyd. Don Rogers was probably the finest uncapped player I've ever seen. There was a lot of feeling between Swindon and Oxford in those days, and getting a result over there was a tremendous achievement. It was a typical derby. I don't suppose I had more than three kicks of the ball and two of those were kicking in.

Nick Harris: We used to go to a lot of away games then, but I particularly remember a Friday night at Stockport. United won 4-0, and I remember Colin Harrington having a marvellous game. That virtually clinched promotion. It was a marvellous night. Mickey Bullock was centre-forward. I remember he scored some very important goals for United at the time.

Colin Harrington: Don't kid yourself, going through the promotions at Oxford was a very arduous and really mentally difficult time. It's always easy to be at clubs and just win and lose but to win when you had to win, that is the difficulty, and it's the character that counts. When you've been through these promotion hauls, it's a shared experience, it's a binding feeling.

The Second Division, 1968-69

Ron Atkinson: Colin Clarke was a great character. He was a super player as well, Clarkey, but he was a great character. We'd just won the Third Division, and the following season we were going into our first Second Division match. On the Friday morning the television people were coming up to do a little line on us. So we're knocking a few balls about, waiting for the cameras to come, and Clarkey said, "I'm fed up, I'm going in." So he went in, and we didn't see him again for about three weeks. He went home to Scotland. He's supposed to have gone home for his mother's cooking or something.

Colin Clarke: I was a bit impetuous. There was no two ways about it. I'd met a nice girlfriend in Prestwick, near the airport. She was an air-hostess. We spent the summer together and I came back to pre-season training. I was a bit love-sick. After a week or ten days I was a bit bored by it all. I was getting a bit miffed by the same old routine, going up Shotover hills and all the rest of it. I just wasn't in the right frame of mind. Being a bit headstrong, I thought, "Well, they won't miss me for a couple of days," and I just jumped on a plane. I flew up to Prestwick to see this girlfriend, thinking it wouldn't be a big deal. I didn't realise the commotion it would cause. I'm up there in Prestwick and I phoned my Mum to see if she's alright, and she says, "There's ten press-men outside the door. They're banging the doors down. Where are you?" I had to jump in a car and drive to Clydebank where my Mum was and explain to the press-men. Of course the following day, the headlines were, "Soccer player goes back because he's missing his Mum's cooking." I had to live with that for the rest of that season and far beyond.

Ron Atkinson: He came back and we played against Aston Villa at Villa Park. We get a free-kick on the edge of the penalty box, and I'm shaping up, because I used to like taking the old free-kicks, and Clarkey comes running up and says, "I'll tell you what, Ron, I've been practising this one in Scotland all summer." I said, "What are you talking about?" He said, "Come on, I'll show you." It was in the days before the Holte End at Villa Park was covered, and he hit a shot that virtually cleared the whole of the Holte End. It went further than those astronauts went from Cape Canaveral. I said, "That's what you've been practising," and he just burst out laughing. He was an excellent player, but sometimes he was a bit zany.

John Shuker: In the Third and Fourth, if you were winning 1-0 or 2-0, you always won the game. When we went in the Second Division, the teams never gave up. You knew you had to play for 90 minutes, and we lost a lot of games when we were winning, and we thought, "The game's all over, five minutes to go," and bang, bang, we end up losing.

Fred Ellis: I saw Jim Barron bundled into the back of the net, and it's the only goal I've ever seen like that. I can't remember the chap's name, but I remember that it was in the first days of substitutes and he ran from that bench to the goal just as Jim Barron was collecting the ball and knocked him into the net and got a goal out of it.

Jim Barron: We played Bury. We were defending the bottom end and they got a corner. There wasn't a Bury player anywhere in the area, and the lad took the corner and I went out, and caught it, and I thought, "Good catch, Jim." I looked around, and Alex Dawson was running at me. He must be one of the ugliest players who has ever played the game, and one of the strongest. I'm sure people remember it as well. He hit me as my feet touched the floor in the six-yard box and I never touched the ground between the six-yard line and the goal. Whether that was the slope or the way he hit me, I don't know, but the referee gave a goal. He'd be sent off these days. That was a painful experience.

John Shuker: We played Southampton in the Cup at the Manor, when Southampton had Mick Channon and Terry Paine and those sort of players and we were leading 1-0 with about 20 seconds to go. Ken Skeen was centre-forward at the time. Jimmy Barron had the ball in his hands and for some unknown reason we'd pushed up to the halfway-line and Ken Skeen decided to run back to the edge of the box and pick the ball up off Jimmy...

Jim Barron: I threw a ball out to Skeeny on the right-hand side, and he got robbed and it was crossed, and Davies scored. Well, they keep saying he scored, but he didn't score actually, because I still think I saved it. The referee gave a goal anyway and it meant a replay and we got beat down at Southampton the following week. Ron [Atkinson] wasn't too pleased in the dressing-room at me for throwing the ball out to Skeeny. I remember him nearly dropping me. He's done things like that. I remember him getting Kevin Keelan, the goalkeeper at Norwich, over a wall once at the bottom end at Oxford, because somebody had had a go at Graham. If anybody was in trouble, Ron was the first person there. I think, as captain, he looked upon it as *his* team.

Tim Sparrowhawk: I remember the signings that weren't so good. The infamous one of Ray Gaston comes to mind. I think the *Oxford Mail* report said that United had snatched him from under the noses of Manchester United and Everton. That was a bit worrying in itself. I think the evidence on the field confirmed the worries. Probably one of the worst players I've seen in a United shirt, along with other strikers such as Adrian O'Dowd and Ollie Kearns.

Jack Fallows: Oh, Ray Gaston. Oh, my God. He was from Coleraine. I remember we went down to Southampton in the Cup. There was a substitution, and Ray Gaston came on. "Come on, Ray, up Coleraine." And he hit the corner-flag.

Colin Clarke: We found it hard, early doors, in the Second Division, because a lot of the players had peaked and were starting to go over the top at the same time. Had they arrived at that point three or four years before, they would probably have taken us on again, because they were First Division players in my eyes. We were struggling, and we didn't have the back-up, so that season was hard. Maurice Kyle dislocated his shoulder at Southampton, against Ron Davies, which was the beginning of the end for Maurice. He really didn't recover from that. I got good press after the game, saying that I'd handled Ron Davies very well and looked a natural for the position. Arthur then came to me and said, "Would you play the position?" I said, "While Maurice is injured, I'm happy to help the club out, but I don't want to be thought of as a centre-half long-term." But things just went from there.

John Shuker: Colin played in midfield on the left, and he'll probably tell you himself that he wasn't a midfield player. He didn't like the running that was involved in it. I remember once when I was left-back and "Nobby" [Clarke] was the left-half. We'd only been playing 20 minutes and I went down the left wing. He gave me the ball, I centred it and the 'keeper caught the ball and kicked the ball out. As I ran back, I ran past Nobby and shouted at him to get back. His words were, "You must be joking, Shuke, I'm knackered." And that was after 20 minutes.

Colin Harrington: I tend to remember, more than the good times, some of the bad times. When we came back from Cardiff after losing 5-0. I couldn't believe it. Five-nil. We never even got into their half of the field. It was unbelievable.

John Shuker: Before the game at Cardiff, Arthur Turner said to Colin [Clarke], "Look, this Barrie Jones, stick on him, he's a good player." And Colin said, "Look Boss, that's not my game." So he went to Ronnie [Atkinson] and said to Ronnie, "Look, Ronnie, this chap Jones, you stick on him." "Alright, Boss," he said. Unbeknown to those two, he'd also gone to someone else and told him to mark this lad Jones, who was a good player. Well, when we get on the park, I'm left-back and as we lined up I've got three men stood in front of me. They looked at one another and said, "What are you doing?" "I'm marking Jones." "Well, so am I." In the end nobody marked him and he scored a hat trick.

Colin Harrington: We did that trip on the cheap. We went down in a coach – directors, first team, reserve, all the ancillary staff – and it was standing room only. Cardiff scored within a minute of the kick-off, and Arthur Turner blamed that on Kenny Skeen and he was only a substitute!

John Shuker: It was a little bit icy and we all went out before the game and decided what studs we were going to wear. Jimmy Barron was in goals, and Jimmy had decided to wear rubbers for some unknown reason. We hadn't been playing more than two or three minutes and Jimmy decided he was going to change his boots, so he signalled to the bench. Arthur and Ken Fish said, "Ken, give him Jimmy his boots," and Ken Skeen went off round the track. As he got just behind the goals, Cardiff scored from about 30 yards. While we were kicking off, Jimmy changed his boots. As Ken got back, Arthur gave him a rocket, saying it was his fault that Jimmy had let one in, that he was talking to him behind the goals at the time.

Arthur Turner: Things were alright and then one director resigned and another director came on to the board. He knew more about the game than I did, sort of thing. It went on for a while. There was no animosity, but I couldn't take that. I was the manager. Eventually it happened. I went to one of the board meetings, and he suddenly decided that I should become general manager and they should employ a team manager. The incredible thing was that I was already general manager and I was already the team manager. I had been in control. Eventually they split the job. I became general manager, and they appointed a team manager to take over the whole football side. Although I stayed for several months, I would never accept that, because I was a tee-totaller and I never intended to mix drinks in the board-room and the tea-room. I wasn't having that, so then I used to go to watch players at other matches.

Under Ron Saunders, 1969

Gerry Summers: In the January they decided to advertise for a manager, and there were three of us involved. I never found out the third person, but Ron Saunders was definitely one, because we chatted at the football club before they interviewed us, and he got the job. I always remember the old chairman, Ron Coppock, who was a great fellow. I don't know what he said to Ron Saunders, but when I was in for the interview he said, "I don't expect you to perform a miracle and keep us in the league." But Ron did. He performed a miracle.

Colin Harrington: Ron Saunders came when hope of staying in the Second Division had really gone. I think we were five points adrift of Fulham and the confidence had gone in players – they were getting ready for the Third Division.

Colin Clarke: He was a shock to the system because Arthur had always been so laid back in his manner. Blunt but laid back. We more-or-less just got on with it. When Saunders came he was a disciplinarian, and tremendously hard, physically. The intensity of the training was hard on older players, who'd had a part-time existence some years before. He implemented a very basic system which involved sheer endeavour and hard work. It was a modern-day Wimbledon effort where we just booted the ball up and squeezed. But it did the trick. It was a long slog, but we finally avoided the drop. And we were all grateful for it in the end. It stabilised the club and we survived for the next seven or eight years in the Second Division, which we would never have done had Saunders not arrived at that point.

John Shuker: Ron Saunders came with about 10 or 12 games to go, and I went back up front and fortunately started to score a few goals. Ron's idea of the game was that we would not lose, which we needed at that time. Myself and Ken Skeen were up front, and he used to say to the midfield players, "Just push it up front, let Shuke and Skeeny run," and the back four were not allowed over the halfway-line, so it meant that me and Skeeny were running for 90 minutes non-stop. I remember one particular time. I think it was Hull, away from home. Jim Barron kicked the ball out of his hands. I went up with the centre-half, and headed the ball on, and the shout from the bench was "Now you've headed it, *chase* it." I think I could have been an Olympic runner that year! But everything worked out right at the end of the season.

Colin Harrington: When we got into the Second Division Shuke came into his own. A tremendously versatile player with incredible service. He did a lot of his good time during the really difficult times in the Second Division.

Sandy Brewer: It didn't matter where John Shuker played, he always seemed to do quite well. I remember him most for a game at Fulham. I didn't very often go away but I went to this game at Fulham because it was a crucial game – both teams were in the relegation battle. Shuker was playing centre-forward that day and he scored quite early in the game. And Fulham absolutely bombarded the Oxford goal for the rest of the game. How Fulham failed to score I shall never know. Oxford won 1-0. They saved themselves at the end of that season and I think Fulham got relegated.

Jim Barron: Possibly at the time the team wasn't good enough for the Second Division, but we stopped in, again by the skin of our teeth. I remember a game at Fulham where we scored in the first minute and then defended for 89 minutes. I saved a header off Cliff Jones, well into the second half when I think if they'd have scored then, we could have struggled. It was possibly one of the best saves I ever made.

John Shuker: I think I scored two on the Good Friday against Blackburn at the Manor. I scored seven or eight in about eight games, which were really the most important goals I scored for the club because those goals kept them in the Second Division. They weren't spectacular goals. They were tap-ins, most of them, which I was fortunate to be on the end of.

Colin Harrington: It went right up to the last match of the season against Sheffield United. We won it 1-0. I think the 'keeper was Alan Hodgkinson. I think we played reasonably well, but only scored one goal, and that was it. I didn't score that many, but I remember I did score a goal that day. I think Ken Skeen was a bit upset about it, because it only dribbled in!

Colin Clarke: Ron Saunders promised us that everything was going to change, that the contracts would be looked into and we'd all be given good rises if we could survive and stay up. He dangled that carrot all season. At the end of the season he wasn't forthcoming with the rises he had promised, but he badgered and bullied the players into signing contracts. A lot of players at that stage of their career were quite happy to do that, but I didn't. I rebelled, as I often did in those days! He said to me, "You're the only one left to sign. When are you signing the contract?" I said, "I think I've explained to you. I'm not signing that contract as it stands. I think I'm worth more than that. If you want to review your situation, I'm happy to help you." He said, "I don't think you understand what I'm getting at. I want you to sign that contract as it stands." So I said, "I won't be signing it as it stands." He said, "Let me rephrase it. If you don't sign that contract, you'll be back every day during the summer, running on that track." I said, "In that case, don't phone me, I'll phone you." And he leapt across his desk and tried to grab me by the throat. The veins in his neck were popping out. I turned and sprinted out the door, ran straight down to the London Road end, round the back of the stand and out of the ground. He frightened the living daylights out of people. He was a menacing figure when he got angry. The lads were in hysterics when they saw me scampering down and he was screaming after me. That was the beginning of the end of our relationship. In fact, he left about a week or ten days after that.

Ron Atkinson: We were training up Shotover one morning and he got a phone call. He cleared off and left us up Shotover. And he'd gone to Norwich.

Colin Clarke: We had a meeting on the Tuesday, I think it was, saying there had been speculation about his future but he had pledged himself to the club and we could look forward to the future together. Then it was the Wednesday or the Thursday that he held a second meeting. He said, "Well, lads, I know we had a meeting the other day, where I stressed that my involvement with the club would be for the next however-many years and we looked forward to a future together, but there's some things in life that have come to me easily and some things that haven't. I've got a wonderful wife and a lovely family. I enjoy the work that I do. But there's one thing missing, and that is money. Norwich City have just offered me a lovely contract, so I'll be saying goodbye to you." With that he presented us all with a little pewter tankard, inscribed, "Thank you, from Ron Saunders." And he walked out the door.

Penalties

Colin Harrington: We never had a consistent penalty-taker. The person who always should have taken penalties was Cyril Beavon, a wonderful striker of the ball. The trouble with penalties, they arise at inopportune times, they're never when you're winning 4-0 or 5-0. It's always when it's 1-0 to the other side and this will give you the draw. After you've missed a few penalties it becomes very difficult.

Ron Atkinson: Bev was quite a good spot-kick taker, but funnily enough, I think he missed a couple. I remember him missing one at Reading in a big game one night. I think he stubbed his toe and the goalkeeper had to walk forward and dive on it. I took one, sent the goalie the wrong way but missed. Skeeny took one against Birmingham and missed that.

John Shuker: We were kicking towards the nurses' home end, as we used to call it, the Cuckoo Lane end, and we had a penalty. Skeeny picked the ball up and he said, "I'll take this, I'll take this," so we all said, "Go on then, Ken, you take it." He ran up and he hit the ball well. He hit it so well that it was still rising when it went out of the ground.

The Mascot

Eric Kowalski: My Dad, Frank Kowalski, was the mascot for years. He started out as a cheerleader in the early 1960s, going round the ground before the game and at half-time. He used to sell badges, rosettes, lottery tickets, gollywogs, anything that made money for the club. His life revolved around Oxford United. One time my Dad was coming out of

Pressed Steel and he was knocked off his push-bike. He was concussed and it turned out that he had a broken arm. Someone found him and rushed him off to the old John Radcliffe Hospital. They kept him there, set his arm and put it in plaster. As he'd been concussed, they wanted to keep him in, but United had a Wednesday game so he discharged himself. My mother was frantic, worrying about where he was, and then he arrived home at 7.30 with his arm in plaster. Mother said, "My God, what's happened?" He said, "I haven't got time now – I've got to get changed and go up the Manor." It wasn't until ten o'clock that night that she found out what had happened.

Pranks and Superstitions

Colin Harrington: In football you spend an awful lot of time looking at the clock, either waiting for three o'clock or waiting for half-past seven. If you can imagine, you go into a hotel and you're in there at say five o'clock and you're hanging around and the clock goes slowly. The players who make all the difference are those who take your mind off things and get things in the right perspective. Later on in my career we used to meet at a hotel just off the Iffley Road. We used to get there just before 12 for lunch, watch television until half-past two and then drive to the ground. That was putting a more professional image on things. Players always used to be playing tricks on one another and – I suppose it was wrong really – they tended to pick on certain players. One of the really good players was Davie Sloan, a right winger. He was only sort of 5 ft nothing but scored a tremendous amount of goals with his head. Very brave and quite a devastating player, but he was the typical Irishman. I remember them saying to David that one of the shops down in Oxford was giving players an offer on shoes. David rolled in there, tried these shoes on, and then he proudly announced, "I'm from Oxford United." And the bloke said, "Yes?" They used to catch David out no end of times.

Ron Atkinson: His wife said, "Don't ever trust anything Ron tells you in future." We used to have him turning up on Sundays for training. We told him that after training we were all off to Brighton for a few days' special training. He'd pack his bags and turn up, and everyone would start laughing at him: "What are you doing, Sloany?" I remember somebody putting pebbles in his hubcaps. Then he said, "I've got something wrong wi' me car." We said, "Take it to the garage, there's a friend of ours called Mick Annic. He'll look after you." So he's in the garage looking for some bloke named Mick Annic.

Colin Harrington: People like Graham and Ronnie, Tony Jones, that was their whole modus operandi really. They'd be laughing until maybe five minutes before they went out and then they'd focus. The other thing I remember was them taking their false teeth out, the last thing before they went out. None of them had a full set of teeth. They took them out and there was a great big gap there, which always amused me.

John Shuker: Everybody is superstitious in their own little way. I always liked to come out last, but when I was captain I had to come out first. I think Graham liked to come out near the back. We all had our own little superstitions. You'd put your boots on last or you'd put your shorts on last or you wouldn't put your shirt on until you were coming through the door.

Jim Barron: If we'd been on a winning streak, I'd wear the same suit, the same underpants, the lot, for each game. Before the game I always used to draw a line, from the middle of the six-yard box down to the goal-line, touch the floor, touch the bar and kick both posts. I always did that before the game. I think I created a record once because I got booked for drawing a line before the game started. That was at the bottom end at Oxford.

Five-a-side

Colin Clarke: We were a bit like country-hicks in the early days. We were invited to our first indoor five-a-side tournament, and we knew nothing about it until Ron Atkinson came in and said to a few of us, "Clarkey, Colin Harrington, Mickey Bullock, Davie Sloan, Graham, myself, Maurice Kyle. We're going down to Bracknell. We're hiring a mini-bus and Colin Harrington's going to drive it." "What is this? It sounds like a right old bodge-up." "No, all the top clubs in the country are in this indoor tournament." "Indoor? I haven't played any indoor football." We all turned up and sure enough the skip was already packed. Colin Harrington drives us all the way down in this mini-bus. We get in this big arena. Sponsorship was creeping into the game then so players were wearing flashy yellow-and-blue and red-and-white shirts, glossy shorts, and brilliant Adidas black-and-white trainers. We're looking at the teams warming up in the arena, thinking, "Look at the kit they've got, I wonder what's in store for us." We're lugging this skip in there. Ron goes in and says, "I won't be playing today, I'll be acting manager. I'll pick the team. Clarkey, open the skip. Get the kit out and hang it up." I was the youngest. I couldn't believe it when I opened the skip. It's got the old faded orange shirts with the round necks, but the elastic had gone in the necks, so instead of them being tight round the neck, they were dropping on the shoulders. Like women's halter-neck things. And the sleeves were so short they were up to our elbows, because they'd shrunk so often in the wash. Then I looked at what we'd got for shorts. I dug further down the kit and out comes these butterfly shorts, nylon shorts that hang about three feet off your legs, flapping. We had cotton socks that had shrunk so many times in the wash that you could hardly get them on your feet. You couldn't wear them up to your knees because they weren't long enough. You had to roll them down across your ankles. So Ron's in hysterics because he doesn't have to wear them. The trainers are old white plimsolls that were so dirty that Ken had to do a quick bodge-up job and dubbin them black. That was the kit we had to wear. Ron had opted to sit it out. I think he must have known something about the kit. We looked like a bunch of farmers. I think we played Colchester in the first game, and I was seriously hoping that we would get knocked out because I felt embarrassed in the kit we'd got. The first ball came to Maurice and he was so nervous and embarrassed that he actually booted the ball nearly out of the arena. And worse was to come. We won that game so we had to play again. In the same kit. I can still remember Ron laughing – the tears were coming out of his eyes – when he saw us putting that kit on, because we looked diabolical.

8 *"We pass the ball to each other"*

SECOND DIVISION SUCCESS, 1969-72

Gerry Summers succeeded Ron Saunders as manager in July 1969. Long-serving John Shuker took over as captain in 1971, Roy Burton established himself as first-choice goalkeeper, while Nigel Cassidy, Dave Roberts and Hugh Curran proved popular signings. It was a buoyant time, and gates averaged over 10,000. Fans were rewarded with good League results – United briefly topped the Second Division in October 1970 – and exciting Cup runs. A win at First Division Nottingham Forest brought a League Cup quarter-final in 1969-70, and First Division Burnley were beaten in the FA Cup a year later.

THE ARRIVAL OF GERRY SUMMERS

Gerry Summers: Ron Saunders left the club suddenly during the summer. They immediately came back for me, and I went again to be interviewed. I was interviewed twice for the same job and then got it. I think they wanted somebody to take over quickly, because they were nearly into the season. I went down on the day they played Wolves in a pre-season match. I took a friend down with me, and they lost 5-1 to Wolves, who weren't a particularly good side, and the fellow turned to me and said, "Are you sure, Gerry, that you should come to this club?" It was my first managing job and the chairman Ron Coppock was tremendous. They gave me my contract, and I realised I had to do something in that year, i.e. keep them in the league. They'd just survived the year before. They'd come through very quickly. They'd come from a Southern League club to a League club, from Fourth to Third to Second. They'd gone too quickly, really, because they'd outgrown everything – the ground, the facilities and the players. Ron Saunders had kept them in the league by being ultra-defensive, working tremendously hard, and just nicking a goal. Then here was me, a new fellow coming in, wanting them to play football, which caused a few surprises. I always remember my first game. We played at home to Huddersfield and we lost 2-1. I caused a sensation that week by dropping Ron Atkinson. I didn't realise what a sensation it would cause, but it did, because he hadn't been dropped before, and he was the captain. The next game was Birmingham away, which was going to be a very difficult game because they were a big club and were expected to get out of the league. I brought Ron back, and played three midfield players, with Ron in the middle of them, and we won there and went on quite a good run.

Colin Clarke: I was going through a bad period. I hadn't signed my contract. I was still trying to negotiate a better contract. We played Portsmouth on a boiling hot day and they were murdering us. We were totally disorganised. And I felt that we weren't really working hard enough as a team. I dropped my head a little bit, because I was so angry that we weren't getting up to them and getting the ball off them. Gerry Summers had seen me drop my head for a mere minute, even though I'd worked really hard up to that point, and he decided he was going to sub me. I was furious, because I felt that there was a few on the pitch that day that could have been off a bit earlier. I was on the other side of the park, and I stormed all the way across in this soaking wet shirt, and I took it off, and threw this shirt full-blooded and it's smacked Gerry Summers straight in the face. I can just remember him shouting, "You daft bugger." As I've come off the pitch, John Evanson's already come on and they've restarted the game. I think Graham Atkinson slung this 35-yard ball out to Evo and, as he was prone to do, he let it bounce under his foot. So the crowd, as one, "What the hell are you bringing Evanson on for, taking off Clarkey." So he's getting absolutely slaughtered. And Evo's head dropped. I remember that being a terrible time for John.

Tim Sparrowhawk: John Evanson was a very good midfield player. I remember a goal he scored off his backside once. The goalkeeper kicked it out, it hit his backside, ballooned over the goalkeeper and went into the net.

Colin Clarke: Evo was one of those who'd beat six players, but if you put a pass across the face of goal for a simple tap-in, he would hit it over the bar or fall over the ball. He was so frustrating. I remember Alan Harris phoning me. He was at Fulham at the time. He said, "Quick, could you tell me about Evo." I said, "He's a tremendous athlete. A very fit boy. Two wonderful feet. Tremendous body-swerve. Tremendous crosser of the ball. Tremendous passer of the ball. Got a great shot." "Bloody hell," he said, "You fancy him a bit." I said, "Oh no, he's a pain in the backside." He said, "What do you mean?" I said, "He's a tremendous passer of the ball but he never passes to our players. He's got a tremendous shot, he never hits the target. He's a tremendous crosser of the ball but he never crosses at the right time. He's a tremendous athlete but he never runs in the right places." He said, "Oh Christ, I think I've got the picture." He subsequently signed him. He played with George Best and Rodney Marsh, and he had three good years at Fulham. I can imagine them three together.

League Cup, 1969-70

John Shuker: I remember the Swindon game in the third round. I think we won 1-0 and Sloany scored a header from the edge of the box. The games we had against Swindon were always good games. We didn't win many against Swindon.

Gerry Summers: We beat Notts Forest, who were a First Division club, in the fourth round. That was one of the early flurries in the League Cup, which helped the club and the confidence of players. We got involved with Carlisle in the quarter-final. It was the ideal fixture. Carlisle, like us, were a Second Division side, and they had one or two injuries when we played at home. There was a full house that night. It was a draw, but we should have won. We had 90 per cent of the play, and we just couldn't get the all-important goal. Ken Skeen got clean through and the goalkeeper came out, and he took the goalie on and rolled it past the goalkeeper and everybody thought it was the winning goal and it bobbled and bobbled and bobbled and went past the post. I remember that one.

Colin Clarke: We went up to Carlisle for the replay and we were playing well at that time of the season. We loved the big pitch at Carlisle as well, and we were murdering them. It was 0-0 and we should have been in front, and I was defending a long ball with a yard and a half start on a lad called Bob Hatton. There was only he and I in the picture. I went to play it back to Jim Barron and as I went to play it Hatton caught the back of my heel, to click my heels, so I haven't made contact with the ball and I've fallen over. The referee was well behind play because we'd been pressing in their box. The referee never gave it, and the linesman never gave it. Hatton then went on to run up to Jimmy and try and round him, and Jimmy was forced to bring him down, and they got a penalty-kick. They won the tie with a penalty-kick. We were the victims of a diabolical decision. Had that not happened I believe we could have possibly got through to the Final of the League Cup that year. We had a good side and we were playing well at the time. That was one of the biggest disappointments I had in my time at Oxford.

Coaching

Gerry Summers: I'd always been very much a football man. When I say "football", I mean that we pass the ball to each other. I went to Oxford brimming with ideas. I knew they would work if I was given the time. Now, this is one thing that managers don't get. Luckily I survived that first year. Not only survived, but did well for the club, and then I had the cushion of a three-year contract. Then you can start, can't you? All my early work was done with the ball. We spent a lot of time on team play and trained at the ground a lot, which upset people behind the scenes. But I could see that it was the only way I could get over ideas quickly. Ron Atkinson certainly took on a new lease of life in that central position. Ron wasn't the most mobile of players, though he was one of the most aggressive and most wholehearted. I used to call him "the poor man's Malcolm Allison" then, because he was always a very outgoing person, and that was before he started as a manager. Playing in the centre, he had Graham Atkinson, who was a very skilful player, on one side. We relied a lot on Graham getting forward from those positions with Ron staying in the middle to be strong, and we'd got David Sloan working on either flank.

John Shuker: Gerry was obviously a totally different manager from Ron Saunders. Ron Saunders was a hard man – "Chase, chase, chase" – and Gerry wanted to play football. We played some good football in the Second Division, with a team that wasn't really good enough to win the league, and barely good enough to stay in the league.

Goalkeepers

Jim Barron: I'd never really had any goalkeeping coaching, apart from forwards shooting at you, until I came to Oxford. Gerry Summers was the first coach I knew who took notice of goalkeepers and took them to one side to give them special training. Now, every club in the country does it.

Gerry Summers: I inherited Jim, and Jim was a very good, agile goalkeeper, but he wasn't the best kicker in the world. As a manager you have to do things very quickly, and when I went there I could see that he wasn't the best thrower in the world. I have a theory about goalkeepers: when they make a very good save, they're always liable to do something ridiculous straight after. In the excitement of making a good save, they're liable to either throw a bad ball or kick a bad ball. Jimmy fell into this category – he would throw bad balls. After about three games, we had a meeting, and I said, "Jim, you are not to throw any more balls." He said, "This is impossible." I said, "It's going to happen. Until I feel that you can throw a ball properly, you're not to throw any more balls." He was a bad kicker off the floor, actually. He was a good kicker out of his hands, but not off the floor, and we used to have to position Ron Atkinson in a place about 12 yards off the halfway-line to flick 'em on. Jimmy was a good 'keeper, and he worked hard to improve. I think he was one of the better 'keepers in England at the time Forest came in for him.

Jim Barron: When I went to Forest it was the biggest transfer deal at Oxford. I think it was £35,000, which was a lot of money in those days. At the time, Oxford had Mickey Kearns and Roy Burton, and Gerry Summers obviously thought he could let me go, which I appreciated because I wanted to play in the First Division.

Colin Clarke: A story I remember about Mick Kearns goes back to Les Bateman, the groundsman, another character fondly remembered by all the people who have been at Oxford. Les used to limp around the ground and pick out all the weeds and observe everything. He was always watching. This day, we had a "Possibles against Probables" match. It must have been in the early seventies. Anyway, Mick Kearns was in goal, and Ron and me are in the Probables and we're playing the Possibles. And Kearnsy always had this mannerism whereby, when he placed the ball for a goal-kick, he would throw his hands up in the air, which meant "All of you can get up to the halfway-line because I kick it miles." So we recognised this gesture: "Up, up." And he'd flick his fingers in the air, and we'd turn our backs on him and go up to the halfway-line because he'd kick it into their half. Then he would walk backwards and make his long run and boot the ball. Unbeknown to him, Leslie had been weeding behind the back of the goal, and had left his wheelbarrow and gone up to sit in the stand to watch the game. So Mick's shouting, "Up, up," and the next thing we heard this "Aaaarrrgghghgh". We turned round and the wheelbarrow has turned upside-down, Mick's stuck in it, lodged against the wall, so his legs are hanging over the wall just at the back of the goal, and he's screaming obscenities at Les Bateman, the groundsman. We had to extract him from the wheelbarrow. Well, we couldn't start the game for ten minutes because everybody was lying around laughing. A 6 ft 4 in goalkeeper upside-down in a wheelbarrow, hanging over the back of the wall. It was unbelievable.

Gerry Summers: Mick Kearns became the first-choice goalkeeper. I could see a bigger and stronger goalkeeper taking over from Jim. Although Mick played for Ireland in the finish, he didn't quite live up to what I thought he would be, because I thought he would be one of the very best.

Colin Clarke: We played Stoke in the League Cup and they had a good side at that time with big Ritchie and George Eastham and Peter Dobing and all that lot. I think we were leading 1-0 and giving them a good pasting. So Mick Kearns has come out well to dive full-length at Ritchie's feet. Ritchie's stumbled over him and on to the cinder-track at the London Road end. Now Mick has taken an eternity to get up. By the time he's got up on his feet again, he's forgotten that Ritchie's behind him. Ritchie's dusting himself off at the back of the goal. So Kearnsy does his little stunt again, which is, "Up, up, up," and he's rolled the ball at his feet. In the meantime Ritchie senses that he doesn't know he's there, so he sneaks round the front of him, taps it in the net and Kearnsy is still shouting "Up, up." I think we drew that match and lost the replay 2-0.

Tim Sparrowhawk: Jimmy Barron, who had been a great favourite with the fans, went to Forest, which was a great disappointment, and then this local chap, Roy Burton, comes in and makes good. Roy Burton's backside was famous at the London Road end, we usually saw quite a lot of it during a match. At one time, as a shotstopper, I would say there were few better than him. I remember one horrendous mistake he made at Peterborough in an away match. It was a big punt upfield and he came out to collect it and didn't quite gauge the trajectory right so it bounced in front of him and over his head and into the goal. I suppose that happens to all goalkeepers.

John Shuker: Roy Burton came from Wantage. In fact I was the person who recommended him to Gerry Summers. Being a local lad, he hadn't been out in the big wide world, as we say. He used to speak as a country lad. He had no flashy things. He used to come out with shorts halfway down his bum. He was a bit of a clown as well. He always got on well with the supporters. They took to him, and why not? He did a good job for Oxford, didn't he? He had the biggest pair of hands I've ever seen anybody have in my life. The only time he ever struggled, I think, was when he had to think about things like long crosses – whether to come or go. But the biggest weakness that Roy had in the early days was that he wouldn't communicate as much as Jimmy. Jimmy would shout if he was coming. If the goalkeeper shouts that he's coming for the ball, the defenders should get out of the way and cover his goal in case anything happens, and if he's going to hit anybody he's going to hit the centre-forward. Roy didn't shout. He'd just come and clatter the first men that were there, usually the defenders. He'd say, "I caught the ball," as you were holding the back of your head or your knee or your back. That was his biggest fault, but he was a good goalkeeper. I don't think there was a lot between him and Jimmy in the end.

Gerry Summers: You must have heard stories about the goalkeeper, Roy Burton. He was a tremendous goalkeeper, and he made this save this day, and he broke his arm as he made the save, and, typical of him, as he came off on the stretcher, he still had the ball. He wouldn't let go of the ball.

Fred Ellis: I can't say enough about Roy Burton. I'll never know how he made some of the saves he made, especially one at Luton from Dave Roberts. Dave Roberts headed the ball back to him so hard I think it would have burst the back of the net but Burtie just put his hands up, caught the ball and kicked it out. It was one hell of a back-pass, believe me.

Making Progress

Gerry Summers: The chairman Ron Coppock was tremendous in that first year, because I had problems within the club, a young manager coming in, and he was 100 per cent. He was only chairman for that year, because he was a very ill man. He stepped down the following year. He stayed on the board, but unfortunately he died three or four months later. Working with him I could see why Oxford United had come from Headington United through the leagues, because he was such a strong man to have on your side. That first year I turned down an offer from Watford to go on the short-list there. The board thought that was tremendous because it was showing loyalty. I said, "Yeah, it's showing loyalty but you have given me my first year, and you have given me a better three-year contract, and, as I can see, I think this club is as good as Watford and can be better." Gradually we got players in. The club gave me more money as I went on. Mr Gibbs, the company secretary, would tell me how much money was available. If he said you'd got £15,000 to spend, you knew you'd got £15,000 to spend.

Ron Atkinson: Gerry was a totally different kind to Ron Saunders. He was an excellent coach but he didn't get particularly close to his players. I think he made a mistake there. I think he'd be the first to admit now that he got a bit worried about the senior players, of which I was one, and he thought we were the boys to clear out. By the time he'd realised, it was maybe too late. But he was an excellent coach. He was certainly the best manager we ever had for looking after us contract-wise. He was very fair in that way, but just lacked that bit of personality. At one stage, we were playing ever so well and we went top of the Second Division, and we were playing like continentals really because we didn't have a big centre-forward. I think Arthur Turner was still scouting, and he went to watch Scunthorpe play. He went to watch Nigel Cassidy, and he came back and said, "Well, if you're going to spend £35,000, don't buy him, buy the little number seven." We bought the big number nine, Cass, who was a useful player. The little number seven then went on to Liverpool and became one of the greatest players Britain's seen – Kevin Keegan. Then, after that, we changed our style and tried to play long ball to Cass and it disrupted us. If we'd continued to play the way we were playing, I think we'd have gone up.

Gerry Summers: I didn't know enough about Kevin Keegan to sign him. Anyhow, he was out of my league. I think he went for £30,000. We couldn't really compete at that. You talk to all managers and they'll tell you about the players they nearly got or could have had. We bought one or two players. We bought Cassidy. I think that was about £20,000. Dave Roberts, a young player at Fulham, was one of our best buys. I think we bought him for about £2,500. He was playing against our Reserves, for Fulham, and he played particularly well. Mick Brown was my assistant then, and we talked and said, "We must look at this fellow again."

Mick Brown: I'd been to watch a few games, Fulham Reserves, and I couldn't understand why the blond-haired guy playing for them wasn't in their first team. Then one day I got wind that he was maybe moving to another club for a small fee. I'd been plaguing Gerry to go and get this fellow, and now I said, "If you don't get him by this afternoon, he's going." It was about two and a half grand. That seems silly now, doesn't it? Gerry said, "Do you fancy him that strong?" I said, "Yeah, I do." Gerry gave it the okay, because he couldn't get in touch with all the board members, and we agreed to pay £2,500, and there were certain board members who were up in arms about this, because they hadn't been consulted about spending £2,500. We got Dave Roberts as a result of that and he did very well for us.

Gerry Summers: In 18 months he was in the Welsh under-23 side and then he became a full international. He was a tremendous servant to the club. He was an out-and-out defender, tremendously wholehearted, and, though he was born in London, I think he could play for Wales because of his Welsh father. He became very pro-Welsh, and he'd have tapes of all the Welsh songs. I went to see his first international – against Poland at Cardiff – and he was singing along with the national anthem. I think he even learned a bit of Welsh.

Colin Clarke: Rodney Smithson and I had maybe two seasons together as centre-backs. Rodney was a good player and we were a nice complement in the sense that he was right-footed and I was predominantly left, so we balanced each other. Both of us former Arsenal. But I always felt that Rodney, without maligning him, could have done better, because he was so laid back. None-the-less, he was there for 11 years and I bet he played 200 games for the club. He was followed by Dave Roberts. Dave was a good player, and we had the ideal complement, because I had all the skill and he had all the aggression! That should get back to him. No, Dave was better in the air than I was, strong in the tackle, and I think Gerry Summers would be the first to say that we were a very good combination in the Second Division, and we had a good run together, maybe three seasons before David went to Hull for £80,000.

John Shuker: Dick Lucas was there. Dick played over 200 games for the club. He came from North Leigh, a local team, and got in the first team. Unfortunately he had a bad injury and had to finish. He was a good professional. He always did a good job for the club.

Gerry Summers: It was a very lively dressing-room, with Ron Atkinson and people like that. The professional dressing-room is a very cut-throat business. There's great camaraderie, but there's also egos there. When you're a young player, you have to suffer a bit before you can get out of it. Dick Lucas was a young lad, a very promising player. Dick had a lot of ankle trouble which stopped him going on, but he was a good lad, and they used to tear strips out of Dick. I kept saying, "Dick, you've got to come back with something that's going to hit them, to get them off your back." It's all done jokingly but it can become too much. I could see this happening to Dick. He said, "Yeah, I always think of the thing to say back, but it's too late then. The whole thing's finished." I said, "You've got to work on it." Ron was a very wholehearted bloke who used to give people stick. People never dare come with a new suit or a flash tie. You'd get done. And he was issuing forth at Dick this day and, I always remember, Dick hit him back with something and stopped him in full flow, and never did anybody say anything to Dick again. You can see this happening throughout every club you come to. I remember Ken Skeen, a wholehearted player, a very funny lad as well, a great lad to have in your dressing-room. The referee used to come in the dressing-room to talk to the players. Ron Atkinson always used to say to them, "Are we allowed to swear?" This was his one question. At this one game, the referee turned round and said, "Yes, I'll turn a deaf ear to any swearing," and Ken Skeen, quick as a flash, says, "Which is your deaf ear?"

The Manorettes

Tim Sparrowhawk: The Manorettes were based on American cheerleaders. I think they sold programmes as well. I was probably just a little young to appreciate them fully but I think it was an era when Oxford were getting very gimmicky, and I think that was one of the gimmicks. I remember bands playing before matches and I saw Brinsley Schwarz and Ace, who had a top-ten hit at the time.

Alison Kinnear: There was an advert in the *Oxford Mail* for 18 programme-sellers. Thirty-five turned up, and there was a meeting in the Beech Road Stand. They didn't want to disappoint anyone so they took on all thirty-five. I remember they asked us what size shoes we took. The uniforms were paid for by a £200 gift from the supporters' club. We had to go to Webbers, a shop down the High Street, and they measured us and we went back at a later date for the uniform: blazer, skirt, black boots and socks, and hat and blouse. We looked a bit of a shambles walking round the pitch. I remember trying to keep step. We tended to look down at our feet and we never practised. Frank Kowalski led us round. It was a bit cold and some girls complained that they had cold knees, so they gave us trousers. They were black, flared, and had a yellow stripe down each side.

Pat Giles: It was Arthur Turner's idea, and they took us on away trips as a thankyou for selling programmes at home. I remember some bad incidents. Coming out of Aston Villa we were stoned. We did a very foolish thing and marched round the Millwall ground, the Den, and we were spat upon and attacked by a group of girls when we came out. The best memory I have is when we played Nottingham Forest in a midweek game and we went up there and won 1-0. Kenny Skeen scored. There were about half a dozen of us from Milham Ford School. When we went to Nottingham, the headmistress gave us time off to leave early but only if we dressed up in our uniforms and went to her study before we went off to the match.

The Reserve Team, 1971-72

Mick Brown: We finished second in the Football Combination, which was a major achievement when you consider the Arsenals and the Tottenhams. Ipswich Town had a very strong team, the nucleus of their first team throughout the seventies. In those days teams carried far bigger staffs than they do now, so it wasn't uncommon to go and play Chelsea and them have six or seven household names in the team. To finish second that year was a great achievement, one I'm very proud of.

Arthur Turner's Departure, 1972

Edmund Gibbs: He had been there so many years and done so much for the club that no-one wanted to get rid of him, so they made him general manager. Gerry Summers was the team manager and Arthur couldn't resist interfering, and so, in the end, Gerry said, "I'm not putting up with this any more," and he was quite right. Arthur was bitterly upset.

Arthur Turner: For me, general manager was a job for nothing. Mixing drinks and stopping in the tea-room and the board-room didn't appeal to me. Eventually it had to happen. The old chairman, Mr Coppock, had died, and Peter Playford had taken over. He came to see me. They called a special meeting and they told me I was getting the boot. I was out. But I must say this, very, very sincerely, I had a lot of respect for Oxford, I really did. I had a happy lifetime in football. I like to think I gave something back to the game. It was good to me, and I met a lot of good people. I met people in the game of football who I think were some of the best people I've ever met in my life.

9 "Is this going to cost me my two best players?"

PEAK AND DECLINE, 1972-75

In June 1974 six directors resigned and Tony Rosser took over as chairman. Rosser supported the £75,000 record signing of Andy McCulloch but extensive redevelopment of the Manor Ground caused financial pressures, leading to the sales of Scottish international Hugh Curran (to Bolton) and Welsh international Dave Roberts (to Hull). By the end of 1974-75 only three players – Roy Burton, Colin Clarke and John Shuker – remained from the successful Second Division side. The 1975-76 season started badly and Gerry Summers was sacked in October. However, Summers had taken the club into a new era with improved coaching, a successful youth policy (under chief scout Fred Ford), and trips to Europe for the Anglo-Italian Cup.

"The Three Cs"

Chris Fallows: When I first started going up there my favourite player was

Derek Clarke. He wasn't everyone's favourite. My second team was Leeds, and I really liked Allan "Sniffer" Clarke, and of course Derek was his brother. Derek had the same actions, and he looked the same. And he did score one or two goals. Only one or two. There were the three Cs – Clarke, Cassidy and Curran.

Gerry Summers: Of the Clarke brothers the main one was Allan, but I always thought that Derek would be one of the top players because he was a very skilful player. Unfortunately he had injury after injury. I signed him, and it caused a sensation, because I spent about £18,000, which was a lot of money in those days, and didn't play him. Nobody could understand that I'd bought this fellow and he was not playing in the first team.

Tim Sparrowhawk: Cassidy was again the big centre-forward. He'd got the image – the big droopy moustache. I think he milked the support of the crowd really. If you draw an analogy with cricket, he reminds me a bit of Dennis Lillee. The same image. The same rapport with the crowd.

Peter Foley: Nigel Cassidy was a hero in those days. Pancho, I think they used to call him. Big moustache. Black hair all over the place. About two stone overweight though.

Colin Clarke: The goal that gave me the most pleasure was the Watford goal, because at that time we could see Wembley [FA Cup fourth round 1971]. That was a diving header. It was behind me, so I had to jack-knife and thrust my neck forward, and it flew in. I remember doing a lap of honour. Oh, a funny incident. As I picked myself up, all ecstatic, I've run to the west side of the ground, and Cass is sprinting after me, saying, "Clarkey, Clarkey, the cameras are the other side." I've done an about-turn and sprinted the full width of the pitch to run on the stand side where the cameras were, with Nigel on my back. That was typical of Cass. He'd remember that type of thing. I remember scoring a goal against Swindon, diving full-length to head a free-kick, right in the corner of the net. And Cass did a lap of honour shouting, "I did the decoy run." That was typical of Cass.

Chris Fallows: Hughie Curran was another character. He scored a lot of goals for us and then he went away, and he came back for a testimonial. I can't remember who's testimonial it was, but at the end the fans poured on the pitch. They ignored whoever's testimonial it was and carried Hughie Curran off shoulder-high. And next season he came back to us because obviously the fans loved him. He carried on scoring goals for the second time.

Tim Sparrowhawk: The song that used to be "Nice one, Cyril". Well, it was "Nice one, Hughie." That was the Oxford version.

Peter Foley: After training, Hughie Curran and Burty [Roy Burton] used to have a little competition. Hughie would line up six balls outside the penalty area and we used to sit behind the goal on the bank on the training ground and watch this competition. Hughie Curran used to whack these balls, and Burty would be everywhere stopping them, top corner, bottom corner, and they used to wind each other up all the time. If Hughie scored Burty would go mad. If Hughie had had his six shots and hadn't scored then he'd be going mad. It was brilliant watching them.

Mac: When I was about 12 the manager of my football team arranged for about four of our team to have a week at the Manor – cleaning the boots and sweeping up. It was great. I watched the players train and trained with them a bit. I had a penalty competition against Roy Burton. He scored all his five and then saved all my five. Five or six years later, I thought, "Why couldn't he have let one in?" I remember Hugh Curran practising overhead kicks with Roy Burton in goal. Someone was crossing the ball and Hugh Curran was spot on with every one. It was amazing to watch. One of them was the hardest I've ever seen anybody hit a football, from over his shoulder, and it was hurtling into the top corner. Roy Burton just stood still, reached out and caught it in one hand. Hugh Curran stood up and went, "You **!*!*! *!*!" Roy Burton just threw it back out to the winger: "Next."

The League Cup, 1972-73

Gerry Summers: One of the big games was the Manchester United match. We're playing them at home in the second round, and we're playing the full Manchester United side. Bobby Charlton, Best, you name them, they're all there. We've gone a goal down in the first few minutes, so we're expecting the worst because they're coming at us, but we battle through and we somehow contain them and get an equaliser. Then we outplay them in the second half, and we're going down the hill, which is always worth a goal to you, I suppose, and we're battling away and we get the winner, so we think, with seven minutes to go. I always remember turning to Mick Brown and saying to him, "This is going to be the longest seven minutes you and I ever sit through at a football match." Now Manchester United come back into it, and we're in the closing minutes. We've cleared a ball into their half and Bobby Charlton's picked it up right in the centre-circle and they've caught us on the break. Ken Skeen goes to put him under pressure, and Ken Skeen gets cramp, just as he's closing in. I can see him now, going full length with the tackle and not being able to move. And Bobby Charlton went forward and hit a ball from 30 yards that nobody saw. It hit something and came out of goal, and I think if we'd played on we might have got away with it.

John Shuker: I don't think anybody knew it had gone in. I'm sure the referee didn't. I think it was the linesman who saw it. We all thought it had hit the bar, but it had hit the back of the net and flown out again. We lost the replay 3-1 and Geoff Bray scored.

THE ANGLO-ITALIAN CUP, 1972-73

Colin Clarke: We got into Europe and started experiencing a better standard of football and a better standard of living, because we were travelling to good hotels. We hadn't done that before. We had always scratched around in transport cafes and places like that. Now we were starting to come into the big world. We were getting good kit. The Anglo-Italian, for me, was the first sign that we'd really come out of the country-hick stage. We played Bologna and that was tremendous. They were top of the Italian League at the time, and we dominated the game. We played our best football on that day. We dominated the game but couldn't score. They played a weird system with no wide players at all. They literally played up the centre of the pitch, and allowed us to have the ball on the flanks. We could cross the ball all day long, but they always had nine players in the box to head it out. That was a new experience for us, but we couldn't crack them, and we drew 0-0.

Nick Harris: I was one of the founder members of the *Oxford Journal*. I was distribution manager, but within a few weeks I was writing stuff about United. Tony Rosser was the boss of the *Journal* and he wanted to be chairman of United. The first time I ever had to report on a United game, he sent me to Italy to cover United versus Bologna in the Anglo-Italian Cup. To me, now, it sounds very simple, but in those days it was a shock. I went to the office on a Monday and he said, "You're going to Italy tomorrow with United to cover the game in Bologna." I didn't have a passport or anything, but off I went. I was very well looked after by United. The lads were very kind to me. A lot of practical jokes. Then I went to Rome with them. I was an old hand by then. I was reporting on my second-ever football game. Quite a funny tale. They had played Torino in the game at Oxford, and Nigel Cassidy had given the Italians quite a rough old time. They'd said to him, "When you come to Italy you're going to be sorted out." Nigel Cassidy had a mystery injury just before we went to Italy and he never went. When we arrived at Rome airport, there was a lot of press activity, waiting for United. The lads told the Italian press that I was Nigel Cassidy and I remember being interviewed. The Roma game was one of my great memories of United. They played in the Olympic Stadium. They beat Roma, 2-0, who were a real top Italian side then. Sad there was only 5,000 people there, but Hughie Curran, who was a real favourite of mine, scored both the goals. We had a marvellous night out in Rome afterwards. It was just fabulous.

Gerry Summers: I thought it was magnificent just to get Oxford into a European competition. The directors were wholeheartedly behind it, but one director happened to say, at a meeting at the end of the season, "That tournament's cost us £1,000." I said, "Well, for £1,000, we've got £100,000 of publicity, and it was tremendous for the players." I always remember that they were very worried about going over there midweek and then coming back to play, but the thing was so well-organised. We had to go out on a Tuesday, play Wednesday afternoon, come back Thursday. I always remember, after the Roma one, playing at Swindon, the local rivals. We never used to do particularly well at Swindon but we went out and beat them comfortably, and I can see the team running out now after beating Roma: "What are Swindon? This is going to be a doddle." And that's how it proved.

Fred Ford and the Youth Team

Gerry Summers: Fred Ford came as chief scout. We'd got this youth side coming together. We had a very strong Scottish contingent because I met a an excellent fellow called Jack Gilroy while I was at Wolves, and when I came to Oxford he used to bring boys down. Unfortunately he was killed in a car crash not long after I left Oxford. But he brought a whole group of young players. He was a teacher, and most of them were former pupils. Hugh McGrogan was one of the youngest players to play for Oxford. He played against Manchester United. Matt Busby came down with Manchester United and opened the new dressing-rooms, and on the afternoon we beat them 1-0. I don't know how we beat them because they had 90 per cent of the play, but we did, and Hugh McGrogan played his first game as a 17 year old. I thought he would have been a far better player than he was. Billy Jeffrey was a good midfield player. Andy Bodel played a few games. There was a person who worked in the north-east who used to take all the players to Burnley, and Mick Tait and Les Taylor had been to Burnley and they were umming and aahing, and they came down, and I offered them apprenticeships straightaway. They were amongst the first youth players, with Billy Jeffrey, Hugh McGrogan, Andy Bodel, all coming together, so Fred Ford's first year was with a very young youth side in the Midland Midweek League. I said to Fred, "Fred, you'll have problems this year, but next year, when they're at their right age, under 18, we'll see what happens." Well, the next year, half of them were in the first team anyhow, so they didn't play in that youth side all that often!

Mick Brown: The biggest thing about Fordy was his intensity, his sheer intensity and his passion and love for the game. I think that came over to kids and parents alike. He didn't have to sell himself. He just naturally did that. Everybody who came into contact with him respected him for that. Many is the time that I found that he'd slept at the ground in his office, having come back from Doncaster or York, or somewhere like that, the night before. It worried me a little bit. "No, I'm all right," he said, "I've got things to do in the morning." The schoolboys loved him. He was like a Dad or an uncle to them. And the parents also knew, without having to be sold on the idea, that if their son signed for Oxford United, he would not fail because of lack of care and attention from the people at the club.

Gerry Summers: Fred was very much like Ken Fish in the stories you'll hear about him, and you'll have to believe all of them. He was a tremendous fellow, a tremendous enthusiast. The youth side were playing at Aston Villa one day, and they lost heavily. He got them in the dressing-room afterwards and he was telling them what had gone wrong, talking to them, and there was a box of biscuits that had been left in by the home side for the lads to eat. The box was near Mick Tait, and he took one of the biscuits, so Fred went berserk: "You can't do that, I'm talking to you, don't eat the biscuits. Put them down. I'm talking." Off he started chatting to them, telling them what they were doing wrong, and he turned round and there was Mick Tait again with one of the biscuits. Fred got the biscuit tin, turned it upside-down in the middle of the dressing-room and jumped up and down on these biscuits. "Now, will you listen?" Jason Seacole was another young player who came through. Jason was from near Oxford. I had him with the first team to train and I said to Fred Ford,

"That's the best one I've seen, you must sign him." Jason wouldn't sign for a while, and Fred used to pop in occasionally to his house, just to talk to him and have a cup of tea, trying to get him to sign. That was a very proud moment for Fred when he came and said, "There's the form there, he's signed blue forms." When I'd left Oxford Fred rang me up. I'll always remember this. He said, "I've found the best schoolboy I've ever seen." I said, "Better than Jason Seacole?" He said, "Yes." I said, "Who is it?" He said, "Mark Wright."

Mick Brown: You'd get somebody like Kevin Brock, who was the hottest property in schoolboy football. Manchester United, Tottenham Hotspur and Arsenal were queuing up to sign him, but he signed for Oxford United. That's a measure of Fred Ford. There's a saying in football, "Judge yourself by the club you leave behind, and the state you find it in and the state that you leave it in."

Gerry Summers: Fred Ford was a very good tennis player. When he had problems with players on their contracts, he often used to take them for a game of tennis, give them a good thrashing, and he found out it was psychologically good because when he talked to them again he usually got them to sign. He told me this, and you have to smile about him. Some time later I'm trying to sign McCulloch from QPR. He was a big centre-forward. I'd seen him play quite a lot, and he ummed and aahed about the move. Now, you knew at Oxford that if you didn't nail them straightaway you'd have problems. One of the problems was that if they came round and looked at the ground, they'd think, "I don't know about this." And he was from QPR and he was a First Division player, but I said, "We'll go and have a bit of lunch." We're walking out of the ground and there's his car, and he's got a squash racquet in the back. I said, "You play squash?" He said, "Yes." Now I played squash, so I said, "Come on, we'll have a game of squash." We went straight down to Highfields, and we played squash, and he wasn't bad actually, but I wasn't bad and beat him. Then we had lunch, and I thought, "I wonder if this works, what Fred told me." And we started talking again, and he was far more receptive, and finished up the afternoon signing the contract. So I said to Fred, "Fred, it works with squash as well as tennis."

Financial Trouble, 1974-75

Gerry Summers: Unfortunately we had to sell Dave Roberts, when the club was in very bad financial trouble, when Rosser took over and spent a lot of money on the ground. I remember saying to him, "Is this going to cost me my two best players?" He said, "No." He pulled the whole of the stand out and made new dressing-rooms, which wanted doing because the dressing-rooms weren't up to standard, but in the finish it did cost me my two best players, because Dave Roberts had to go to Hull, and we had to sell Hugh Curran, who I bought from Wolves, to Bolton. That was disappointing.

Edmund Gibbs: I signed every cheque the club ever issued from 1949 to 1974 so I knew every penny that ever went out and had a firm hand on the income. I went to London for three days and left a cheque with my chief clerk. I signed the cheque in advance to buy national insurance stamps for about £14 or so. Whilst I was away Rosser came into my office. He demanded that the cheque was handed to him. My clerk let him have this cheque under protest and reported to me as soon as I got back. Rosser took this cheque and signed a player for £20,000 without the knowledge of the manager, and this was money that had come in for the conversion of the Beech Road Stand. I was so incensed by this that I resigned. When Rosser drew that cheque he shoved us over the limit and that was the first time I'd ever been over the limit. The bank was on to me the next morning and I had to say, "Well, I'll fix it within seven days." I made sure that money was available to cover that cheque and resigned. None of this came out in public of course. I just said I'd had enough.

Colin Clarke: The team was getting a little younger. We were starting to lose some of the key players. Graham Atkinson had a tremendous season or two. John Shuker was another player who had a tremendous career at Oxford. I think he still holds the record for the most appearances. I feel that John, Graham and myself were really instrumental in keeping the team together in the Second Division when the club had no finances. We had to bring in the young players. In came Bodel, who played alongside me, Bill Jeffrey, Colin Duncan. Jason Seacole was a tremendous prospect before the injury which cut his career short. These lads needed a lot of nurturing. I think John and Graham, particularly, gave tremendous service to the club in allowing them to go through that period when there was a tremendous gap between the senior players and the youth players that Fred Ford had brought to the club. We hung on and hung on, to subsequently get relegated, but there was an inevitability about it. We'd lost a lot of good players and we couldn't keep plugging the cracks. We were really coming apart.

Gerry Summers: We had a happy mix of senior players and young players coming through, but suddenly when you had to sell two of your senior players, and there were no incoming players because transfer money was not available, it threw too much emphasis on the young players. When I left, Mick Brown had more-or-less the whole youth side in there, at 18 and 19, which was a bit difficult, and that's one of the reasons that they went down.

Colin Clarke: Jimmy Light played full-back for a few years. He was always slide-tackling 40 yards away from players, sprinting up the line and running into touch. He had to do everything at 100 miles an hour, Jimmy, but he was a tremendously willing worker. Gerry Summers' hands were tied in terms of finance. Brian Heron was about £15,000, which was not a lot of money at that time. Trevor Aylott was a free transfer. Colin Duncan came through the youth policy. He was a Wantage boy. He made tremendous strides in a short time. As did Billy Jeffrey. They had to come in and learn quickly. And thankfully they did, and we just managed to salvage things. But prior to them breaking through, Brian Heron had a good season at the club but unfortunately he broke his leg twice in a year. He was a talented Scot but a bit wayward in his performances. I once wrote a poem about Brian. It had quite obvious connotations in it: "The Bird on the Wing." The heron. And he's still got it today. He keeps it in his wallet. He was a character. He was one of these blokes that you could write something about. The poem was virtually done in broad Scots. It referred to the Friday session. I can remember little bits of it. "Friday came, yellow bibs for all to see." Yellow bibs were a sign that you weren't in the team. I've written it in Brian's voice, and he goes on to say, "Help ma bob, jiggy bunnet, he's handed wan ta mae" which was a reference to the fact that he was sub. Then it finishes, "I canna believe it, the crowd will be sparse; What? Nae bird on the wing, they'll know it's a farce."

BBC Radio Oxford

Nick Harris: Radio Oxford came on the scene and said, "Would you like to help out reading the results." My first game as a commentator was 0-0 against Blackpool. It wasn't much of a game. John Evanson was playing for Blackpool. I remember I interviewed him after the game because there wasn't too much else to talk about. I was very nervous indeed. Even more nervous doing the after-match stuff, interviewing people, and coming back to the studio. It was quite daunting at the time. People trying to put you off as well. I can remember reading out my considered piece in Radio Oxford and a colleague hid under the desk and set fire to my notes. I'll never forget. I'm reading, and my notes are slowly burning. And I'm reading quicker to try to avoid them disappearing out of my hands.

Colin Clarke: Gerry Summers called me one day and said, "Friday morning, can you go down Radio Oxford's studios, you're on a quiz programme." I said, "What is it?" He said, "Well, sport, I think. I think it's mainly football." So I arrived and I found out it was a general quiz, with the highlights being music, and classical music as well. Also some sports, but not really football-orientated. So I got in there, and there were four of us. I couldn't believe the questions they were asking. I'd been in there 15 minutes and I hadn't said a word. I was getting a bit hot under the collar. Anyway they finally asked about the only piece of music I'd ever recognise, so I got on my buzzer: "It's 'the Big Country'." "Yes, Colin, well done." Then I never spoke for another 15 minutes and the programme ended. It was the most nerve-wracking thing that I'd experienced in football.

v Sunderland, April 1975

Colin Clarke: The goal that everybody seems to remember was against Jim Montgomery when we beat Sunderland who were top of the Second Division at the time. I scored from about 30 yards with my right foot, and it flew in the top corner and that was about four minutes to go. That was special because they were going for the title and there was a big crowd there.

Nick Harris: I was a very, very green reporter and United played Sunderland at the Manor, and I think if Sunderland had won they'd have got into Division One. Their directors had gone to a secret Lakeland hide-out to discuss what they were going to do in Division One, as it was then, and United scored in the last minute and beat them. I was very, very naive, and I ran on the field after the game and tried to do an interview with Bob Stokoe, the Sunderland manager, who was leaving the field, and I won't repeat what he said to me but it was about placing a microphone in a very uncomfortable position. That was extremely embarrassing. A very silly time to try to interview somebody.

The Departure of Gerry Summers, October 1975

Les Bateman: I can always remember when Gerry Summers went. Tony Rosser rang up on the telephone in the referee's room and I went over and he says, "Les, see if you can find Truscott." He was secretary at the time. He said, "Tell him I want to speak to him." And Truscott had the privilege of telling Gerry Summers he'd finished. That was how Rosser carried on.

Gerry Summers: As a manager you can only spend so long at a club. I'd been there about seven years. My last 18 months became very difficult with the new chairman taking over, bringing his own board in and spending a lot of money, and we got a bit topsy-turvy, with better players having to be sold just to pay the wage bill. I thought we could survive with the young players, but it threw a tremendous pressure on them. We were into the season, and I suppose the manager's always the last to know, when he gets the sack. I think we went up to York and lost our sixth successive League game and suddenly they decided that I was going to go. It was around the end of September. You're brought up in football and you know what goes on, but the first sacking! Joe Mercer rang me up, and said, "You're not a manager until you've been sacked the first time," and I said, "Yeah, I know, Joe, but it still doesn't make it any easier." It's a hard bang at your pride and what you've done. I think most people would say that I'd kept a lower-league side in the Second Division, playing quite attractive football on very small gates. At that time, I was the manager to get them in the highest spot in the Second Division.

Colin Clarke: Gerry was misunderstood by some of the players because he was a little deep in his thinking. He did an awful lot of good for the club, and his manner of leaving was a little shoddy. He transformed us into a professional outfit; we were better organised, our diet was better, our kit was better, we had tours, we had trips, we had a higher profile and he made us aware of a new world in a lot of ways. I won't be thanked by others because a lot of other lads maybe didn't like him as much, didn't like his team selection or some of his coaching, but you have to recognise a lot of the things he did. Personally he encouraged me to take up coaching, to a point where he literally pestered me into taking my preliminary badge and subsequently taking my full badge, so I'll always be grateful to him.

10 *"They all had to call him Mr Fish"*

KEN FISH, TRAINER AND PHYSIOTHERAPIST, 1964-88

Ken Fish arrived in 1964 and stayed for 24 years. As trainer, coach or physiotherapist, or more simply as a wise man, he was an inspiration behind Oxford United's rise through the divisions and consolidation in later years. He was also one of the club's great characters. A South African amateur international and World War Two veteran, Fish played for Aston Villa, Young Boys (Berne) and Port Vale before serving as trainer to Port Vale and Birmingham City.

KEN FISH

Arthur Turner: I had one of the best trainers in this country when I had Ken Fish. I'd tried to get Ken Fish when I was at Stoke City and he was at Port Vale. Then I got him to Birmingham. And I got him from Birmingham to Oxford, and he was one of the best signings I ever made because he could handle men. He could handle players, he could train them, he could get them fit. They'd respond to him. He didn't have a big whip, like some trainers might have. I never interfered with him. I never had to. I put him on the same wages as the players. Ken Fish got the same bonus when we won. Ken Fish got his share of any perks that were going, which in my book he was entitled to. The club bought a house for him, 33 Osler Road, overlooking the ground. All he had to do was come down the garden and he was on the field. That was where he lived all the time he was at Oxford. I couldn't speak too highly of him. A great fellow.

Ken Fish: On my first visit the taxi-driver dropped me off in London Road and I thought, "Blimey, what the hell's this?" The office was a wood-and-iron hut, with a galvanised roof, about six yards wide. Ken McCluskey, the secretary, showed me round the ground. We went in the home dressing-room and you could just about get 12 players in the bath. The visitors' dressing-room was as bad. The referees' room was a hole about the size of a small toilet. I thought, "Where do we go from here?" He showed me the treatment-room and it was out of this world. It was the width of a bed and underneath the slope of the stands. It had a seven-and-sixpenny lamp for heating. I thought, "This is an education." I said to the secretary, "What hotel do I stay in tonight?" We went back to his office and he said "Could you manage in this room?" I said, "Yes." There was a camp-bed, and he pulled the camp-bed out. You know, the ones you have in the army. And there was a chair to put my clothes on. I thought, "Bloody hell, this is a great welcome." Well, at that time the team used to travel away with a tea-urn and sandwiches, and the players thought that a "short corner" was an hors d'oeuvre. Any set-piece was strange to them. But the chairman said to me, "I know you've come from a First Division club to a Fourth Division club, but I want you to realise that we want to be professional."

John Shuker: Ken Fish came along and worked there for 20-odd years. Ken did everything. He ran the training, looked after the kit, worked out the schedule for travelling, worked out what we wanted to eat and went in the hotel kitchens to tell them what we wanted. A big figurehead for the club, always there, always available for players to chat to.

Ken Fish: When Ron Saunders left to go to Norwich, he said, "You're coming with me." I said, "No, I'm not." He said, "I'll double your wages." I said, "No, I'm not. I'm staying. I'm under contract and I'll see it through." When Jim Smith went off to QPR he wanted me to go along. He said, "We could still be in Oxford and go in by car." "No," I said. "It's out of the question."

Gerry Summers: I always remember the first day I was there. Ken came to see me, and said, "Am I staying or going?" Those were the first words he said to me. A very forthright fellow with tremendous experience. I enjoyed working with Ken.

Ian Greaves: Fishy is a legend, isn't he? Everybody in football knows Ken. And his missus, who's a lovely lady. Ken used to put his spikes on on a Friday afternoon. He'd pack the gear for an away game, and four o'clock, he'd put his spikes on. He was in his sixties, and he was sprinting up and down the touch-line. I thought, "That's incredible. I don't believe it."

Peter Foley: I used to go and see Mr Fish, get my ankles strapped up, and he'd give me a little rub. He'd always have a quiet little word, tell me how good I was and how many goals I was going to score. Ken was great. He was there years and years before I got there, and he was there years after I left. He was Oxford United. I honestly thought that when he left the club, the club would fold, because he was such a part of the club.

Jim Smith: I came from a First Division club, Birmingham, to Oxford, and ground-wise and facility-wise, it was a bit depressing, but the one thing that was First Division was Ken Fish. He looked after things in my office, made sure there was a bottle of wine and beer in for Saturdays. He made sure all the kit was spotless and the referee's room was made out right for match-days. The treatment of injuries, and cleanliness of the place, which is important, was down to Ken Fish, and he kept the standards up. He was like a Sergeant-Major really, which I think is a good thing. I'm talking particularly about the apprentices. They all had to call him Mr Fish, and they all had to stand to attention and wait until he inspected all their respective jobs.

Maurice Evans: I didn't realise until I came here how important Ken was to Oxford United. He did virtually everything, and he didn't want anyone to get involved. I remember saying to him, "Ken, I think now is the day when you need to start taking it a bit easier, and I'm going to start taking a few jobs away from you." He said, "No, don't do that, that would finish me." Eventually he did agree to one or two things. Yes, he would let the apprentices pack the skip and do one or two more things for him. And he still enjoyed it. Ken was fantastic.

Before Ken Fish Arrived

Colin Harrington: Before Ken arrived we used to go on road runs and if we all arrived back together that was a masterpiece. They'd be up London Road swigging tea, coming back in buses, you say it. That was the sort of discipline at the club at the time. Jack Shelton was the trainer. Jack was one of these blokes who would come in, put his tracksuit over the top of his clothes and stand outside the dressing-room entrance. He'd say, "Do a lap." They'd do a lap and come back. "Right, another lap." He'd puff on his pipe and say, "Two more laps." When it was foggy they used to sit down the bottom and he had no idea who was training and who was not. I didn't like that indiscipline, really, I must admit. Sometimes, when we were having a training match and Jack didn't think things were going right, he'd pick up the ball and say, "I'm going in now," leaving 22 players out on the pitch.

Cyril Beavon: We used to do road runs. We'd split into two groups and Jack wouldn't know which group to go with. I remember one time when we went up to Green Road roundabout. Jack sent us off and said he'd catch us up. Well, we disagreed with him going on his bike, so we all ran like the clappers to the Green Road roundabout, and went down the subway on the other side and back to the ground. Jack was up Green Road roundabout, asking people, "Have you seen my players?"

Ken Fish: Speaking to a player one day, he said it wasn't road-work it was "dodging-work". I said, "How do you mean?" He said the trainer used to go out on the bike and then they'd lose him and one or two would even get lifts on a lorry. When they came back, they came back too early. So there was a house on the corner where some of the lads lived and they'd go and have a game of cards.

Ken Fish at Work

Ken Fish: I went into the drying-room and had a look, and there was kit hanging up, never laundered, in a shocking state, and I thought, "You'll never be able to get players to play in that type of tackle." It was out of this world. You couldn't possibly have it. So I said, "That's ready for the fire then. I'm going to burn that if I decide to come here and stay." This was on the visit. And there were a couple of potato bags full of football boots, and one or two of the boots had gone green.

Arthur Turner: Ken wasn't the type of fellow that saw every morning as a repetition. He could get players doing "novelty training," as I call it. Ken

Fish would introduce little training games, which would make it all enjoyable, and the players used to lap it up.

Ken Fish: Five to ten I would ring the bell in the referee's room. That would ring in both dressing-rooms. I would go out and check that everyone was out. One lap round the track before we started training or going on the road or whatever we were doing. The first day pre-season we did eight miles on the road and the next day we did ten and the next twelve. In the afternoon, training was all ball-work and physical work on abdominals and that sort of thing. At the beginning of the season some of them were doing 200 sit-ups. I wouldn't ask them to do anything I couldn't do. I worked seven days a week and took training on Tuesdays and Thursdays for the amateurs and part-timers. You have to make training interesting, not boring. I'd put in brain exercises where you'd take your right leg out sideways, your left arm would come up, and of course the lads had never seen this. Touch your nose with your thumb. The laughs that went on.

Ron Atkinson: There was a clock outside the old dressing-rooms, and the first day he came he got up on this big ladder and we're all watching him and he stuck sticky-tape or something over the clock so we couldn't see what time it was. He was very, very unorthodox. I remember him training us one day in a very confined indoor area, and his teeth fell out, and Colin Booth turned round to us all and said, "Look at him, his teeth have fallen and they're still chattering away even though they're on the ground." He was brilliant, Fishy, he looked after us. He was fabulous.

Nick Harris: Before I was involved in journalism, I worked for a local sports shop, and we used to supply kit to Oxford United, so I got very friendly with Ken Fish. I used to take the match-balls up to Ken and he would roll them along the floor in the dressing-room and if one wasn't right he would just throw it out the window. He wouldn't give them back to you, he would throw them out the window. But what a gentleman. What a really nice man.

Ron Atkinson: He was so reliable. If you said to Fishy at the start of the season, "In March, I want to change my left boot" or something, you wouldn't have to ask again. In March it would be done. He was so precise, so exacting in detail. And yet I had a testimonial night at Clanfield, and he forgot to pack the shorts. Ah, I tell you, did he take some flak off the players? They slaughtered him that night. That was an affront to his pride.

Nick Harris: When Ron Saunders was in charge, United played at Hull, and they had to wear the change-strip and they didn't have the socks. It was the first time he'd ever come in the shop and they wanted these socks by "tomorrow" because first thing in the morning they were going to Hull. And the next day I got to the shop late. My motor-bike broke down at Cumnor and I arrived at the shop at ten o'clock. I got to the Manor, delivered these socks, and he gave me the biggest dressing-down in front of everybody. It was the first time I'd met the team or anything. I remember Ron Atkinson saying, "Come on, Ken, give the chap a chance."

Peter Rhoades-Brown: I remember when I was injured once – I think it was a thigh strain – and I came back to fitness. It was a Reserve game. Ken was stood on the far side and I didn't realise. Ken had been with me for two or three weeks in the treatment-room, and as I was running up and down the far side I could hear this Ken Fish voice from the stand, talking to me, and I'm thinking, "He's haunting me. I can't get rid of him." And he was stood behind one of the boards on the far side. Obviously you're not allowed to coach from the sidelines, even in Reserve games, and he was stood behind there, coaching me, telling me where to run and how to run with my bad leg. It was only in the latter years that I was allowed to call him Ken, actually. Everyone had to call him Mr Fish.

Colin Clarke: Fishy was treating Colin Booth, another great player. At that time he only had a little cubby-hole at the end of the stands. It was down at an angle so you had to duck your head in under the stand ceiling. Ken had to operate in this little room, and Colin Booth was in there getting treatment Sunday morning, and Ron, myself, Cyril Beavon are looking at Ken rubbing Colin's knee and talking about the previous day's game. I think ultrasound was just coming in then, and he was sticking it on his knee and rubbing and rubbing, and he's been treating him for 15 minutes on his right knee, and Colin's gesticulated to us that it's the left knee. Now it's 15 minutes, so we're shaking away. Eventually Colin couldn't suppress himself. He said, "Ken, you know, it's my left knee." "Of course I know it's your bloody left knee, you fool, I'm just trying to gauge the two of them together. You can't work on one without gauging the strength of the other one." And he never batted an eyelid. He just said, "Yes, I think that one's okay, I'll move to your bad knee now." We were falling all over the place. Fifteen minutes.

Nick Harris: Going to Italy for the first time, to Bologna for the *Oxford Journal*, he looked after me so well. He wrote "Scoop" on all my luggage labels – "Scoop" Harris.

Gerry Summers: Bologna was the first game. Though it was a Wednesday afternoon there were quite a few people in the stadium, and he said, "We must get the supporters on our side." I said, "What are you thinking of doing, Ken?" He said, "Leave it to me," and I wondered what he was going to do. He went off and bought flowers, had them all done up in little bouquets and gave them all to the embarrassed players and they ran out and threw them at the crowd. The crowd were all ready to have a go at us, thinking, "These English people," and "Who the hell is Oxford United anyhow?" and here's these players throwing flowers to them. Then we had a tremendous reception. It took the feet from under them. Ken was liable to do that sort of thing.

Colin Clarke: I always liked a prank or two pre-season. A new stand had been developed and the changing-rooms were now under the stand. But there was always a light problem there. It was always dark when we went into training. I had bought a mask in Scotland. It cost me quite a few bob, and it was a grotesque mask with a big wart on the end of the nose. It was gruesome. It really was frightening. So I thought, "I'll bring it in, I'll wind up a few of the players and I'll probably wear it during the team-photo call." I got in early in the morning, and waited for everyone to come in. And the lighting was really bad in and around the dressing-room. I hid behind the door, and when each one came in, in turn, I stepped out and went, "Boo!" Now, you can't imagine the fright they would get. They were actually jumping in the air, and jumping across the room. I scared the living daylights out of some of them. And it's hysterical, because all the ones I've done it to are now queuing up behind me to see the reactions of everybody else. Everyone's in hysterics. So I know that Ken Fish has got to come in at some point. Ken walked in, and I got in front and I went, "Boo." And he never batted an eyelid. He said, "Get that bloody mask off, Clarkey, you're like a bloody kid." I tell you, that was a bigger laugh than anything else. The place was in hysterics.

Gerry Summers: We were always keen on warm-ups and Ken used to have them with six footballs in the old dressing-room, passing the ball and doing all sorts of things, getting them warmed and psyched up. Ron Atkinson had this thing where he had to get ten headers with a partner before he'd go out. Sometimes it was 20 keep-ups, and on the day the nerves were going, and they can't keep the thing up, and the game's being delayed until they've got these ten headers in. Ron used to tackle the concrete walls with a ball and they used to go out very motivated, self-motivated and motivated by Ken. As a young manager, I always remember walking into the dressing-room to motivate the players before the 1969 League Cup quarter-final, the most important game the club had played at that time, and I found that it was too much for me, because I was quite keyed up. I thought, "I'd better get out of here and leave it to Ken."

Maurice Evans: He used to have players jumping up and heading the wall, that sort of thing. I thought that was a bit strange when I first came and saw them jumping up and Briggsy heading the wall. I thought, "I can't really see this" but that was Briggsy, that was how he played as well. The players loved Ken. It was a great atmosphere.

11 *"The bank were returning cheques for players' wages"*

THE MICK BROWN ERA, 1975-79

Mick Brown took over a young team, and United were relegated to the Third Division in April 1976. Poor performances, the hooliganism crisis and an impending recession caused home gates to fall to below 5,000. Club finances worsened but United stayed in the Third Division. Clubs were also hit by the new freedom-of-contract regulations and expensive ground changes to conform with the Sports and Safety Act. United suffered a further massive blow – the tragic deaths of Peter and Sally Houseman in a car accident in March 1977.

MICK BROWN APPOINTED, OCTOBER 1975

Gerry Summers: I'm talking to my staff, telling them I'm going to go, and Fred Ford and Mick Brown said, "We'll pack up as well." I said, "There's no need to do that. One out of work is bad enough, but having three out of work is harder still." I really talked them into staying, and said to Mick,

"Just get on with it. You just have to get on with what happens." Mick then took over. He was well-qualified for it, for sure, and I don't think he did badly. Though they went down, I think really it was a problem of finance more than anything.

Mick Brown: Gerry said, "I've got a strong feeling that they'll offer you the job, and I'm recommending it, so it is pointless you putting yourself on the scrap heap." He was happy that I stayed and that was very, very important to me at the time.

Colin Clarke: Mick was a completely different type to Gerry. A bubbly type, an infectious type who would kick every ball with the team. He had to win. If you played five-a-side he had to be winning it. He'd stay out all day or he'd cheat to make sure his side won it. It was a big job for him and he handled it well. He took over at a time when the club were down and out financially, and maybe a little bereft of talent. Too many youngsters had to fill the gaps. He had a hard task. He and I had a couple of up-and-unders but in the end we got on with it. I left during his period, because I felt that 12 years was plenty, and I'd been through some battles in that time and maybe felt, rightly or wrongly, that I wasn't given the respect that should have been afforded me. That may be arrogance on my part, but I did feel that at the time, so I left by going to a tribunal, from which I was given a free transfer. Although I left in a little bit of a cloud, as it was, it didn't take away the fact that I enjoyed the 12 years.

Relegation to Division Three, 1975-76

Mick Brown: The club had got nine points at the end of October, and nobody had ever recovered from such a bad start as that. But if you take the period from then to the end of the season, our League form would have put us about halfway up the table. I remember we went to Portsmouth and won, and we went to Notts County and won, and we won home games. We won three games on the trot and never moved a place in the table. As I went about the country watching games, other managers and coaches would be saying to me, "Hey, what do you think you're doing?" All of a sudden everybody was panicking – there was Oxford coming on a bit of a charge when they considered them dead and buried.

Mac: The first time I went to the Manor was during the relegation season. I couldn't believe that so many people could be in the same place at the same time. It was Plymouth at home. We drew two-all. Mick Tait scored for us, and Paul Mariner scored for Plymouth. 1976. It was the year that Southampton won the Cup and I remember an away match at Southampton towards the end of the season. We lost 2-1 and someone nicked my scarf off my wrist. There was about 18,000 at that game. It was terrifying. But really exciting. John Shuker scored a penalty and Colin Clarke scored an own-goal. The ball was curled in by Peter Rodrigues, I think, and Colin Clarke's leg went one way and the ball went the other way. Roy Burton just held his face in his hands. I remember John Shuker very well. Whenever we played football in the park, my mates were all "Allan Clarke" and I was someone like "Peter Foley", but when we got a penalty I'd run up and go "Shuker" and it would go right in the corner. If I didn't say "Shuker" I'd miss.

Tim Sparrowhawk: I remember an away game at the old Eastville Stadium. Bristol Rovers. I think we were under the cosh for about 89 minutes. Then Roger Gibbins popped up with this goal. You can never say the game is dead with Oxford. There was this match at Orient that we lost at the end of the season, and I can remember the Oxford fans calling for the team to come on the pitch as if they'd just got promotion. The team sheepishly had to come on the pitch and acknowledge the cheers of the fans.

Peter Foley: The dressing-room was a horrible place, and some of the senior players were very disappointed, players who'd been at the club for a long time, and had risen from the Fourth to the Second, only then to get relegated back into the Third. But we had five or six of us aged only 18 then, so we were probably too young to know what was happening.

The Fans

Colin Clarke: They were a little bit critical at times, the Oxford fans, but they were very loyal. They turned up as regular as clockwork. I was always "Old Clarkey, Old Clarkey." I think I got on fairly well with them. I never got any stick in all the 12 years. You were part of them, because you played for Oxford. You were a little bit of their property. I always found I got on well with all the old boys, and I used to drink in all the pubs. You got pestered of a weekend if you went out. You had to explain why you gave this pass-back and this, that and the other. But by and large they were a loyal lot and they kept turning up. I got a letter once from a guy who more-or-less said I was the best thing since sliced bread and they should make me manager when I hang up my boots and all this, so I was a bit chuffed. It was handwritten, and he was very literate, and it was obviously a very intelligent letter. I just happened to show it around, and I hadn't looked at the address. "Oh, look at this, guys, somebody saying what a wonderful player I am and how when I finish my career I should become manager, take over the club and take them into a new era, and this sort of thing." They've taken one look at it and it's addressed "Littlemore". They said, "It's a blooming inmate. He writes to all the lads and writes that stuff." And I was so deflated after this big build-up. I've still got that letter. It was really nice.

Peter Foley: As a striker it's a love-hate relationship. If you're scoring goals they love you. If you're missing chances they hate you. But that's part and parcel of the game really. I know there have been one or two players who have gone to clubs and have been absolutely crucified by supporters and have had to leave the club because of it. I don't think, in all the time I was at Oxford, that a player there ever had so much abuse that he had to leave the club.

Fred Ellis: I think in those days Mick Brown, who's now the club secretary, did a lot of good unpaid work for the club. He started the London Road Club, which was a fantastic idea.

Mick Brown [supporter, later club secretary]: My first away match was at St Andrews, where we drew 0-0 against Birmingham City [2 October 1971]. There was 32,000 at the game. Quite a big crowd for my away debut! It opened my eyes to perils and pitfalls of going to away matches. I got streetwise, so to speak. It just snowballed from there. I started running coaches to football matches about 1974 or 1975. Because there was fairly widespread trouble at football matches in those days, a number of people ran coaches to Oxford away matches and I was just one of a number. As coach organisers, we were invited to a meeting of the Thames Valley Crime Prevention Panel – quite a mouthful – of which Jim Hunt sat on the committee, together with senior people from the police. They suggested that more organised travel arrangements were made, and the London Road Club was effectively formed there. Our first match was the fixture at Cambridge, where unfortunately there was a lot of trouble, although our coaches, because of the traffic, never arrived until after kick-off, so we weren't attributed to the trouble. That would be about 1976 or 1977. The London Road Club, I'm pleased to say, has thrived from thereon, and is still offering what it was always intended to – cheap transport. My involvement, and my enthusiasm for the club, came to the notice of the board of directors at that time, and I was invited to join the club in a commercial capacity. Peter Marsh was on the board. Peter was involved in various crowd-psychology projects.

Peter Marsh: It was a very strange experience, being a director. Here I was as a struggling academic and somehow I found myself on the board. It was basically through Desmond Morris, who's an old chum of mine. Desmond had been seduced on to the board, and later to vice-chairman, and felt a bit lonely among dentists and butchers and people like that, so I think he wanted a kindred spirit. It did seem very strange at the time. It seems even stranger now in retrospect. I was not only a supporter but I did my PhD thesis up there on the terraces [published in 1978 as *The Rules of Disorder*]. The London Road fans in the mid-seventies were really no different from other fans. Although they got labelled as hooligans and savages and demons, and the image of the London Road was that it ran with blood most Saturdays, that didn't actually happen at football games. There's a lot of talk about it but it never quite happens in the way that people imagine.

Chris Fallows: I had trouble against Sheffield United once. These blokes piled out of a mini-bus and laid into me and a couple of my mates. They didn't particularly hurt you, but you thought afterwards, "What is the point of going up there for that?" I went for the rest of that season, but the next season, for the first few games, I couldn't be bothered. I thought, "I might as well stay in the pub, have a drink with my mates, rather than go up the football with the fear that I might get some idiots jumping on me."

Mac: Spectators could walk round the ground. I used to stand in the Beech Road while the captains tossed up, then stand behind whichever goal Oxford were kicking towards. At half-time I would walk round to the other end. The manager's dug-out used to be on the Osler Road side. I think it was because they used to swear so much that they didn't want the Beech Road to hear it! The managers had to come out before the players so they could walk across the pitch and get to the dug-out on time. It seemed like it was always raining. I don't remember any sunny matches at all! I remember a 3-3 draw with Peterborough. The Third Division days were like a permanent three-all draw.

The Third Division

Mick Brown [manager]: With young players you're never quite sure how they are going to react. You might think that they are looking like being decent players but until you actually throw them into the lion's den, you're never going to know. Also, when a club is on a slide, it's very, very hard to arrest that slide. Going down a division isn't necessarily the sanctuary that you think it is. You can very quickly slip through the net yet again, and I was always aware that that was a strong possibility. The first thing to do was to try to stabilise the ship. We managed to do that, and what pleased me most was that wherever we went people always respected that we tried to play football. In fact, that was a criticism of us, if you like. A certain manager once said to me, "Of course, you know the trouble with you?" I said, "No, but go on, you're going to tell me." He said, "You play too much football." I said, "Well, I'll stand accused of that. If that's the worst thing they can say about me, then I'm happy with that one."

Peter Foley: A lot of us had come through the youth team together so we had a great spirit amongst us. Billy Jeffrey got in the first team when he was 16. At the time I think he was the youngest player to represent Oxford United in a League game. Billy was a great passer of the ball, short passes or long, a typically determined Scot. There were some good young lads at the club at the time. I felt maybe we didn't benefit because we all got thrown in together. Les Taylor later captained an FA Cup Final team [Watford in 1984]. What higher honour can you get than that? Les was another tigerish player. Up and down, up and down. He was a good tackler. He could pass the ball. And he scored a lot of goals from midfield.

Mac: Les Taylor used to live in digs opposite where I lived in Barnes Road, Cowley. He was a really good player. His landlady's garden backed on to a park and we used to purposely set up goal-posts right in front of the garden and hope that Les Taylor was out there, sunbathing after football, so that he could spot us and have a word with the manager, who'd sign us all on, so we'd be playing in the same team as Les Taylor a week later. You've got to put yourself in the shop-window, haven't you?

Peter Foley: Taity [Mick Tait] was a good player. He could play everywhere. He scored goals for the club and defensively he could do a good job as well. He always got one or two red cards a season, Taity, because he needed a rest every now and then!

Mick Brown: There was the day at Blackpool. Blackpool were always a useful outfit, but there was no reason to know what was going to happen. John Shuker got sent off. That was rare enough in itself, for John to be in any sort of trouble. It happened out of nothing, and all of a sudden we had three players sent off. There was nothing leading up to it. We weren't that type of a team. Peter Houseman was one. One of their players spat in his face or something. The ball was out of play. The next thing Peter hit this fellow with a left hook. It was a nightmare day. To be fair, Mick Tait was always a bit of a volatile character, and you could see that happening with Mick, but you didn't think so with Peter Houseman and John Shuker.

Peter Foley: Gary Briggs was there in the early days. Briggsy was the first player to come through an independent tribunal. He was a great servant for the club. One of the hardest players I've ever seen in the Football League.

Mick Brown: I think, in the record books, Lacey of Tottenham is down as the first one recorded as *going* for the tribunal, but on the day they changed the thing round and he became the second one to go through. I always maintain that Gary Briggs was in fact the first player ever to be transferred under the tribunal. I'd seen this young fellow playing for Middlesbrough Reserves and he had impressed me. We eventually persuaded them to let us have him on loan, and he came and played the first month and everybody was so taken with him they said, "Buy him." I said, "But they don't want to sell." John Neal was the manager of Middlesbrough, and he had been a player at Hull when I was a young player. John must have got fed up with me ringing up and saying, "Well, come on, let's agree a fee." "No, take him for another month." They were quite happy to have one of their players playing in a League team and doing well, where they could keep an eye on him, his value going up all the time. Our directors wanted to get him signed as quickly as possible for the very same reason, but I was the ping-pong ball in the middle. John said, "Take him for the full three months, to the end of the season." I said, "John, he's not going to want to come back. He's going to want to stay, and then you and I will have to go to a tribunal." It made a bit of an enemy of John, because he wasn't very happy at the outcome. I was mandated to agree up to £30,000. I told John we'd do that, but if it got to a tribunal situation, we were in a totally different ball game, and that would not be my offer. We went to the tribunal and I did a lot of work with the directors, sitting down, planning our offer, and we actually put in an offer of £12,500, and the tribunal came out with £12,500, so in the end I'm very, very pleased with the job of work we did there because Gary went on and did 10 or 11 years. Yeah, I'm very happy with that one. And David Fogg. I signed David on a free transfer from Wrexham and he's another one who did ten years.

Peter Foley: They used to say that Foggy was "the best free-transfer ever". I only ever saw him get roasted twice. He got roasted by the same player twice – Mossy [David Moss], who later became the assistant manager at United. He roasted him once when he was at Luton and once when he was at Swindon. But apart from Mossy, I never saw anybody give Foggy the run-around. He was a good professional.

Mick Brown: When I brought Hugh Curran back, he was actually running the bar at Bolton Wanderers. He came back to Oxford and scored something like 12 or 13 goals. He could hardly train with chronic knees, and sometimes he couldn't play as regularly as I wanted him to. There was a classic match where I had him as sub and we were a goal down. We got a free-kick and I thought, "Go on, get on, see if you can whack this." He didn't take the free-kick, but the ball went in, came out, and all of a sudden he whacked this ball and it went in the net and in doing so he got injured and had to come off. I bet he'd not been on the field a minute and a half.

Peter Foley: Hughie was my minder for a couple of seasons. If anybody was giving me a bit of a kicking, Hughie used to sort them out. He was a player of the highest quality, a Scottish international. He could head the ball harder than most of us could kick it. He gave me lots of tips, and always encouraged me. My best season, when I scored 23 goals, was playing next to Hughie. Hughie was strong in the air and I used to follow him around and get on to things quickly when they dropped on the floor. He was sent off once at Chesterfield. We had two players end up in hospital, Hughie got sent off and I was limping on both legs, but we managed to hold out for a 1-1 draw. They were all going to beat us up in the supporters' bar afterwards, because they were so incensed at Hughie. We went in there afterwards for a drink, and they were all gunning for Hughie's head, so we had a quick pint, back on the team bus and home. The old pros always looked after us: Shukes [John Shuker], Burty [Roy Burton], Hugh Curran, Brian Drysdale and Colin Clarke. Colin Clarke was a good player. The left foot was the wand. He used to say, "You just show me the channel and I'll deliver it in there with the wand". He had a lovely left foot. He probably had too much skill for a centre-half because they're usually a bit big and dopey, but Clarkey was a very intellectual jock. He gave me lots of advice and always encouraged me. He was also a great goalscorer ... a great own-goal scorer. We played Port Vale one day. Port Vale was a bloody horrible place to go, dull and dark and the mud's really black. I was only a young lad and I think I was playing right-side midfield, totally out of position, and hating every minute of the day. What I do remember is that somebody crossed the ball, penalty spot, and Clarkey volleyed it into the top corner. Burty never moved an inch. One of the best goals I've ever seen. Definitely the best own-goal I've ever seen. Clarkey will deny it if you speak to him, but I saw it with my own two eyes – Colin Clarke, own-goal. I remember a game at Hull. I scored a volley from a corner. It went like a rocket and I wasn't the best striker of the ball. Most of my goals were tap-ins, typical striker goals, but this day I hit one at Hull and it flew in the top corner. It was Gordon Hodgson's first game for the club. We signed him from Mansfield and he became a great friend of mine at the club. We won 1-0 at Hull that day and I think he thought that he'd signed for something special ... but he hadn't!

Penalties

Peter Foley: I've never known players so frightened to take penalties. I don't know what it was about the club but we always used to miss. One day we played Hereford at the Manor. I think we won 5-2. In the second half, we were going downhill towards the London Road, the crowd were going mad because we're winning, which was a bit of a rarity in those days, and we had a penalty, so up I stepped, yours truly, and I think the goalie saved mine. Anyway, the game carried on, and inside a few minutes we got a second penalty. Up steps Hughie Curran, puts the ball on the spot, struts back in the way Hughie used to strut, runs up to the ball, a little dummy, and the goalkeeper's dived to his left. Hughie's lent back and nonchalantly knocked it about ten yards over the bar. You can imagine the crowd's feelings there. Two penalties. Against Exeter I scored one and missed one. The first one I ever missed was at Tranmere. We were 4-0 down at half-time, and Mick Brown threw a wobbly and resigned on the spot. We went out for the second half and we had a penalty and it was about six inches of mud all over the place, and it was horrible. I always used to stick them to the goalie's left, and I don't know what happened this night but I chose to put it in the other corner. By the time it got to the goal I think the goalie could have done ten press-ups and picked it up. That was the first one I'd missed. Then on the Monday Mick was training and things continued as normal, and the resignation was never mentioned again.

Cup Games

Mick Brown: Obviously I remember the one at Manchester United [FA

Cup third round 1976]. Tommy Docherty's side were having one of those spells when they were beating everybody. I don't think anybody had gone to Old Trafford and given them such a hard game as we did, and to my dying day I maintain that we got done on two of the dodgiest penalties that have ever been seen. A couple of weeks later Gerry Daly wrote an article and said that the most embarrassing moments in his life were striding up to take two penalties that he knew weren't penalties against Oxford United. We got beaten 2-1. I was really, really gutted, because I don't think we could have done any more. That was hard to take. And I can remember Andy McCulloch going through and being brought down in the box, clearly inside the box. The whole crowd went quiet, and the referee, I can see him now, said, "Play on." There's not many brave enough to give that sort of a penalty at Old Trafford. I remember walking out the door with tears in my eyes, feeling for the boys, and some reporter said, "They must be the worst two decisions you've ever seen in your life," and I went, "Yep." Of course, the Sunday papers were, "Brown slams referee – 'worst decisions I've ever seen in my life'." I ended up getting a letter from the FA, charged with bringing the game into disrepute, which I thought was rather ironical after everything that had gone on, but I got off that. Nevertheless I had to go through the whole process and bite my tongue.

Colin Clarke: Although we established ourselves in non-League circles, as Headington United, we were subsequently punished when we met non-League teams in the Cup from our position as a League club. We had a terrible record: Bedford [1966-67], Chelmsford [1967-68] and Kettering [1976-77]. Derek Dougan came and scored the winner for Kettering from four inches. A four-inch shot. That was another bad night for Oxford.

Peter Foley: We lost against Nuneaton [1977-78]. We played Notts Forest in the League Cup one night, and they came down with this star-studded team – Birtles, Woodcock, Robertson, Larry Lloyd, Viv Anderson, McGovern – and they beat us 5-0 and we didn't touch the ball. They were magnificent. The game started and I worked my way into position and Larry Lloyd came next to me. I looked at his legs, and I swear that my two legs together weren't as big as one of his legs, and I remember he clattered me, and I hit the deck. I thought, "My God." In all the years that I'd played I think that was the hardest I'd ever been tackled. I was, "Hhhhhhh, hhhhhhh, give me some breath."

Mick Brown: I think we had played Plymouth in the round before. We drew at the Manor and Malcolm Allison made some statements about what they were going to do to us down there, and I used that in my team talk down at Plymouth. I gave a cutting to Jason Seacole, saying, "That's what Malcolm thinks about you." Jason Seacole got us the winning goal that day. We had the right to play Nottingham Forest, but we'd got a load of injuries and a couple of YTS lads playing in that game. They gave us an exhibition of why they were the best. I'd got a couple of bottles of champagne, and I went to take them to Brian Clough, just to say, "It was a pleasure to watch you play." As I arrived at the door, Peter Shilton said, "Come in," and I went in and all the big name players were there, and Cloughie sat there, holding court, and I felt like a schoolboy who'd been called up in front of the headmaster, and all I wanted to do was give him two bottles of champagne and say "Well done" but it's not quite as easy as that with Brian. He had to hold court, lecture us all, and not one of their players said a word.

Financial Problems

Mick Brown: I knew the problems better than anybody else in the town. Clubs bent over backwards to keep their financial problems out of the public eye, and yet Oxford became one of the first clubs to go public and tell people what the situation was: "The Inland Revenue are going to close us down next week; bills have got to be paid and if we don't then we are talking about days." Once that started to happen, it became a fashion up and down the country. All the other clubs suddenly came out and let it be known. It became a question of having to sell our better players and promote another kid. It was very difficult for the supporters to stomach that. It was very difficult for me as a manager, who wanted to get on and be somebody. It was difficult for players who wanted to stay but knew that they had to move. The whole situation was a difficult one and it needed strong people to see it out. Fortunately we did, and the club then went on to better things. But there was very, very serious danger of it going under. It got to a stage at one time where you couldn't even think of taking a player on loan. It was just simply paying the wages, and the bank were returning cheques for players' wages on Friday. You have done your Friday morning work, trying to prepare the players for the match on the Saturday, they've gone off to the bank and come back and knocked on your door, saying, "Hey, the cheque's bounced." Well, that's hardly the greatest preparation for going out and fighting relegation the next day. We had board meetings until three and four o'clock in the morning and trying to be fresh and prepared to do the business the next day was extremely hard, but it was an apprenticeship that you couldn't have bettered anywhere.

Peter Houseman

John Shuker: Peter Houseman came to the club from Chelsea and he hadn't been there very long before everybody realised what a good player he was. He had so much skill it was unbelievable. I used to play left-back at the time and he was mostly on the left wing, and he used to say to me: "Look, John, even if there's a man marking me, just give it me, don't worry." I used to give it to him, and he was so skilful that he would just get out of trouble with no problem. He was also a very good friend of mine.

Colin Clarke: Peter was well-loved and amazing for team spirit. He'd be the first one in the dressing-room, shaking hands with the players before the game, and giving you a pat on the back: "Come on, let's go for it." Personally, he was a good friend of mine. He was so warm and we had a lot of common interests. From time to time Pete and I would go out for a meal together. We would wait until the hard session of the week was finished, the Shotover session on a Tuesday. We'd sit there and think, "Thank God that's out the way," and we'd sip our Chateaubriand and talk about his Chelsea days and talk about football, and we'd do that maybe once every six weeks or so.

John Shuker: I lived in Aston and Peter bought a house in Witney. My wife, Lynn, and Sally [Houseman] got on well together. Peter and I used to travel in together. The families went out together, and their children played with ours. On the night that Peter and Sally died [in a car accident] we had a do at Cowley works. They went with two neighbours and we took a couple of friends from where we lived in Aston. We met them there and stayed together all evening.

Mick Brown: The terrible irony was that it was another one of those functions that we'd put on to raise money for the club. All the players had done very well in attending these functions. Peter's neighbour's wife, who drove the car, never had a drink at any stage. I still remember coming home that night, and seeing blue lights flashing and one thing and another, and thinking, "Oh, some poor soul has had an accident." I got home and it wasn't long afterwards when police called. I find it very difficult now to talk about that, because it brings it all back, but at the time I was absolutely devastated. That was a bitter, bitter blow.

Colin Clarke: Peter really was a larger-than-life figure. He exuded such warmth and vitality. He was a huge figure in the dressing-room, and on the pitch. We didn't really recover from Peter, because, far apart from his ability, which was enormous, he was a person we looked forward to seeing in the mornings. He would always be holding parties for the kids. He'd invite the Dads round, he'd separate the kids and we'd go into the other room and have a good drink and reminisce. He brought the club together in a lot of ways. He brought the players together. He was badly missed.

John Shuker: I'll never forget Peter and Sally, and neither will my wife. We still go down to the grave, and put flowers there. It was a big loss to football and everything really.

The Backroom Staff

Mick Brown: I was extremely lucky in that I had two of the finest men in football to lean on as a young manager – Ken Fish and Fred Ford. Two lovely men. I don't think I could have seen through those four years without their help and guidance. They should have got the freedom of the city of Oxford. Then we got Ray Graydon. He'd been at Aston Villa and been quite a big name and gone off to the States. Ray did very well, even after I left. He loved Fred Ford, and he learned an awful lot from Fred. Ray wanted to learn and I think he followed Fred around all day, finding out what Fred did, and it fired his enthusiasm. I took Bill Asprey on to run the Reserves. I knew Bill as a player, and we'd been on an FA coaches tour to Zambia. Then, when I left, he took over as manager.

Mick Brown's Departure

Mick Brown: Ron Atkinson suddenly came on and said that he needed a new assistant manager at West Brom. I think it was right for me and right for the club. I'd done just short of ten years. Sometimes you can overstay your welcome and I didn't want to do that. The club actually got a transfer fee for me. Can you believe that? It was called compensation. I only had a little to do before my contract was up, so it really wasn't an issue, but West Brom paid money for me. It worked out fine because we had two good years at West Brom and that led on to Manchester United.

12 *"It was like a magician using his wand"*

UNDER BILL ASPREY AND IAN GREAVES, 1979-82

Bill Asprey's managerial spell (1979-80) included an FA Cup defeat at non-League Barking, but his signing of Malcolm Shotton was one for the future. Bottom of the Third Division in December 1980, United's playing fortunes improved dramatically when Ian Greaves arrived as manager. A financial crisis led to the intervention of Robert Maxwell in January 1982. A week later United won 3-0 at First Division Brighton in the FA Cup, but Ian Greaves resigned soon afterwards.

UNDER BILL ASPREY, 1979-80

Chris Fallows: Bill Asprey and his team were getting a bit of criticism from the supporters. Rightly so. We had a poor team then.

Peter Foley: I think supporters throughout the country are the same. If the team are doing well and you're playing well, they think it's great. If they think you're not playing well, and the team's not playing well, then you get the abuse. Over the year that I was scoring all the goals they used to sing that I could walk on water. Then there were other times when they would sing "What a load of rubbish." I remember one game. Bill Asprey was the manager and he took me off. I didn't feel I was doing that bad that night, but the crowd were giving me a bit of stick and the Boss took me off. Next day I went to see him, and I said that I felt that the crowd had made the substitution. Anyway he disagreed, and I asked for a transfer. In one of my moods! He put it in the press that that was the last time I played for him, and it all got a little bit nasty. Anyway, with a few injuries and a few bad results, he decided to put me back in, but it was as substitute. We played Plymouth Argyle at home. We'd been going about 70 minutes and the manager said, "Warm up." So I've gone running down to the London Road end to warm up, and suddenly there's this huge shout from the crowd, "Eff off, Foley, eff off, Foley." I went on, scored within two minutes and we won 1-0. At the end of the game I was walking on water again. That's how it is as a forward.

Chris Fallows: They had a very poor team then but you still kept going. You used to moan that you were never going up there again and you were wasting your money, but then you'd still go again. Then you could see the rise when Ian Greaves took over. They were bottom of the League at Christmas and he got them out of it. I think he formed the basis for the team that got in the First Division and won the Milk Cup. Not because of the players, but the attitude.

Ian Greaves Appointed, December 1980

Ian Greaves: I'd been sacked from Bolton in January 1980 after spending six years there and being very successful. I'd been helping out a pal at Hereford, looking at matches for him and things like that, then someone from Oxford contacted me and asked if I would like to have a word regarding the position there. I accepted the job on Christmas Eve. The other person involved was Bill McGarry, an old sweat like me. One of the most vivid memories for me was going to my office the first morning. There were trees there. We don't have trees around football grounds in the north, we have big iron mills and smoke and things like that. But the most marvellous thing was a squirrel running along the wall. I couldn't put the two together. How could a squirrel be running along the wall of a football ground? It was too nice a place. I thought, "Oh, my God there's some shaking up going to have to be done here." In a way, that squirrel was as responsible as anything for the way I shook up things at Oxford. I remember arriving there on New Year's Eve and they were having a New Year's Day or New Year's Eve lunch, and I cancelled it. I just said, "This is not a Christmas club from today on. This is a football club." It didn't endear me to too many people around the place but I made it clear right from the beginning that I wasn't there to be loved, I was there to get success. The club had been months upon months without a victory, to the point where they were bottom of the division by x number of points.

Nick Harris: Ian Greaves came along, and he turned things round in a matter of a few weeks. It was a marvellous experience being around him. He instilled such confidence in the club. He put faith in the youngsters. Ian Greaves must really take a great deal of credit at United. He brought a lot of fun back to the game, and a lot of fun back to the Manor. I thought he did a very good job.

Ian Greaves: I remember that our first game was against Charlton, who were top of the table. We beat Charlton at home 1-0, which was like the shock of the day in football. I think we went to Reading for the following match, which I discovered was a vicious local derby, and we beat them 1-0, and from thereon in we went 29 games and lost about four. Over the two half-seasons to when I left – Christmas to the end of the season, and the start of the next season to the February – I think we played something like 49 games and lost nine. If you had put them two half-seasons together you'd have been promoted, wouldn't you? I got the credit because it was like a magician using his wand, but I give so much credit to the lads. They were superb, great to work with. It was difficult to know in the first month, because I'm a very hard lad if people don't do it my way. I get very annoyed very quickly, which Briggsy and Shotton and people like that, big as they were, found out. I did it my way, and them two in particular were superb. I changed the style of play completely. I changed it to a northern style of football – tough, argumentative, niggly. Yeah, I got us niggly, I got us argumentative as a team. I didn't want us to have our names taken. I didn't want people sent off. Big Shotty got sent off and got the full verbals from me. That was the only time anybody got really in trouble with me. I was a bugger for things like that.

Peter Foley: He made us defensively a very difficult club to beat. Most of the training was not so much what we did with the ball, it was what to do when the other team had the ball. We all had our little jobs to do. It wasn't complicated. We became a very, very difficult club to beat. I think we went 14 or 15 games one season without losing, having lost loads the year before.

Ian Greaves: We brought big Roy Burton, the goalkeeper, back from nowhere. He played superb, and he'd been given a free transfer a couple of years before. He had been brought back from somewhere as a second 'keeper and he played out of his skin for the year I was there. It was just marvellous the way the lads reacted. Billy Jeffrey. Everybody told me that Billy had gone, but he was absolutely superb in my time at Oxford. John Doyle, the right-back, had done practically nothing prior to me arriving. All of a sudden he's playing like Alf Ramsey. Don't ask me why. I have got some ability as a football manager, I do know that, but I wasn't Midas. I don't know why they reacted as they did. They reacted to the point where they were almost pushing for promotion when I left, which was quite ludicrous with the squad that we had.

Peter Foley: Ian Greaves turned a side that couldn't win very many games into a side that lost very few games, with the same players. He was a great manager. He was dead straight. You knew exactly what you had to do and if you didn't do it you were out. If you did it, you got a good pat on the back and "Let's look forward to the next game". He got me going again. I'd had a couple of years where I'd gone off and was very stale and maybe needed to move. Once Ian came to the club, he gave the club a bit of a shaking-up. I think I benefited, and started scoring a few goals again.

Ian Greaves: When I arrived, Foley had stopped scoring, stopped running, stopped playing, and inside a couple of months he looked like an international. He was going where I asked him to go. He was running in areas where he hadn't run in his entire career. All of a sudden he looked a really good player. Big Joe Cooke, the big black lad up front, looked a good player for a couple of months. Andy Thomas, the young kid, did well. I stopped playing him up front, I tucked him in behind the two strikers. He was a slim lad. You just blew him and he fell over. I just tucked him in so no-one could tackle him and he couldn't stop scoring. He was lazy but talented, so you use them in a different way, don't you?

Sandy Brewer: I was always interested in Thomas because I'd been along to watch him playing for the Oxford youth team. I thought there was an international in the making. I often wonder whether he would have made it if he hadn't broken his leg down in the West Country. In his very early days he was a centre-forward who scored a lot of nice goals. I saw his first Reserve game at the Manor. I used to park in Lime Walk, and I was about a minute late and by the time I'd got in he'd already got one. I think he went on to get another two or three in the same game.

Cup Games, 1981

Ian Greaves: The one I remember most was at Everton [League Cup third round]. I don't know why, other than we should have won it. It was just before Howard [Kendall] got it going again at Everton. We went up there flying, and we went 1-0 down. To this day I can remember that Keith Cassells missed two sitters. We were like blood brothers, me and Cass, and I later took him with me to Mansfield.

Jack Fallows: We went to Everton with the London Road Club, and of course the native police are very strict at Everton: "Right, form two queues if you know what two queues are. Get your money ready." Anyway, we all filed into the Everton ground, and that night we did really well. We lost 1-0. Joe Cooke was down the far end of the ground and we all thought it was in for the equaliser and it didn't come off, but it was a great game. The Everton supporters clapped United off, I shall never ever forget that.

Ian Greaves: We went to play a non-League team on the coast in the FA Cup first round. Was it Dover? The Friday night I'm with Doc Morris at the studios in London. The following day we go to Dover. The lads are already down and I go and join them on the Saturday morning. I hadn't done my homework. I hadn't checked up. Do you know, they hadn't won against a non-League side for years? They were scared. It was only on the Friday night that Doc Morris said to me, "Oh, that first goal tomorrow, Ian, we need it badly." I said, "What's up with you?" He said, "We haven't won against non-League clubs for years." We beat Dover 2-0, no problem, but I could smell the fear in the dressing-room.

Nick Harris: United played at Aldershot [FA Cup second round] and drew 2-2 and beat them in the replay when Keith Cassells got a hat trick. I was going to interview Ian Greaves. I'm not very good with equipment, and I remember him rebuilding the tape-recorder for me before we could actually do the interview.

Maxwell the Saviour, January 1982

Peter Marsh: The state of the club in the late seventies was really the state of virtually all other struggling Third Division clubs. I think we needed about 11,000 through the turnstiles every other Saturday just to break even, and were getting between 4,000 and 7,000, so quite clearly, as a profitable exercise, it was a non-starter. Increasingly, like a lot of other clubs, it began to rely on promotion departments, lotteries, peripheral things like that, and various people chucking in bits of money from time to time. Although the bank was threatening to pull the plug on Oxford United, the club's assets were in fact rather larger than its debts. It was a viable going-concern. There was some basis there for actually running the club. But, yes, we were in trouble, and the bank was on the verge of calling in the overdraft, so we were faced with getting new injections of capital or getting a new chairman or new directors. There were very few options left open to us.

Jim Hunt: We'd got an overdraft of £162,000 and we'd got a facility for £150,000. We also owed something in the region of £30,000 to people outside of the bank, and the bank could not forsee any improvement, having done a budget for the next 12 months. They told us, at Christmas 1981, that they would close us down if we couldn't repay the £150,000. Well, we couldn't repay the £150,000 and they gave us 14 days' notice that they would not cash any cheques after 31 December. So, if we didn't do anything between 1 January and 14 January 1982, the wages wouldn't be paid. It was then that I was asked if the board of directors would like to speak to Robert Maxwell. And that's how it all started. Maxwell was on holiday in the West Indies at the time and he just told the bank to hold everything till he came back.

Edmund Gibbs: Well, the phone went one day. Olive answered it, and it was Maxwell. He'd been approached by the people who were running the football club. They'd got into this kind of bankruptcy situation. The bailiffs were coming in on the following Monday and they'd asked Maxwell to rescue the club. When he spoke to me, he didn't know whether to go ahead with it or not. He'd got a management-consultancy report saying, "Don't touch it with a bargepole." So I went up there merely to see if it was possible, financially, to do it. I went up there on a Tuesday and he shoved this report in front of me and said, "You'd better read this," so I read it. He said, "What do you think?" I said, "They don't know anything about running a Football League club. What's the total indebtedness?" So he said what it was and produced a great list of debts that the outgoing chairman had given to him. I said, "It can be made to pay but you've got to change things quite a bit." He said, "Would you come back and assist me on this?" I said, "Well, for six months, on certain conditions."

Jim Hunt: Robert Maxwell became chairman of the club and bought shares. I understand there is a rule somewhere – and you can check this out – that you had to have 75 per cent of any shares to enable you to transfer any tax losses to other subsidiary companies. Oxford United had quite a lot of tax losses that he could take. That's how I understand it anyway. He paid about £121,800. I'm not sure of the exact figure. He paid £1 each share. I said to him, "Everyone's paying £4 a share." He said to me, "Do you want £121,800 or don't you?" And obviously the board of directors decided that £121,800 at £1 a share was better than nothing at all. And nobody else looked like coming forward. Then the first thing Maxwell did of course was to change our bank from Barclays to Nat West.

Edmund Gibbs: So we switched banks and he guaranteed £250,000, which we didn't use in my time because we didn't need it. He paid in £121,000 and said, "Why do you want me to put this in?" I said, "Well, if it goes wrong, you're going to lose it. I want to make sure you're committed. A loan merely makes the £100,000 debt into a £220,000 debt and that's no good, and I don't want to be involved if that's the situation." They'd lost £100,000 in the six months up to that January and the next six months we made £200,000, partly by selling players, mostly through the pools again.

Jim Hunt: Funnily enough, if we had known that some few weeks later we would sell Keith Cassells and Mark Wright to Southampton for something like £160,000 maybe we wouldn't have needed him anyway, although I do believe that, had we not done that, by the end of the following season the club would have been back where they were in the first place.

Peter Marsh: I had my own reservations, which I expressed at the time. I'm not trying to wash my hands of that whole episode, but I did argue very strongly that maybe Maxwell, with his Board of Trade record and so on, was not the ideal candidate for us. But you have to accept that Maxwell came in, put the money in when the overdraft was being called in, and financially rescued the club. And that's why I think our decision was unanimous, including me, to invite him to be chairman. Maxwell bought the whole thing, lock, stock and barrel, for 120 grand, which must have been a bargain by anybody's judgment.

v Brighton, FA Cup Fourth Round, January 1982

Peter Foley: We went there, a Third Division side, and I think Brighton were placed about sixth in the First Division. They were the highest-placed First Division team still in the FA Cup, and were one of the favourites to win it. We went down there and we blitzed them. We played out of our skins, and the manager fancied us to win as well. Keith Cassells scored a fabulous first goal. He may have fouled the Brighton defender. They were both chasing the ball, and I think Keith may have nicked his ankles a little bit, but the referee waved play on, and suddenly he struck one in the top corner from about 25 yards. That was a great start. Then within 10 minutes, Billy Jeffrey knocked the ball over their back four, about 16 yards out, and I just ran in and sweetly knocked it on the volley and it flew into the bottom corner, probably one of the best goals I've scored. Of course that put us 2-0 up. From that point onwards, the more they tried the worse they got, and everything we tried came off. And the second half, a rarity, I scored a header. It wasn't a classic, it was just a bobbly thing that went over the goalie's head. Then, afterwards, the Oxford fans wouldn't go home. They stayed on the terraces for ages and ages and ages. It was excellent. That was maybe the turning-point for the club. That got the name of the club going again.

Mick Brown: We not only ran coaches to Brighton but we hired trains from British Rail. Nobody expected us to do anything and we came home convincing 3-0 winners. It was shortly after Maxwell had taken over, but we were still involved in fund-raising. We had a "Save Oxford Soccer" committee to raise money. We'd arranged a stag-night at a club, and I'd arranged buses to pick us up from the "football special" and take us up there. Unfortunately the stag-night took second stage really. Having won, against Brighton, the majority of people there were supporters, and it was just a celebration. That was a good night, certainly one that sticks high in my mind from my days connected with the club.

Ian Greaves: I'd been on television in London, I'm coming back in a taxi to Oxford, going to give it a big trip with a nice meal, a nice night-out and a few bevies, and I look on the billboard and it doesn't say "Great win by Oxford United at Brighton", it says "More places in university this year." I thought, "They're not giving us a mention and we've just beaten a First Division team." Now that shocked me. That had something to do with me going. From Maxwell arriving, I knew it was time to go. I went home one night, picked up the *Oxford Mail* and Maxwell was quoted as saying, "I spoke to the manager today and I told him that we mustn't get promotion this year but it must be next." We'd never had a word between us. I went straight down to Pergamon Press. The board table was as big as this room. I'm sat at this end and he's about 40 yards down there, and he said, "Oh, you're the best chappie for this job. I know you are a good man." And I thought, "Hey." I got up out of my chair and walked round and plonked the *Mail* down in front of him, underlined by me. And he went, "Ha, ha, ha, ha, licence, old boy, licence." I said, "I don't work like that, I can't work like that, I am leaving." He sat me down and phoned the Duke of Marlborough at Woodstock. He were trying to impress me. Then another call comes in and he's at it: "Yes, one and a half million." If I was going to go before I arrived there, I was certainly going now. I wrote out my resignation, put it on the table and said, "Look, there's not much point in me hanging around and messing about, you've got my resignation." I hadn't signed any contract at Oxford.

Peter Marsh: He didn't want to leave. The idea that he deserted Oxford for a better deal was really very unfortunate. If you're a manager and you have the strength of character, almost bordering on arrogance, in the positive way, that he had, then you're not going to take any crap. You're going to find somewhere else to move to very quickly. I think the lack of understanding amongst our fans, who villified him when he left, was very unfortunate. I think Ian would have done a tremendous job. I had a great deal of admiration for him.

Chris Fallows: Jim Smith gets all the praise now, and rightly so, because he was a good manager, but the basis of it stemmed from Ian Greaves. You could see the whole thing changing. You could see the success coming.

13 *"Well played, Mr Shotton"*

THE RISE TO THE SECOND DIVISION, 1982-84

New manager Jim Smith inherited a promising side and then bought players wisely. In April 1983 chairman Robert Maxwell angered fans with his attempt to merge Oxford United and Reading. The following season United won the Third Division and set the Milk Cup alight by beating Newcastle United, Leeds United and Manchester United in a second replay. A late equaliser by Everton's Adrian Heath marred the quarter-final and United lost the replay 4-1.

JIM SMITH APPOINTED

Jim Smith: As much as anything, I joined the club because I was out of work, and I needed to work. It's strange, life's coincidences. I was manager of Birmingham and on the Saturday we drew at West Ham. Unbeknown to me I was out of work but I thought I was still in work. We went out for an evening meal with Ron Atkinson and his wife, in Stratford-upon-Avon, along with Paul Reeves, a director of Oxford, and his wife Yvonne, who were very good friends of Ron. That was Saturday evening. On the Monday I got the sack. On the Tuesday Paul rang me and asked if I would be interested in joining Oxford. Within two and a half weeks of leaving Birmingham I was working at Oxford. I didn't know a lot about the club. I had played for Aldershot against the team that had Ron and Graham Atkinson and Colin Booth. I knew Ron Atkinson very well, and he told me what a lovely place it was to live. I jumped in quickly and probably made a wrong career move, but in actual fact it was the best move I made. I had a lot of publicity during those three or four years, but above that was the personal satisfaction in achieving the success at Oxford, particularly in the manner we achieved it, the football we played. We had a fantastic set of lads and we had a great time together.

Maurice Evans: I rated Jim very highly as a manager. He was very hard but he was very fair. I thought he handled players very well. Most of all, it's about players. Players win matches, managers don't. Jim was one of those that allowed players to express themselves. He got the best players that he could possibly get, within his budget, and let them get on with it. Everything gelled. There was a great atmosphere at the ground, people interviewing Jim every day, and it was tremendous. It was certainly the best years that Oxford have ever had. There were three or four years of success, which is very rare for a small club.

Peter Foley: Jim Smith introduced his new players and got everybody playing his way, which is a pure footballing way. Jim likes good players. He likes players who can pass the ball well. He likes players that can express themselves, and Jim got some high-quality players to the club.

Peter Rhoades-Brown: He was Hurricane Andrew, I think. Very passionate, Jim. He hates to lose, which is a good thing. George Lawrence pulled me aside one day and said, "Because you're playing on the wing, you're closer to the dug-out, and you're the only person who can hear the manager, so be careful, don't take any notice of what he says." Jim used to hammer the winger. He's driven a couple of players to tears at half-time. Obviously you go out and prove him wrong in the second half.

Peter Foley: Jim could throw a few cups of tea around the dressing-room, but that was his frustration at the lads not doing exactly what he wanted, but he'd be telling jokes on the way home, so it would all be forgotten very quickly.

Jeremy Charles: One day we were losing 1-0 at half-time and Jim Smith was in one of his purple-head moods, chucking cups around the place. And Mr Maxwell walked in and said to Malcolm Shotton, "Hi, Skipper, how's the family?" And Smithy's just looked at him. So then he put locks on the doors so Mr Maxwell couldn't get in.

Peter Rhoades-Brown: It was quite interesting, because when Robert Maxwell wasn't there Jim used to eff and blind, and pin a few players against the wall, but when Robert Maxwell was there, Jim used to mellow a bit. So, I think, unbeknown to Jim, we used to invite the chairman in, just to keep him quiet! I remember playing at Wimbledon when I'd just moved up from London. In the first half I think I crossed every ball behind the goal. I was just trying too hard. I couldn't do a thing right. We got into the dressing-room at half-time and he spent 15 minutes having a go at me, and he actually gave me 10p to ring home to get me house up for sale again. He said, "Just go and ring home and tell her to put your house up for sale, because you're having such a bad time you'll end up playing for Hillingdon or Southall." I said, "Give me ten minutes. I'll go and prove myself." I went out, and the first thing I did was chase somebody and clatter him. I got booked. I put another cross behind the goal. Then Smithy brought me off. I went and sat down, thinking he was going to absolutely slaughter me, and he patted me on the back and said, "Well played, son." That's just the way he was. He put Steve Biggins on, and we actually scored straight from the free-kick when he brought me off. And he said that was probably the best substitution he'd ever made.

Building a Team

Jim Smith: Playing resources were quite good. Ian Greaves had had a fall-out with Mr Maxwell and had the chance to go to Wolverhampton Wanderers, but he'd done a good job here and left the basis of a good side. In fact we nearly got promotion that first year. I started with about 16 games to go [in 1981-82]. I think we ended up with three away games, and I think we had to win all three to go up. The first was Swindon Town. They were attacking our goals and there were two smoke-bombs and one arrived at the feet of Roy Burton, the goalkeeper. He was kicking it away and they scored. It was amazing. The linesman flagged, but the referee allowed the game to go on. It was an amazing goal really, and we lost that game, and lost our chance of promotion. Because Mr Maxwell was chairman, we had freedom to bring one or two players in without actually selling, although we did sell Mark Wright and Keith Cassells. We bought people like Mickey Vinter, Steve Biggins, Steve Hardwick, Trevor Hebberd and George Lawrence. George came on loan at first and then we eventually bought him. People talk about Mark Wright going for so little money at that stage, but nobody knows what that money was because we got Trevor Hebberd and George Lawrence out of it. Trevor was sold for £300,000 at the end of the day, so Mark Wright, an 18-year-old lad, was sold for the equivalent of about £400,000, so it was still a good sale for Oxford United.

"Thames Valley Royals"

Chris Fallows: Robert Maxwell pumped money into the club, he saved the club, he was a larger-than-life figure, he had a lot of contacts, he gave us publicity, we give him publicity, but I think he was publicity-seeking, I don't think he had the supporters at heart. He tried to take Reading and Oxford and merge them to Thames Valley Royals. Reading fans didn't want it and Oxford fans didn't want it, but he was going to do it no matter what.

Jim Hunt: One Sunday Maxwell rang me and asked me for the home telephone number of the chairman of Reading. Everything was done on a Sunday with Maxwell. When he was chairman of Oxford I had a book and I used to jot down all the home numbers I could find, in case I was ever asked by him. I gave him the phone number of the Reading chairman, but I didn't know what it was about. I thought we were going to bid for Kerry Dixon. About two months later, towards the end of the season, we were playing at Doncaster and the secretary of Doncaster said, "Jim, your chairman wants you on the telephone." Maxwell then told me that the news was going to break on television the next day.

Peter Marsh: The idea of merging Oxford and Reading struck anybody who even had a passing interest in football as being perhaps the most stupid thing anybody could try to do, but Maxwell boasted that only the Thames flowing backwards would stop this deal going through. What some people call a pitch invasion, and other people call a peaceful protest, marked the start of the game after this deal had been announced [v Wigan on 23 April 1983]. I think even Maxwell, looking on with his family, and seeing the strength of opinion amongst fans, must have thought that he'd made a bit of a whoopsie. It was really a lack of understanding about what football was about. Not just at the fan level. I think the commercial level as well. Football League regulations say, very sensibly, that you can't run more than one club at a time.

Jim Smith: That was a down part of my time at Oxford. I got labelled as a turncoat because I supported Maxwell. If your chairman says you're going to amalgamate with another club and you're a professional manager you have to go along with it. Maurice Evans [the Reading manager] was in the same boat to some degree. Maurice was going to be my assistant. They fought the situation. They thought there was something wrong with the shares. Mr Maxwell was led to believe it was all tied up, which it wasn't.

Maurice Evans: I just couldn't possibly see it working with the two clubs being so far apart and such great rivalry between the supporters. I don't think Mr Maxwell appreciated the rivalry between local clubs. Reading and Oxford always had that, and Swindon and Oxford. I always remember Mr Maxwell at the meeting that we had at Lancaster Gate [FA headquarters]. He gave his talk about the amalgamation of Reading and Oxford and, at the end of it, said, "Now I would like the two managers, Jim Smith and Maurice Evans, to say a few words." I always remember we were playing away at Huddersfield the following day, so it must have been a Friday. I said, "Quite honestly, Mr Maxwell, I'm not particularly interested in the merger, I'm more interested in the game tomorrow, at Huddersfield, and I wouldn't like to say anything further on the subject." He came up to me afterwards and said, "Maurice, you should have been a politician."

Peter Marsh: The commercial failure was tied up with Maxwell not actually having the shares in Reading, or the proxies, that he thought he had. You would have thought that he would have checked that first, before he started making grand announcements.

Third Division Champions, 1983-84

Sandy Brewer: I thought it was the best Third Division team I've seen in my life, and I've seen a lot of them. They showed it by going through and topping the Second Divison as well, with very little change.

Jim Smith: John Trewick came in to midfield, and we set off in the Third Division and won the Championship. Bobby McDonald came in at left-back, and, just before the deadline of that year, we added John Aldridge to the squad. Trevor Hebberd, particularly, was an outstanding player for us. Gary Briggs and Malcolm Shotton were the foundation of the team, and it enabled the likes of Kevin Brock to blossom, and Andy Thomas, who unfortunately broke his leg when he looked to be an outstanding young player.

Peter Foley: Brocky was a class player. He should have played for England with his ability. I think he played for the under-21s. He had as much ability as you'd ever see in any pro, I think, but maybe at times you just felt that Brocky needed a bit of a kick up the backside. I think he played his best football when Bobby McDonald played behind him.

Jim Smith: Bobby McDonald was probably the best value for money because we got him on a free transfer. He was always a character. He'd had a few problems in the past at Man City and Aston Villa and Coventry. Ray Graydon had been with him at Coventry and Villa. He said, "He's a super full-back. He's getting a bit more mature. We're not on the big-city scene. Maybe let him have his few beers in the local pub and nobody'll know about it." That's what we did. To me he was an outstanding player and very influential in making Kevin Brock the player he was.

Chris Fallows: I've never known a player blow so hot and cold as George Lawrence, but all the fans loved him for it. He didn't know what he was going to do, so, if *he* didn't know, the defender certainly didn't. He came back to the Manor with Bournemouth and of course they gave him a standing ovation, and he got the ball from about 30 yards out and walloped it into the top of the net. Great goal. The 'keeper never saw it. I think the crowd probably lifted him too much!

Peter Rhoades-Brown: For some reason I remember the clash at the top of the Third Division when we played Walsall away, probably because it was my goal that won it! Steve Hardwick saved a penalty in the first half and we played ever so well. We took a lot of supporters up there – we were top of the table – and the atmosphere was electric, and I scored a volley, I think halfway through the second half, and we won 1-0 and it was just magnificent. I think that result, and a few results after that, really saw us up for good.

Jim Smith: Briggs and Shotton were there when I first came to the club. I'd had Colin Todd as a centre-half [at Birmingham]. Then I saw Shotton and Briggsy play, and I thought, "Crikey, we'll never get away with these two. They can't play." In all fairness, they got better and better and better. They were as brave as you could be. Not many centre-forwards are brave these days, so they didn't like going in that box where Briggs and Shotton were or they might get a lump on the back of their head. Briggsy never enjoyed a game unless he came off with his eye bleeding! He banged his eyes that much that he had a scar-tissue problem, but it never bothered him. He just put a plaster on, or some Vaseline, and off he went out again. I don't know how many times he'd had his nose broken.

Nick Harris: I think you realised there was something special when they started buying players that you thought were definitely beyond their reach before Robert Maxwell was in charge. The year they won the Third Division they bought John Aldridge from Newport, under terrific pressure from Sunderland and lots of other clubs.

Jim Smith: Newport were one of the few teams to beat us at the Manor Ground, and John stood out for me. The club paid a fee of £75,000, but it was Mr Maxwell's decision that we would give the money "now" instead of as a spread, and that enabled us to get John before anybody else did.

Chris Bishop: My favourite player at that time was Mick Vinter. We always used to call his name out and he would wink or give us a wave. That means everything to a little lad. When we sealed the Third Division Championship, against Rotherham, he scored the winning goal to make it 3-2. That was only a couple of minutes before the end. We all stormed on to the pitch. It took about five minutes or so to get it cleared, to play about a minute, and then we stormed on again.

Jim Hunt: I always remember when we won the Third Division and we were presented with the trophy on the pitch. Maxwell grabbed the mike and was congratulating the club on winning the Third Division and he couldn't remember Malcolm Shotton's Christian name. He said, "The trophy will now be presented to Mr Shotton." During the game, that afternoon, Shotton kicked the ball into the stand, and some voice from the Beech Road Stand shouted, "Well played, Mr Shotton."

The League Cup, 1983-84

Sandy Brewer: I think the best football I ever saw there from an Oxford team was the first half of a replay against Newcastle. Kevin Keegan was playing for the opposition. George Lawrence was outside-right for Oxford, and he led them a merry dance. They were kicking down the slope, and they absolutely overwhelmed the opposition. They should have been about four up at half-time, but it was one of those games where the ball wouldn't go into the net. They finished up winning 2-1.

Jim Smith: Newcastle at the Manor Ground in the first half and the Leeds United game were identical performances. Both reached fantastic levels of play really and we would have beaten most teams in the country on them performances. Having drawn up at Elland Road, 1-1, the replay against Leeds was in doubt through frost. Eddie Gray, the manager of Leeds, didn't want to play and let us know he didn't want to play, so we were quite delighted. We knew they'd be a bit apprehensive. It was not treacherous but it was pretty hard and I thought the performance under the conditions, and everything considered, was probably the best while I was connected with Oxford United.

Nick Harris: Commentating on big grounds was just a dream come true. I suppose that League Cup replay at Old Trafford was one of the biggest dreams, when United drew and Kevin Brock scored that goal from a free-kick, when he chipped it over the wall. Fabulous. Though Manchester United scored about a minute later.

Jim Hunt: On the Sunday morning before that replay, I had said to Maxwell, "What if we draw at Manchester, and we toss for choice of grounds and win the toss. Do we play it at Manchester and get three or four times as much money than if we played at Oxford, or do we play it at Oxford where we've got a better chance of winning?" And Maxwell said, "I shall be there." I said, "But supposing you're not?" He said, "We'll play it back at Oxford." We drew 1-1 at Manchester United, and Ron Atkinson was their manager. After the game, I was standing at the bar with a Manchester United director, and I heard someone mention something about the next replay. I said, "I spoke to my chairman on Sunday and he said that if we won the toss we'd play it back at Oxford." Ron Atkinson said, "Well, I'm not going to toss then." I said, "You've got to toss, Ron." He said, "No, if I don't toss, where would you rather play it? Here, where you'll get four times as much money, or somewhere in the Midlands like Aston Villa, where you'll get very little." I said, "When do we get a chance to play it at Oxford then?" He said, "You don't, do you?" The deputy secretary of the Football League was in the room and they called him over. He said, "If the two clubs don't toss, the Football League have to decide where it will be, and it will be in the Midlands obviously." I said, "I can't agree to that, because that doesn't give us a chance to toss." Anyway, I got back home at three in the morning, after leaving there quite late with the team. I went in about quarter past nine in the morning, a little bit later than normal, and this deputy secretary of the Football League was on the phone. He said, "Jim, I'm sorry, I made a terrible mess of things last night. I really quoted the book without having it with me. You were right. The fact is, it's only if both clubs agree not to toss, then we would decide, but if one club wants to toss then you've got to toss."

Maxwell then got on the phone to the Football League. Graham Kelly was the secretary then. He said, "I want you to toss and I will call," and Maxwell called right. He said, "We'll play at Oxford." And we played it at Oxford and won 2-1 in extra-time when that Steve Biggins goal went up and up in the air and looped over the goalkeeper and into the net.

Jim Smith: I remember winning the third game against Manchester United because it was an extra-time goal and when that went in we knew we were through. I remember the tremendous atmosphere that evening from the fans and everybody concerned. That game put us on the map as much as anything we'd been doing in the League. Having beaten Man United we got Everton at home.

Chris Fallows: When we drew with Everton that night, in the quarter-finals of the Milk Cup, I remember we got the free-kick on the left, and I've never known such noise from a crowd. It was crossed over and McDonald scored. I remember thinking at the time that the crowd virtually got them that goal, and then the commentator said it on the telly so I must have been right! Then, of course, ten minutes to go, it comes to Kevin Brock.

Chris Bishop: We were all celebrating. We thought, "What a big scalp" and Kevin Brock did the backpass, and little "Inchie" Heath scored ... ooh, it's just a terrible feeling, knowing that you come so close to beating a big club like Everton.

Jim Smith: There were three incidents in that game. One was when Trevor Hebberd was done by Irvine. Not intentionally. He got a bad injury and had to come off, and if Trevor Hebberd had stayed on I'm convinced we'd have won, regardless of Kevin Brock's backpass. Then, we were overconfident really. Reidy was all over Kevin. It was a definite foul, but we didn't get it. Kevin turned back, passed it blindly back and, to be fair, Heath took it very well under the conditions but Kevin should have gone down at that stage, got the foul and stopped the game. But, the one nobody ever mentions is that Steve Biggins missed an open goal. He should have headed it into the back of the net with literally the last touch of the game. In the replay I underrated Everton. I thought they were an ordinary side and that we had a great chance, even at Everton, but something happened for them on the night. I think I should have gone there a bit more defensively. If you look back in history, it was Howard Kendall's year, Howard's chance to be a top manager rather than being an out-of-work manager.

CELEBRATION

Peter Rhoades-Brown: We went up for a little presentation at Pergamon House. All the wives and girls were invited up. Robert Maxwell came up to me and said, "Have you moved in okay? How's things?" I said, "Yes, fine. Everything's fine. I've moved house." All the lads are walking past, thinking, "You're in, Pete. He obviously knows you and everything's fine." He said, "Have you enjoyed the season?" I said "Yes, I've had a great time. Everything's good." He said, "How's the car going?" I said, "Fine." It was just trivial chat, but I'm thinking, "This is great, I'm in with the chairman." He said, "How many goals did you score last year?" I said, "Well, not enough, possibly, but I'm creating a few and I'm doing okay." I must have been there for 20 minutes, him talking to me, and all of sudden he said, "Anyway, Mr Aldridge, nice to see you, we'll be talking later on." He obviously thought I was John Aldridge. I went and told John Aldridge, and he said that if Robert Maxwell came up and called him "Pete" he was going to slaughter me.

14 *"You will get promotion this season"*

SECOND DIVISION CHAMPIONS, 1984-85

In 1984-85 Oxford United won the Second Division Championship in style. It was the first time that a team had won the Third and Second Division titles in successive seasons. But manager Jim Smith departed in the summer of 1985.

Champions Again, 1984-85

Peter Rhoades-Brown: We went in with eyes open, thinking we would have a consolidation season in the Second Division, and we just walked straight through. We didn't lose many games. Jim Smith did a good job in keeping everybody together, and it was such a good family club. All the wives and girl-friends and kids and everything. We used to have socials on a Saturday night after a game, and coffee-mornings for the wives, which is all part of the club as well.

Jim Smith: I bought David Langan from Derby County to Birmingham for £300,000. As an attacking full-back he was one of the best I've ever been involved with. When I left Birmingham David had back trouble. Ron Saunders actually said to him that he'd never play again, and gave him a free transfer. Well, David didn't want to stop playing. I invited him down on trial, pre-season, and he did alright, but we had Paul Hinshelwood, who'd had a very good season in the Third Division. Paul was definitely going to play in the first game of the season. The weekend prior to the first game of the season we had a reserve game, down at Brackley I think, on the Friday and a first-team game at home to Reading on the Saturday. Dave played at Brackley and got through the game okay, and Paul was playing against Reading. Paul went down with a tummy-bug on Saturday morning, and Dave had to play in the last pre-season game. He'd already played the night before but he was outstanding. I had to play him in the first game. We went up to Huddersfield and won 3-0, and poor old Paul Hinshelwood, who'd done well, never got another smell.

Nick Harris: I remember going to Huddersfield. I think it was the first game United played in the Second Division, and they won 3-0 and Aldridge scored a couple of goals. I remember thinking then, "This is the first game, but this looks to be a very, very useful side." They'd bought Billy Hamilton and it all seemed to be gelling.

Jim Smith: Billy Hamilton had impressed me when he played for Burnley. I'd known him for a long time. I spoke to John Bond about him, and John said, "He can't play but he'll get you 20 goals a year." I thought, "I'll settle for that, 20 goals in a year," but Billy could also play. Anybody who played for Northern Ireland, regularly, must be able to play, and he was a much better player than I anticipated, and was a great asset for the fans and for the team in the first half of that campaign in the Second Division.

Peter Rhoades-Brown: John Aldridge scored goals left, right and centre, with Billy Hamilton. We just enjoyed playing together. Most of the time I never used to look up. I used to cross the ball knowing that either Billy or John was going to get there. More often than not, one or the other would knock the ball into the net. So they appreciated me doing my job properly, and I appreciated them finishing off my crosses, and it made me look good. They're international players. Great lads. The fans knew them quite well as well, because they used to mingle with the supporters in the supporters' club.

Jim Smith: David Langan was a dream for Billy Hamilton, because when he got down the line, that ball would come across. I always remember that goal against Arsenal in the League Cup when Billy seemed to be about 10 foot above the crossbar when he headed it in. Then of course Langy scored the winner against Arsenal, from 35 yards or something.

Chris Bishop: I saw the Arsenal game. I think that's got to be one of the best Cup games I've ever seen. Really exciting. They were near the top of Division One at the time, and Oxford matched them. It was 2-2, towards the end of the match, and David Langan's shot was one Pat Jennings could have saved. It just sort of flopped over his hand and went in.

Fred Ellis: Billy Hamilton could receive the ball, protect the ball, pass the ball, and he could score goals. The best combination we've ever had was him and Aldridge. The pity of it was that they didn't play together all that long. I can remember the night that Billy was hurt. He was just warming up before the match and he just turned and passed the ball a few yards and that was it, just like that.

Kaye Ellis: I run a charity shop, and it was going to be opened by a celebrity. I'd asked for one of the Oxford United players to come and open the shop, and Billy Hamilton turned up. I was absolutely thrilled to bits. He shook my hand and came and met the directors of the shop and then we started talking. He was talking about his life in Ireland and how long he'd been playing football. He was a gentleman on the pitch, and a gentleman off the pitch, which says a lot nowadays. He had to stop playing when he had a knee injury. He had a testimonial and you'd probably get about 2,000 people for an ordinary testimonial, but when Billy Hamilton had his, there were 4,500 there.

Jim Smith: Trevor Hebberd was a little bit of a unsung hero. He was a manager's player. I think you'll find that Trevor's played every position bar goalkeeper. He never stopped running. He was a tremendous athlete. Training-wise, he won all the cross-countries and virtually all the sprints. Also, a manager's dream. He never gave you an ounce of problem. He just got on with his job. They used to call him "Smiler" because he'd never smile.

Peter Foley: Trevor was a great team-player. Trevor Hebberd could run and run and run and run. I've never seen a professional footballer cover as much ground. When we used to go running up the hills at Shotover, Trevor would just run off into the distance and you wouldn't see him again for the rest of the session, he'd be so far ahead of us. He was the same on the pitch. He was everywhere.

Maurice Evans: I was scouting that season, watching the teams we were about to play, and I remember saying to Jim, halfway through the season, "I'll tell you what, Jim, you will get promotion this season." He said, "For

God's sake, don't start saying things like that." I said, "No, but I really do think you will, because I've seen every team now in the Second Division, and I'm convinced that Oxford are the best side." He said, "Well, look, just keep it to yourself. Don't tell the players. Don't tell the public. Don't say anything." Of course, as it turned out, they did really well and got promotion. Tremendous.

Chris Bishop: I remember a magical match against Leeds United where Leeds took a 2-0 lead just before half-time and we pulled back to win 5-2. The only thing, it was marred a bit by Leeds fans. There was scaffolding behind the goal, and they started chucking bits on to the field. Steve Hardwick wasn't having a very good time of it, because they were chucking coins as well. Apart from that, that was an excellent match and one of the best comebacks I've seen.

Peter Rhoades-Brown: Grimsby in the Second Division as well, when we won 1-0 in the last minute. I've got into the box and stooped down, and the ball's hit me on the crown of the head and gone in the far corner. Everyone went mad, and it was another important result.

Jim Smith: In fairness, when I look back at the team that got us promotion to the First Division, when we played at our best it was probably one of the best footballing sides I ever managed.

Chris Bishop: I remember the Shrewsbury match when we actually got promotion. That was an evening match. David Langan scored the winning goal. It was 1-0.

Jim Smith: A fantastic feeling. But we knew we still had a job to do to try to win the Championship. We had three games to go. Away at Leeds and Charlton, and Barnsley at home on the last day. We celebrated a little too much on the Wednesday. We lost 1-0 at Leeds United, then drew at Charlton, so we weren't Champions until we beat Barnsley 4-0. Then Mr Maxwell did his organisation bit again, and we were all sat in the dressing-room for 20 minutes while he made his speech, till I had to go up and say, "The lads are ready, what are we doing?" Of course he brought them up the stairs and introduced them, but unfortunately he didn't know the names. He kept giving the wrong names out. That was a bit of a cock-up really, but nobody bothered about it after, when we could celebrate the Championship. When we went round the city on the bus top, it did amaze me how many people turned out. We never really thought of Oxford as a soccer city but it was fantastic to see. I think they really appreciated what we'd done.

Sandy Brewer: When they were Champions of the Second Division, they had a parade which came past this house with the players on a coach. We were sitting eating a meal and we saw them coming so I went out to the door and gave them a wave. I heard Jim Smith talking about it afterwards on the radio. I heard him say that "little grey-haired men and women were coming to the doors and waving to us". I thought, "Hello, he's got me spotted."

Robert Maxwell's Influence

Jim Hunt: When he first came into the office, when he took over, he said to me, "You're Jim Hunt?" I said, "Yes." He said, "And you're secretary?" I said, "Yes." He said, "Well, there's three things I expect of you – loyalty, workmanship and honesty." So I said, "No problem there. I worked at Lucy's 33 years before I came to the football club." He said, "I checked on that." I said, "I think Bill Reeves can tell you that I've devoted myself to the football club and I virtually work a six-and-a-half-day week." He said, "He's already told me. And before we talk about honesty, I'll just say one thing, and that is to remind you that you can only lose your virginity once."

Mick Brown [then United assistant secretary]: To deal with, at the football club, he was quite good, because he let you get on with the job. He didn't interfere. At some clubs the chairman goes in every day, forever looking over your shoulder, commenting, telling you how to do your job. But you were allowed to get on with your job. Obviously he wanted to be involved with major financial decisions, but when there were decisions to be made he made them instantly. He didn't mess about. He certainly didn't have board meetings to discuss them into the early hours of the morning. In most cases those decisions were either proven to be right or you could see why he had made those decisions. He had the capability of looking two or three steps ahead. He made many comments in the football world. He labelled the Football League management committee the "mismanagement committee". He said that it wasn't the right way to work, and that has now changed. There's now a board of directors at the Football League. Similarly, he said that football was undersold on television and should be earning massive sums out of television. Again proven to be the case.

Peter Rhoades-Brown: I'd obviously heard a bit about him, like you do before you come to a big club. People say, "We've got a big chairman, a lot of money, he wears a furry hat and you won't miss him." My debut was against Preston, and I'd done a couple of interviews on the radio. About half past two Jim [Smith] called me into his office, and I thought he was going to drop me. I thought, "Oh, crikey, I've been dropped already and I haven't played yet." I'd never been called into an office before the kick-off. He said, "The chairman wants to meet you." The chairman said, "I'm Robert Maxwell," I said, "I'm Peter Rhoades-Brown, hello, chairman," like you do. I couldn't really work out why I was being introduced, but he liked to get to know the players he'd bought. He took an interest. He said, "Well, hopefully, if you can play football like you talk on the radio, you'll be a bloody good player."

Jim Hunt: He couldn't remember names, and one of the reasons was that he was dealing with so many people. I've seen him conduct four meetings at the same time. I've been down at Pergamon Press and he's gone from room to room, from one meeting to another, and I found that rather amazing. If he was in America he would ring me up at half-past eight their time. Whether he ever thought that it was half-past one in the morning here or whether he thought, "That's what he's paid for," I don't know. Many times I've had a call on a Sunday morning asking me what the result was the day before.

Nick Harris: I used to find interviewing Robert Maxwell a little daunting. I remember interviewing him before that Milk Cup quarter-final against Everton. I asked him, "Are you nervous before such a big game?" He stood up to his full height, looked at me and he said, "Nervous? The last time I was nervous, young lad, was standing in front of a German tank without any shoes on." What do you say after that? I just said, "Well, thank you very much" and that was it.

Les Bateman: Jim Hunt rang me up one Saturday. I was at home that day – I was only part-time – and he said, "We're coming back at half-past five tonight in the helicopter with Mr What's-his-name because he's got to open the ice-rink. Would you go and get all the lights on." So, of course, back I go at half-past five, put the floodlights on, and Maxwell comes down in his helicopter while Jim Hunt and I stood there by the dressing-room. His chauffeur was waiting outside and he walked straight past me and never said anything.

Peter Rhoades-Brown: Robert Maxwell took an interest. He knew everybody's nickname, but, because he was such a big businessman, and in different countries every other day, he sometimes lost himself and didn't know where he was. I remember one day, when I was injured. I was stood in the tunnel area, and he came up to me and said, "Peter, which is the home dressing-room and which is the away?" He hadn't been to the Manor for a while and he couldn't remember.

Jeremy Charles: I remember we played West Brom the first game of the season, and Mr Maxwell couldn't get to the game. There was a little message from him: "If you lose the toss, go for an early goal." I think the best one was when he asked the club doctor when he was going to be fit.

Mick Brown: I remember one particular occasion. It was pre-season. I'd left the Manor at 12 o'clock. I think we were playing somewhere like Charlton away in a friendly, so obviously I was keen to go. The phone rang. It was one of Maxwell's secretaries. Maxwell wanted me to come to Headington Hall to do a job. I got up there and someone had put in front of him a little booklet that Watford had produced and distributed to all the local population. Maxwell liked it, thought it looked good, so he wanted to do exactly the same. He called in a number of people – the commercial manager, the secretary, myself, etc – and said, "I want this to go out this week." This was the Saturday and he wants it to go out on the Thursday, and he wants it as a full-colour brochure. I said, "It's not possible." He said, "Of course it is." We did all the work. We phoned up the team and the manager arranged for a team photo to be taken that Sunday. We worked all day Sunday, and we got it out, a full-colour brochure, and it was delivered with all the papers that week.

Jim Smith: My relationship with Robert Maxwell was pretty much the same all the time, until towards the end. I would probably say that nobody had a "relationship" with Robert Maxwell. You worked for Robert Maxwell and that was it. Depending on how much he respected you, or how high up the scale you were, he let you get on with your job. He didn't ever interfere with team matters. All I had to speak to Robert Maxwell about was finance. Could we afford him? Could we pay these wages? He would say "Yes" or "No". If it was "Yes", you'd get on with it. That was really the sum total of my relationship with Robert Maxwell on a day-to-day basis. You didn't have a social life together. I only ever talked to him about matters appertaining to Oxford United. But our relationship, in the early days, was successful, and I think that's also got to be important when you're working for Robert Maxwell. My relationship, as such, changed when he took over the *Mirror*. It wasn't me that changed. It wasn't the club that changed. He tended to change. If you look at the early copies of the *Mirror*, I think he had his photograph on nearly every page!

A Change of Manager

Jim Smith: I had to do a live televised interview with Saint and Greavesie down at Elland Road about 12.30 and I didn't know but Maxwell had been on television to say that we wouldn't play at the Manor Ground in the First Division. That was the first question they asked me and I didn't know anything about it and I tended to say that was a load of rubbish really and we would be playing at the Manor Ground next year: "Mr Maxwell is a fine political man, he's obviously working at getting a new ground eventually." I then got a phone call at Elland Road at two o'clock to ask me whether I was going to pay the wages because we couldn't afford First Division wages at the Manor Ground and I'd gone against my chairman on national television. All I said was, "If you'd have told me prior to what you said, I'd have been able to answer how you wanted me to answer." That started it.

Nick Harris: I remember coming back from Leeds on the coach, with the team, and Jim Smith was really down. They'd lost 1-0 and he wasn't enamoured by losing in any way, but they still went on to win the Championship. There had been stories that he would leave United and not go with them into the First Division and I couldn't believe them, but I remember that moment then, thinking, "Yes, perhaps there is something in all this."

Jim Smith: Then I had a kit deal. I told Maxwell that Adidas were interested in doing a deal. I told him the deal. It was all the kit for the youth team, first team, reserves, plus boots and balls, and about ten grand a year over three years. He told me that the Adidas deal was a load of rubbish. He said he'd get a better deal, and to cancel the Adidas deal, which I did. He got Umbro. He told me on the Wednesday night we were at Charlton. He rang me and said, "I've got Umbro. £20,000." And I asked him about the boots and balls. He said, "Umbro will provide them." I said, "Well, they don't make them." He didn't even know they didn't make them. He said, "Well, ask Adidas." I thought, "I'm definitely going to ask Adidas when I've just kicked them into touch!"

Jim Hunt: One Monday the phone went just before one o'clock. It was Maxwell. He said, "I want a board-meeting at three o'clock." I said, "A board meeting at three o'clock? That's impossible. Half the directors won't come." He said, "I don't care. As long as you and Jim Smith are there, it doesn't matter about the others." When we got there, Brian Dalton was there. Maxwell said, "This is your new managing-director." Neither Jim Smith or I knew before we walked in that room that he was being appointed, and that hurt Jim.

Jim Smith: When we got promoted from the Third to the Second, I agreed my contract in ten minutes. Then we got promoted again, and I thought, "Now's the time to get a real contract." We arranged to see each other on the night of Liverpool-Juventus in Belgium. I went down to the *Mirror* and I was sat in the foyer three-quarters of an hour. In all fairness, that wasn't unusual with Maxwell. Also, it works your way. If you were late it didn't bother him that much either. We sat down in the office to talk about my contract. I asked him for what I wanted. He said, "No," and what he'd give me. I said, "Is it negotiable?" He said, "Of course it's negotiable." Then his personal assistant came in and said there were nightmares happening in Belgium [the Heysel Stadium disaster]. So that broke up, which I can understand, but I didn't see him again for maybe three weeks. He rang up for me to come up and see him at Headington on a Sunday, which I did. He just said, "That's all I'm giving you. If you want to speak to anybody, just go and speak to anybody." So I thought, "Well, I might as well," so I did. I can't to this day understand why that happened. If he'd have given me the contract I wanted, which was nowhere near the contract I got at QPR anyway, so it wasn't as though I was asking for enormous moneys, I would obviously have stayed at Oxford. One of the biggest regrets I have in football is that I never managed Oxford United in the First Division, even if it had only been for one game. But I don't blame Maxwell for that. That was my own decision. It was something I never thought would have happened in a hundred years. The moneys weren't that far away either, but I just couldn't understand why it was "Take it or leave it, and off you go if you want." I don't know whether he was trying to call my bluff or what. I honestly don't know, and we never will know.

15 *"That was the impossible dream"*

MILK CUP WINNERS AT WEMBLEY, 1985-86

The pinnacle of the club's history came with the arrival of First Division football in 1985-86. Not only did United survive their first season in the top flight, but the team, now managed by Maurice Evans, earned a trip to Wembley for the 1986 Milk Cup Final. United beat Northampton, Newcastle, Norwich, Portsmouth and Aston Villa, and then met Jim Smith's Queen's Park Rangers in the Final. On 20 April 1986, Oxford went to Wembley.

THE RELUCTANT MANAGER

Maurice Evans: Jim Smith had told me that things were not going well between him and the chairman. He was almost certainly looking to move on, and he more-or-less knew where he could go. He asked me to go with him, but I felt a certain allegiance to Mr Maxwell. He, after all, had rescued me from the scrapheap and given me a job and I felt that I should stay. I told Jim that. I said, "I'm enjoying what I'm doing. I'll just stay here as chief scout." Anyway, all the players and the staff went on tour to

Portugal. I got a phone call early one morning in Portugal: "Hello, Robert Maxwell here. Jim Smith has resigned with my blessing and you will be taking over as manager." I said, "Oh, no, I won't, Mr Maxwell, no, no, no." He said, "Why not?" I said, "Because I've finished as regards managing. I don't want to manage any more." He said, "Well, you've got to be crazy. You've never managed in the First Division." I said, "No, I'm not crazy, Mr Maxwell, I just don't want to get back into it." He said, "Fly back immediately, and come and have a chat with me," which I did, on a Sunday, down at Pergamon. He said, "What about it then?" I said, "I've not changed my mind." He said, "Would you be prepared to take over as caretaker until we can appoint someone?" I said, "Yes, I'll do that." So the season started and the first game was away at West Brom, which we drew, and then we were at home to Tottenham, which we drew, and then we played Leicester at home on the Saturday, and we beat them 5-0. Well, of course, everyone was happy, and Mr Maxwell, being the clever man that he was, knew that now was the time to pounce and get me. He said, "Maurice, I'd like you to come and join us for a bite to eat tomorrow, you and your wife." So I said, "Yeah, okay." He said, "Six o'clock then, at Headington Hall." So we turned up on that Sunday and he grabbed my wife as soon as she walked through the door. He'd never met her before and he said, "It's you, isn't it? It's you who doesn't want your husband to become a manager again." She said, "No, it's nothing whatsoever to do with me. He makes his own decisions about football." He said, "Well, that's fair enough, Maurice, isn't it, you can take over." I said, "No, Mr Maxwell, please don't." He said, "Come on, come on." In the end, of course, I agreed, and I must admit I enjoyed it. It was very hard at Oxford in the First Division, but I did enjoy it.

The First Division, 1985

Maurice Evans: I was a little bit worried, to say the least, that we were not going to be good enough. I also knew that it was also going to be very, very difficult for me, taking Jim Smith's place, to change things drastically. The public would have gone absolutely crazy, and probably rightly so. The team had done well, and they deserved an opportunity in the First Division. But my thoughts were correct. We were not good enough, so I had to start trying to get better players. The top fees then were about £600,000, and Oxford could spend probably £300,000. And we could not pay the wages that the top sides could pay, purely and simply because we didn't get the gates and could never get the gates. I found it very hard to convince players to come here. They looked at Oxford as a small club.

Chris Bishop: The average attendance was at least 10,000, and to pack that in the Manor Ground you hardly had any room to move, with the surges and that. It was the best moments of watching at Oxford that I can remember. We didn't have a particularly good season, in the First Division, but the atmosphere made up for it. It was an excellent experience, just to appreciate Oxford being in the First Division, against all the big clubs.

Harold Kimber: Of the 92 League clubs, I think I went to 88 of them [as a director]. I didn't think, when I played for Headington in the Oxfordshire Senior League in the 1930s, that I would later be in the boardrooms at places like Arsenal, Liverpool and the Manchester clubs. I was very proud on those occasions. Very proud.

Maurice Evans: My first signing was Neil Slatter, who I'd watched at Bristol Rovers for some time. He had been very consistent. We needed a defender. He was an international. He'd played in the first team at Bristol since he was about eighteen, so he was very experienced, even though he wasn't very old. Neil did quite well but was plagued by injuries. I remember I could have sold him. He played particularly well at Everton, and Howard Kendall said to me after the game, "What about Neil Slatter?" I think I paid just over £100,000 for him. I think we could have quadrupled that at that time, but I said, "No," because we were building a side to try and stay in the First Division. Ray Houghton had been one I'd tried to sign for Reading. I'd been beaten by Malcolm Macdonald of Fulham. As soon as I had the opportunity to sign him here, I did, because I thought Ray was a very good player.

Chris Bishop: I remember the first game we played against Liverpool at home – the 2-2 draw. I honestly thought we'd be overawed by playing Liverpool, this really big club, but it wasn't any of that. It was a really good performance. I thought in the end we were a little bit unlucky only to draw, even though we got the draw with an own-goal by Alan Kennedy. John Aldridge scored against the team he loved and grew up with. We went wild in the crowd.

The Milk Cup, 1985-86

Peter Rhoades-Brown: I think the first round was Northampton. We won 2-1. That was a scrap. Richard Hill was playing for Northampton then, and he eventually came to us.

Nick Harris: United were very, very lucky to get anything out of the game at Oxford. I remember going to Northampton for the second leg and sitting in the cricket pavilion, with a pair of binoculars to watch the game and commentate on it, and John Aldridge scored the vital goals.

Maurice Evans: Gradually we seemed to be progressing, and no-one was talking about us, and we were certainly not thinking about getting to Wembley and then suddenly we ended up in the semi-final, and there we were playing Aston Villa, away from home first of all. We went up there and we drew 2-2, so all we had to do – all we had to do! – was beat them here and we were at Wembley. We played well up at Villa, but when we came back here I thought we were awful. We were so nervous and edgy in the first half. I remember going into the dressing-room at half-time, and saying, "I can't believe you lads. Most of you are experienced and you seem worried to death. There's people lying in hospital just down the road that are dying and here's you worrying about a football match. What's the matter with you. Get out there and play." And of course in the second half we did very much better, and we ended up winning it.

Peter Rhoades-Brown: Two-nil up. Couldn't believe it. Then it was 2-1 in the last couple of minutes, and we had to defend for our lives, and everybody just busted a gut and defended. People say, "What's the most memorable moment of your career?" and I say, "I think it was the final whistle, against Aston Villa." As soon as that final whistle went, something sparked off in my brain and I just went absolutely barmy. I went running up to the London Road end: "We've made Wembley. This is it. My dream come true. Playing in the First Division, playing at Wembley." It was just mass hysteria, people jumping up and down, yellow and blue, people screaming and shouting and hugging and kissing each other. Everybody was jumping up and down. They probably felt how I felt. I hope they felt how I felt. They just went absolutely mad because they probably couldn't believe that we were at Wembley. We deserved it because we played the better football in both legs.

Maurice Evans: So then we were on our way to Wembley, which was very interesting because on the other hand we were struggling at the bottom of the First Division. If I'd have had a choice I'd have much preferred to have been safe in the First Division and not have got to the Milk Cup Final, but you don't have a choice.

Vic Morris: Everybody realised then that we were at Wembley, and it was all chaos, ticket-wise. We were allocated a certain amount of tickets, and they all had to be sold at the club. They employed lots of casual workers, ex-bank managers, and me and my daughter. I think they had to employ about 20 people to sell these tickets. I went up there on the Good Friday prior to the match, and there was a queue from ten o'clock in the morning. We were supposed to shut at four and we finished up closing at half-past seven at night. I didn't see the end of the queue right from the time we opened the office till night. They completely sold out of tickets. Where everybody came from to buy those tickets I don't know. It was tremendous.

Jim Hunt: Mick Brown was ticket-office manager then. We sold something in the region of 36,000 tickets for that Milk Cup Final, simply because I purchased all the tickets that I could from clubs up north. People in Newcastle and Sunderland and all those places were not interested in Oxford United and Queen's Park Rangers.

Tim Sparrowhawk: Wembley was the trip that produced all the latent fans and the old fans. They all came back together. Thirty-six thousand tickets sold quite easily. As a child, that was the impossible dream, that Oxford would be at Wembley. That was the thing of fantasy.

Jack Fallows: It was a dream to us to be there at Wembley because there used to be a standing-joke. When Ronnie Atkinson was captain, in those days, they said, "Well, Ronnie, when you get to Wembley, you shake hands with the King." But we've got a Queen? "Well, there'll be a King by the time you get there."

Maurice Evans: It was very sad for Billy Hamilton in the Milk Cup Final because he was absolutely desperate to play. I had watched him in training, and knew that there was no way that he was anywhere near fit enough to play in a game as big as the Milk Cup Final. In the end I had to call him in and tell him that he wasn't going to play. And that was hard, because he had probably been one of the biggest reasons why Oxford had done so well in those years. But he was a nice fellow, Billy, a smashing fellow. He was very understanding. David Langan kept pestering me because Langy had been sub against Villa. I'd left him out for some reason. And he kept knocking on the door after we had made the Milk Cup Final: "Maurice, am I going to be playing in the Final?" I said, "Langy, it's three or four weeks away yet, I can't tell you." He said, "I've got people coming over from Ireland who want to watch. I've got to arrange tickets." "Langy, look, I can't tell you at the present moment, but as soon as I've made up my mind I will call you in and I will tell you." I'll never forget when I told him. He was thrilled to bits.

Nick Harris: The year before, at a United function, people had jokingly said, "If United ever get to Wembley, we'll shave our beards off." It was a joke. And of course, it started to take on a reality, certainly with Mick Moore, Nick Johnson, the United commercial manager, and some of the United players. Peter Rhoades-Brown and Jeremy Charles had beards. I'd had a beard for 20 years. My wife had never seen me without a beard. But off it came. Jeremy Charles did keep his on for luck. Poor old Peter Rhoades-Brown didn't play in the Final.

Peter Rhoades-Brown: It was a bad time at Wembley for me because three weeks beforehand I tore my cartilage against QPR and didn't make it, but life goes on.

Jeremy Charles: We knew our team about five days before the game. We stayed for about four days at the Bell in Beaconsfield, and we had a training place where we went in the mornings. We started working on a few things. Obviously we needed to know our formation so we could start working on free-kicks and corners, and picking up people that we thought would be a danger in the QPR side.

Maurice Evans: It was quite relaxed. I can remember sitting the players down, going through the whole team and saying to them, "Right, I want you to tell me what I am looking for from you, and we'll talk about it." So we just sat down and had a chat for about an hour about what I was expecting from them, and what they were expecting from themselves.

Chris Bishop: Oh, I remember the whole day, setting out quite early in the morning, flags and scarves out of every window, going down the M40, a whole mass of Oxford supporters tooting their horns, waving, sticking their thumbs up. It was just an amazing atmosphere. I was only young but I remember it all vividly.

Tim Sparrowhawk: I remember going down the M40 and it seemed full of cars with scarves hanging out. Then this great queue from the M40 into Wembley: would we get there on time? Of course we did. Probably about an hour and a half early in the end, but there was still that panic that you might miss it.

Jeremy Charles: With so many fans going up there, the M40 was blocked. We actually took another route. And everybody was cheering as we went past, going into Wembley itself. We got on to the pitch, and there was the applause, the crowd singing, and everything was brilliant, absolutely fabulous. I think that stands out more than anything.

Jack Fallows: We came off the by-pass to the stadium, and there was the general turmoil and our supporters going one way and Queen's Park Rangers supporters going the other, and the police horses. Of course we were all tensed up. We thought, "I don't know what we're going to do, against Queen's Park Rangers," because Jim Smith was their manager then.

Jeremy Charles: The lads were so relaxed, which I found nice. Usually you get an atmosphere that's a little bit tense and you don't start playing for a half-hour. But we were so relaxed on the day. Ken Fish was marvellous in the dressing-room. He took us for a 20-minute warm-up, an hour before the kick-off. I think Ken was the best because he used to have a little quip at everybody. He'd get the brandies and whiskies ready. Only a small one, mind, not a bottle or anything! He said it was for the nerves, so we agreed with him. Certain players will have superstitions. One of the lads wouldn't put his shorts on until he got to the edge of the tunnel. That was Trevor Hebberd, or "Nijinsky" as he was known to the lads. Some would sit there very quietly. Some would tell jokes. I was terrified. But obviously once you get out on the pitch, and start kicking a ball about, a lot of the nerves disappear.

Maurice Evans: People said to me before we went, "Enjoy it, it seems to flash by and you will not remember it." And it is like that. Although you say to yourself, "I'm going to enjoy this and remember it," you don't really. I remember walking out, of course, with Jim, and I remember the turf being very wet. It had rained during the morning. And you see this sea of faces and most of them seemed to be from Oxford, and I thought, "Dear me, we've got some tremendous support here, I hope we do well."

Jim Smith: It was very, very strange. The strangest point was when we were coming out of the tunnel. You have to wait there, and I was talking to all the Oxford players more than I was talking to my players because they were more my players than the QPR players really. That felt very strange.

Nick Harris: I can remember the day like it was yesterday. Peter Baker [BBC Radio Oxford] and I were at Wembley about ten o'clock or ten-thirty. I was in the gantry, from one o'clock until after the Cup was presented. Peter Baker was involved behind the scenes or on the pitch. I commentated on the game from above with Les Taylor, a former United skipper who had captained Watford at Wembley. It was just a marvellous occasion. But it all went so quickly. I'm sure I would have shed a tear and got quite emotional, but, when you're working all the time, it was getting the work right.

Maurice Evans: We had so many passers in the side, in midfield. There was Trevor Hebberd, Kevin Brock, Les Phillips, Ray Houghton. All those four were very good passers of the ball. None of them were what we call aggressors, or ball-winners, but if we could get the ball enough, we could pass it, and we could outplay teams. I was always a little bit worried defensively, if they got at us and attacked us, but they didn't really because we had the ball a lot more than they did.

Jim Smith: What I really wanted, in an ideal world, was a fantastic game which QPR won 4-3, or something like that. In the early stages of the game, I was more concerned that it might be a crap game and nobody come out with any credit. Whoever got the first goal was going to win and Oxford got it.

Maurice Evans: Trevor Hebberd did particularly well on the first goal. He looked very confident. I remember him checking back, and, when he scored, I thought, "Yeah, we got a good chance here now."

Jack Fallows: He got the ball at a very acute angle, and I thought it had gone the other side of the post. Then I thought, "It's in, it's in," and everyone went up in the blinking air and they nearly went mad.

Kaye Ellis: I lost a cushion and a picture of my idol Billy Hamilton. I threw them up in the air because we scored the first goal, and I threw my Oxford United teddy. The teddy came back to me, but where my cushion went and where my photograph went, I do not know.

Chris Bishop: We were sitting at the back. When Trevor Hebberd scored that gorgeous goal towards the end of the first half, I jumped up for joy and hit my head on a balustrade. I was more careful when the other goals went in.

Maurice Evans: I sat in the stand with David Coates, who was then chief scout. I didn't want to sit on the bench. I had never sat on the bench. In the stand, you can divorce yourself from the game and look at it logically. I remember walking through the banqueting-room at half-time and the stewards stopping me and saying, "I'm sorry, you can't come through here." I said, "Yeah, but I'm the Oxford manager." I came down through the stand and through to the players on the pitch. I looked up and it said about the Milk Cup, "Have you got the bottle?" I thought, "That's just what I need at half-time." I said to them in the dressing-room, "Now then, you're in the driving-seat, have you got the bottle to win it? Because that's all you need. You're there virtually."

Chris Fallows: It was only when the second goal went in, right in front of us, that I thought, "We're going to win this." That was a great goal by Houghton. I had a grin on my face for the rest of the second half.

Jack Fallows: I've never felt so elated in all my life than when the second goal went in. I thought, "Two-nil, I wonder if they'll get back." But then the third goal went in. Aldridge shot and it came out to Jeremy Charles.

Jeremy Charles: You know your players because you've played with them for such a time. If John Aldridge was in that position I wouldn't expect him to pass. That's why he's scored so many goals. All you can do is to follow up, and if the 'keeper makes a save you're there to tap it in, which made life easier for me! To be perfectly honest, I had so much time that I did think, "What if I miss?" Usually, things happen automatically, but there was nobody near me, the 'keeper's just parried the ball, and it was right in front of goal and on my left foot. Fortunately it did creep in! I remember Mal Shotton running up and saying, "That's it, we've won it." I think everybody knew then that the game was out of their reach.

Maurice Evans: I couldn't believe how well we played. You probably don't realise it at the time but looking back on it – I often get the video out and have a look – we played very, very well, and were deserved winners in the end. I remember we went 3-0 up, and after that I was convinced that it was all over, game, set and match, and it was going to be four or five rather than three, so I was very relaxed then. I came down and sat on the bench, and I remember looking at Jim as I walked past and Jim's face was like thunder, and I felt really sorry for him, and I thought, "I shouldn't be really, I should be pleased for myself."

Vic Morris: Poor old Jim Smith, our ex-manager. I felt sorry for Jim because really it was the team that Jim Smith had built. Everybody was shouting, "You should have stayed at the Manor," and all this business.

Maurice Evans: They kept chanting that, and it rang true to me. I thought, "You should have done, Jim, you should have stayed at the Manor, I wish you had." I can remember the players in the last ten minutes, passing the ball about, Ray Houghton, Trevor Hebberd, Kevin

Brock, Les Phillips, and I can remember them keeping the ball and laughing, smiling, and I thought, "Well, this is it, I've never seen this before, where players are having a laugh on the field, particularly with a prize as big as this, the Milk Cup Final."

Jim Smith: I didn't know where to put myself and everybody had to walk off at the Oxford United end, and all the fans sang, "There's only one Jim Smith," which was fantastic and obviously helped me. I appreciated that.

Chris Bishop: Three-nil. I think that was the biggest margin of victory in a League Cup Final at that time. As soon as the final whistle went, we celebrated for about five or ten minutes and we looked at the other end and it was just completely empty. I've never seen a stadium empty so quickly. The QPR fans had disappeared.

Tim Sparrowhawk: Then Maurice Evans sent Ken Fish up to get his medal at Wembley. It was unlikely that Maurice Evans was ever going to be there again, but that didn't matter to him.

Maurice Evans: It wasn't planned at all. I wasn't expecting to win. It wouldn't have been quite the same sending Ken up for a loser's medal! But I felt that Ken had done so much for this club. I was just a newcomer and Ken had been here for years, and had run the club virtually on his own at times, and I felt that he was coming towards the end and it might just be nice.

Chris Bishop: Malcolm Shotton with his hat with horns on, doing his little jig. That really sticks in the mind.

Maurice Evans: I remember going into the dressing-room with the players and just sitting them down before all hell let loose and saying, "Well done, you've deserved it, you've done brilliant," and then Mr Maxwell came in and he said, "Maurice, the press are wanting you, will you go and talk to the press?" I said, "Well, just wait a minute, chairman, I want to enjoy being with the players for a while and I'll come down in a minute." I stayed with the players for probably half an hour, having a laugh and a few drinks, and the press fellow kept coming, knocking on the door: "Mr Evans, the press would like to see you." I said, "Okay, yeah, I'll come along."

Jeremy Charles: Jim Smith actually came in our dressing-room. He'd been with his own team for about half an hour. Then he came and sat with us for about half an hour, which I thought was great on Jim's behalf.

Tim Sparrowhawk: I have a good memory of the cars streaming out. We followed the other cars, not quite sure of the way back to the M40, and about ten cars merrily went into this cul-de-sac. They all had to reverse out, but it didn't seem to matter because it was just great.

Chris Bishop: I remember having these QPR fans in front of us, and they kept on with messages like "Going down, going down." We just laughed at them. We were in a dodgy League position, but we were just floating on air after that victory.

Maurice Evans: At Wembley, at the press conference, you sit in a room behind a desk with a microphone and there seemed to be about 100 press men there. I thought, "Good God, what's this in aid of?" And everyone's firing questions. Mr Maxwell left then. He said, "Before I go, gentlemen, I'd like to tell you that Maurice Evans has got a contract for life." I thought, "Contract for life? What on earth is he talking about?" Of course that was the theme then. They all jumped in on that one. That's the last I remember about the press conference. It went on quite a long while.

Nick Harris: The moment I'll never forget, and the moment I realised United had won the Milk Cup, was coming down the A40, coming down into the dip, towards Wheatley. The sun was just beginning to go down over Oxford and there was a traffic jam of four or five miles. Every single car, every single coach, everything, was all yellow and blue, and banners were hanging over the bridges. It was absolutely incredible. It was like the invading army coming home. Everybody in Headington was hanging out of the windows. It was just amazing. I think I realised then that United had really done something very, very special.

Vic Morris: We went straightaway to the supporters' club and just about squeezed in. If you wanted a drink it was nearly impossible. I think it was the greatest day of my life in football. No-one could ever think that Oxford could win a Final at Wembley. I just couldn't imagine it. I don't really know how it was all done, to be honest. It was like a reward for everything you'd done up there.

Peter Rhoades-Brown: I was injured and had missed out. I had watched the game from the stand with my family. Obviously I was pleased that the boys had won. We went back to the Bell in Beaconsfield and celebrated by dancing on the stage till all hours. Jeremy Charles was singing a few songs. Then we came home. I haven't got a clue when. On our coach we had the players and wives and the trophy – no management. Brian McDermott had taken my jacket during the course of the evening, because we all had the same jackets, and mine had my house keys and car keys in it. Eventually, when we got back to the Manor, the Cup had been handed round the coach by everybody. I just happened to have it in my hand when I was getting off the coach. As there was no-one to take charge of it, I duly placed it up my jumper and got off the coach. Malcolm Shotton was the only one to see me do this. He said, "You deserve to take it home as you missed out." I got a cab and went to stay with Kevin Brock in Abingdon, as I didn't have my house keys. I woke up in the morning in a double-bed with me, Kevin Brock, and the Milk Cup in between us. I don't think the wives were very pleased! Apparently Jim Hunt had a panic because they needed the trophy for the civic reception. He rang Maurice: "Where's the trophy?" Rang Ray Graydon. "No idea." They phoned Malcolm Shotton and, all credit to him, he said, "No idea."

Jeremy Charles: Jim Hunt rang me up the next morning. He said, "Are you okay?" I said, "Yes." He said, "Have you got a headache?" I said, "Yes." He said, "Oh, by the way, have you got the Cup?" I said, "No, Jim, why's that?" He said, "Well, it's gone missing."

Peter Rhoades-Brown: Apparently the first house they rang was mine, but I wasn't there. Eventually they rang Kevin's house, after going through the whole team, and Kevin said, "Of course, Pete's got it, he's in bed with it." And there was a big sigh and cheers from the girls in the office, and they told Jim Hunt that they'd found the trophy. I polished it up and took it to Pergamon, where we met with the rest of the club, and I handed it over with a big grin on my face. I couldn't understand what all the panic was about!

Maurice Evans: Then we went on the open-top bus, on the Monday. When we were outside the Town Hall, we got off the bus and it was obviously very crowded and all the crowd surged round us. I had a handkerchief in my top pocket, which I always have, and I got into the reception and it wasn't there. I thought, "That's funny" but I didn't give it a thought. I looked at the video later and you can see someone whipping it out of my top pocket as we got off the bus, so someone in Oxford has got a nice little memento of the Milk Cup Final – my handkerchief.

Avoiding Relegation, 1986

Chris Fallows: It was our first season in the First Division, and it was imperative that we stayed up, to show it wasn't just a one-off season. It came to the last three matches of the season – Everton at home, Forest at home and Arsenal at home – and we had to win two of those games. Gary

Lineker was playing for Everton and both teams played to the top of their ability. It was an excellent match, but Oxford got on top in the second half, going down to the London Road end. Ray Houghton had a header scooped off the line and Billy Hamilton had an effort cleared off the line. Everton needed to win to keep in the Championship race and there it was, 0-0 with a minute to go, and I turned to my brother and I said, "What a shame, we've played so well, and it would have been nice to have won tonight because I don't think we can excel ourselves like this again," and up popped Billy Hamilton in the penalty area, and he laid it back and Les Phillips drilled it into the net. Of course we all went wild, and we went away happy. We needed a win out of Nottingham Forest and Arsenal. Come the Saturday, we lost 2-1 against Nottingham Forest. We walked out of the ground, and I remember this bloke said, "Well, they'll never bloody beat Arsenal if they play like that." And my brother got quite angry with him and said, "Yes, but if they play like they did against Everton the other night, they will win – you can't have it all ways."

Maurice Evans: I had got to know Cloughie [Brian Clough] well and enjoyed his company, and he came in after Notts Forest had beaten us. I said, "Do you want a drink?" He said, "Yes." But I never had one. He said, "Why are you not having one?" I said, "I'm absolutely sick about that result." He said, "You're not worried, are you?" I said, "Yes, I am worried." He said, "But all you've got to do is beat Arsenal." I said, "It's easier said than done." He said, "You will beat Arsenal. I'm telling you. There is no danger whatsoever. You will beat them." I said, "Well, I wish I shared your confidence, Brian, but thanks very much anyway."

Chris Bishop: I remember the Arsenal game because it was Billy Hamilton's last game and, when he scored in front of the London Road, he did a little Irish jig and sent the fans wild. That was just the icing on the cake. The stadium was packed full. You could hardly move. The matches against Everton and Arsenal were absolutely amazing. Singing everywhere. Even in the family section, where I was with my Dad and my sister. We just got carried away, and sang till our voices couldn't take it any more. Things like "We love you Oxford", "For ever and ever, we'll follow your team, Oxford United rule supreme."

Maurice Evans: We played well again. We had a penalty which I thought was dubious. Mr Axcell was referee – I've got a great memory for referees – and he gave us a penalty. I would not have been very happy if it had been given against us. I think that put us two up. At that time I thought, "We're safe for another season." Arsenal were very disappointed at losing 3-0. None of the Arsenal coaching staff or management came anywhere near the office. I remember sitting in my office on my own. Before I saw the press I always had five or ten minutes on my own, to think about the game and what questions might crop up, and calm myself down before seeing the press. All of a sudden the door burst open. Mr Maxwell came in and said, "Maurice, What the devil are you doing in here? Why don't you come out on the pitch and run round the pitch with me?" I said, "No, Mr Maxwell. I'm not really into that sort of thing." And away he went. I believe he was doing his lap of honour around the pitch. So I sat in here and calmed myself down and went and saw the press. I was probably more pleased with that result than the Milk Cup Final because I think that meant a tremendous amount to the people who had worked so hard to get Oxford into the First Division, and to the crowd as well. I was very pleased about that one, very pleased.

16 *"We've been there for three years"*

AMONG FOOTBALL'S ELITE, 1986-88

United's second season in the First Division ended like the first, with a nail-biting finish to avoid relegation, this time at Luton. Then, in the summer of 1987, Robert Maxwell switched allegiance to newly-promoted Derby County, and his son Kevin took over as United chairman. Mark Lawrenson was appointed as manager in March 1988, when United were almost certain to be relegated, and Maurice Evans became general manager. The Oxford-Derby relationship caused speculation, especially when two United stars, Dean Saunders and Trevor Hebberd, moved to Derby. Lawrenson resigned when Saunders was transferred.

The First Division

Peter Rhoades-Brown: We struggled but we held our own. Instead of playing the Liverpools, Man Uniteds, Evertons and Tottenhams in the Cup every now and again, you're playing against them every other week, and playing against the big names – the Dalglishes and the Hoddles. It was magnificent. I sound quite overawed, don't I? In a way it was like that, but we didn't show too much respect.

Maurice Evans: I knew that defensively we were not good enough. Before long we were going to get caught. Tommy Caton and David Bardsley came in. I got David Bardsley because I thought he was like Langy – excellent going forward. Not the greatest defender in the world, but very good going forward. I thought that would compensate for Langy because I enjoyed that part of the game. I thought David Bardsley was a very good player.

Chris Fallows: There were some characters, like Billy Whitehurst, who's got to be one of the worst players I've ever seen up there. Like a whale. He sticks in everybody's mind because he was a character. When he came back with various teams – he must have been with nearly every team in the League – they gave him some stick, but he took it in good heart and he actually scored against us. He scored a goal *for* us once. It was the first game of the season, against Portsmouth, and he picked it up outside the area and I thought, "Oh, my God, he's going to shoot here," and he curled it with his left foot round a defender and round the goalkeeper, like Michel Platini. You'd never seen Billy Whitehurst do anything like it before, and he never did it afterwards either.

Winifred Crawford: So many players have gone. It upset me a lot when we had to sell our good players. There was John Aldridge. He was very nice to me. And Ray Houghton, my little Ray. He used to sit in the club, a table away from me, after the match. If we hadn't had to sell all our good players we'd be in the top division, wouldn't we?

v Luton Town, May 1987

Jim Hunt: Winning the Milk Cup was brilliant, for a day-out. Whether you were standing on the terraces or sitting in the directors' box, I don't think you could say that you could have had a better day. But I think our achievement of staying in the First Division for three seasons was even greater. We stayed in twice and it was a battle each time. The second year we went to Luton about two games before the end of the season, and we more-or-less had to win. Normally I've never been one to jump around and shout and punch the air, except for that time at Luton. John Dreyer centred the ball and Dean Saunders headed it in, and that was right on 90 minutes, and I knew then that we were going to stay in the First Division. I remember throwing my arms around Nick Johnson, the commercial manager, and I'd never done anything like that before. It was so important.

That stands out in my mind, as much as the Milk Cup Final.

Nick Harris: In the First Division, going to a place like Luton, where there was no away support, I really did feel that everybody in Oxford was listening to my commentary. That particular game was when United had to win to stay up. United were 2-0 up and Luton pulled two back in the last ten minutes, and Dean Saunders scored in injury-time. People I've spoken to since have said, "Yeah, everybody in Oxford was listening to that game." Somebody said their wireless fell in the bath. People were saying how they ran out into the street.

Tim Sparrowhawk: My wife is Japanese and periodically we go back to Japan. It was 1987, the day that Coventry beat Tottenham in the Cup Final, and we landed back in England. At Heathrow you go to the first-stage immigration and show your passport, and the question was, "Did Oxford stay up?" Fortunately, this bloke obviously knew a bit about football and was able to confirm that Oxford had stayed in the First Division.

v Luton Town – Littlewoods Cup Semi-Final, 1988

Peter Rhoades-Brown: I had another chance to play at Wembley just two years after missing the Milk Cup Final. We got to the semi-final again. I couldn't tell you who we played in the early rounds, but I remember the semi-final against Luton.

Mac: The first leg was on a Wednesday night at the Manor. Dean Saunders scored 6.4 for a penalty fall. He scored one penalty and missed another. It ended 1-1. Then I remember splitting up with my girlfriend. On the day we played at Luton in the second leg, her father turned up with a truck and moved all her stuff during the game. I was trying to watch the match on television while all these material possessions were disappearing around me.

Peter Rhoades-Brown: Just before that semi-final we'd played at Luton in the League and lost 7-4, so the television company decided to make it a live match and we lost 2-0. I set the video tape beforehand. I remember having a bad time during the game. Richard Hill and I got substituted. On the way off we both said, "It's the same old faces being taken off." I came straight back home and was that disappointed that I rewound the tape and recorded over it.

When Maurice Evans Stepped Down

Maurice Evans: In the First Division the money goes up and players' wages go up, and players started to think about money rather than football. That really convinced me that it was time I got out of it. Freedom of contract had come in and made management very hard. At the end of the season, if you had five or six players whose contract was up, you didn't know whether you were going to have them the following season or not. So, if you didn't know who you were going to have, you didn't know who you wanted. You had to try and tie players up the previous season. Now, players became crafty. They knew that. So they waited. They said, "No, I'm not going to sign at Christmas, I'm going to sign in the summer when the pressure's on you a bit," so it became very, very hard.

Mark Lawrenson: Due to my ruptured achilles, I was about to be finished as a player, and I got a phone call from John Maddock, who was working for the *People*. He said, "The Oxford job is available. Maurice Evans is currently in charge there, he doesn't want the job, and Kevin Maxwell, who is the chairman, is looking for someone to take it. Do you fancy it?" I said, "Well, I'll certainly talk to him." I went to meet Kevin Maxwell at the Mirror Buildings in London, and talked to him for an hour or two. One of the first things he said was, "Could you still play?" I said, "No, don't be under any illusions, I can't play because of the insurance, I'm just here to manage." Kevin Maxwell sold the club to me really. The job was offered to me and I took it. It was my first job in management. The club were on the brink of relegation. I thought, "The worst that can happen is that we'll go in the Second Division and we can rebuild."

Mac: I was doing some plastering at a house in Eynsham and one of the old boys was an Oxford supporter. He bought a newspaper on the way in that morning and he was really excited about the new manager. He hid his paper behind his back and wouldn't tell me who was the new manager. "You'll never guess who we've got, you'll never ever guess." "Bob Paisley," I said, "Jock Stein." I was guessing names of people who were dead. He told me at lunchtime that it was Mark Lawrenson.

Mark Lawrenson: I'll always remember my first day. I came in, went into the office, closed the doors, sat at the desk and thought, "Crikey, I've got to run this football club now." All of a sudden I was responsible for probably 40 people on a professional basis, so obviously you had to think for other people: the way we were going to play, the team I was going to pick, the scouting. One of the first things I did was ask Maurice Evans to stay in the office with me – I brought another desk in – because I knew that, with his experience, he knew players in the game and he knew managers in the game. He turned out to be very, very helpful. I also appointed Brian Horton as my assistant. I'd known Brian from my playing days at Brighton and he'd subsequently played at Luton and player-managed at Hull. He'd been sacked at Hull, which I thought was strange after what he'd done for them, but I knew him as a person. I'm probably one of those who can step back and see the funny side of things, and I'm maybe not as serious as someone like Brian. Brian likes to shout in the dressing-room. He likes to put people under pressure, a very good motivator, and I just thought that together the two of us would be a good team. Unfortunately we didn't last long enough to prove that a fact.

The Players, 1988

Mark Lawrenson: There was obviously ability in the side – Martin Foyle, Dean Saunders, Trevor Hebberd – and they were also organised. But they didn't have (a) enough good players and (b) enough players who had their heart and soul in it. They were on the brink of relegation, if not already there. There were little things. Tommy Caton, God rest his soul, had played nearly every game for Oxford as a centre-back and he hadn't had a booking all season, and I thought, "This maybe tells me something about the club, that maybe it is a bit too nice. Maybe they don't want to stay in the First Division badly enough." I remember the second or third game we had to play Trevor Hebberd at left-back, which obviously wasn't ideal. We gave Lee Nogan his debut. Robbie Mustoe was still a kid then, and he had to be a permanent fixture in the team. We were really thin on the ground for players, because of injuries, and you couldn't really do anything. I think the first game we drew away at Charlton. Then we drew with Arsenal at home and should have won. I think we drew with Everton down at the Manor, drew with Southampton. We just couldn't win a game, although we didn't lose many. Towards the end probably some of the enthusiasm was on the wane, and we got beat at Watford, which virtually sealed our fate. I remember that was quite a gloomy and doomy day, but apart from that they responded very well.

Peter Rhoades-Brown: We survived for three years, and there's a few that haven't survived for that long. I think the main reason why we ended up being relegated was because we lost a lot of players. Maurice Evans had bought a lot of good players and made them better players and sold them, and we couldn't find anybody to fill their boots, which was a shame, so we ended up being relegated. You can't take anything away now. We've been there for three years.

REBUILDING

Mark Lawrenson: I had a meeting with Kevin Maxwell after the last home game of the season. He said, "Right, who do you want to keep, who do you want to let go?" I gave him a list, and there weren't many that I wanted to keep. He said, "Look, you're really going to have to generate most of your own money to buy players." I think Dean Saunders had maybe a year left on his contract and Kevin said, "I'd like you to get him to sign a new contract for another three years." I said, "Fine, it's going to cost you money, he's going to be the best-paid player at the club." He said, "I don't have a problem with that because he's our prize asset." I said, "That's okay, but if we're going to do that you've got to promise to me that he's not going to be sold within a couple of weeks of the season starting." He said, "No, you've got a season with him." I said, "Fine, at least I know if I've got a season I've got a chance, I can get players and build around him." That could also be a lever in getting other players to the club, saying, "Look, we've got this fellow who scores for fun, basically, come along here, we've got a chance of promotion." My first signing was Mike Ford from Cardiff.

Mike Ford: I'd just finished the season with Cardiff. We'd been promoted and we'd won the Welsh Cup and qualified for the European Cup-winners' Cup. I was getting married that summer. I was sitting in my bath, the morning I was getting married, and the phone rang. I just assumed it was somebody wishing me all the best for the afternoon, but it was the Cardiff City manager, Frank Burrows: "A club's come in for you, we've agreed a fee, do you want to go and speak to them?" I said, "I'm actually getting married today." He said, "I know, they want you to speak with them tomorrow." I said, "I'm flying off on honeymoon tomorrow." He said, "It's Oxford United." I thought, "That's a decent club, it could be very interesting." The next day I went to see Mark Lawrenson. I said, "Can I think about it over the honeymoon period?" He said, "What is there to think about?" I thought, "He's probably right," and I signed.

Mark Lawrenson: I have to smile. He went on honeymoon, came back two weeks later and walked into the ground like a cripple. I thought he was taking the mickey. John Clinkard, who I'd appointed as a physiotherapist, from Everton, came to me, absolutely white. He went, "You're never going to believe this, Boss, he's done his back in on honeymoon." Of course we all roared about laughing and said, "Yeah, yeah, but he'll be fit in a couple of weeks, won't he?" "No, he needs an operation."

Mike Ford: I had these pains in my leg and I thought I'd pulled a hamstring. I phoned John Clinkard and came in to see him straightaway. Slipped disc. I signed on 6 June and I didn't play a game till January.

Mark Lawrenson: Then I had to ring Kevin Maxwell. I said to Kevin, "Look, we're going to have to get a left-back because of what's happened to Fordy, and John Dreyer's gone." He said, "Fine, have you got anyone in mind?" "Yeah, there's a lad at Glasgow Rangers, currently in the Reserves, who used to play at Bolton and Doncaster. An English boy, I think we could possibly get him back down." He said, "Fine, get on with it, let me know." Graeme Souness, my old team-mate, was the manager at Rangers. I rang Graeme and I said, "Jimmy Phillips." He said, "Yeah, I don't think he's going to figure in my plans, a good footballer, 250 grand." I said, "Graeme, I haven't got it." I got on to the Maxwells. I said, "Look, it's going to be 250 grand." "No, we can't afford to pay that." Brian and I saw Jimmy Phillips play, and he cruised a game at Hibs. We met Graeme Souness and I think the final figure was something in the region of £150,000 or £160,000. I said, "Right, I'll just have to ring Kevin to finalise it." I knew that Kevin was away on the ship, the *Lady Ghislaine*, so I had all these numbers to ring. It took me about five minutes to dial them all, ship to shore and everything. The phone went at the other end. This voice said, "Hello." I said, "Oh, Mr Maxwell, can I speak to Kevin, please." And he went, "Speak to me." I said, "Well, I need to speak to Kevin because I'm trying to buy a player." "Speak to me." And of course this was Robert Maxwell, the chairman of Derby. I said, "This is the deal, Jimmy Phillips, Glasgow Rangers, 160 grand, blah, blah, blah." He said, "Fine," and he put the phone down. So I turned to Graeme and said, "Yeah, it's on, no problem." It was very interesting that I had to ask for permission from the chairman of Derby County just to sign Jimmy Phillips. Kevin was great with me. It was just that obviously his father was the man in everything they did together. Trevor Hebberd still wanted to play in the First Division, which he was more than capable of. I got him in the office, and I said, "Look, I can give you a bit more money if you want to stay." I wanted him to stay because he was a good athlete, a good footballer, and he was good to have around the club, but he didn't really want to stay. Derby were in the First Division then, and they did have money, and they came on and said, "Trevor Hebberd?" I said, "Yeah, I'm prepared to let him go, this is what it will cost you." Arthur Cox [manager of Derby County] said, "That's fine, we can let the two chairmen sort that out anyway." I thought, "Here we go again." I said, "Well, have you got any players there?" I already had a list, and Mickey Lewis was one. Brian Horton knew him. I said, "I fancy Mickey Lewis, I value him at this, etc." Arthur said, "Yeah, that'll all be sorted." To be quite honest, I never saw the money, but the managers don't see the money. It just comes in to the club, and, as far as I was concerned, we paid £70,000 for Mickey Lewis and the difference in cash was that Oxford United got 200 grand, which was going to buy me more players. Mickey Lewis did very well for me as an anchor man in midfield – head it, kick it, tackle people, close people down – and Trevor Hebberd didn't want to play for Oxford. As far as I was concerned, it was a good deal.

The Second Division, 1988-89

Mark Lawrenson: We started the season quite well. We had a couple of good results. Up until October, when I left, we were in the top half of the table, probably about eighth or ninth, purely and simply because we had this machine in Saunders. We knew, if we played away from home and kept it tight, he would score a goal for us. That was something for us to build on. I'd had a lot of calls about Saunders, from Graham Taylor at Aston Villa and Howard Wilkinson at Sheffield Wednesday. Graeme Souness was interested. I'd rung Dalglish and said, "Look, at the end of the season this lad's going to have to leave us if we don't get promotion, and there's going to be a queue," so they were looking at him. I knew that we had a gem, but unfortunately I couldn't wheel and deal enough to get the players in that I wanted, purely and simply because I couldn't get the others out. It was frustrating.

The Dean Saunders Transfer, October 1988

Mark Lawrenson: I'd known Coxy [Derby County manager Arthur Cox] for years and years and years, from when I was a kid at Preston. He kept ringing me up about Dean Saunders. I'd say, "Coxy, end of the season, fine, not a problem, if we don't get promotion, get in with the pack." And he said, "You know, obviously, the family connections." I said, "Yeah, but to be honest with you, that isn't my problem because he's not for sale." He would ring quite often and his assistant, Roy McFarland, would ring and we'd all have a laugh and say, "Not you again, that's a shock. It's like having a standing order at Barclays." Saturday we're at home. Blackburn Rovers. I turned up at the ground about 1.30 and Brian was with me. Immediately I walked in the office, the phone went. It was Jim Hunt from the secretary's office. He said, "Can you speak to Kevin, urgently." So I rang Kevin. He said, "Dean Saunders." I said, "Oh, no, not again." He said, "Yeah, he must speak to Derby after the game." I didn't really know what to say. I said, "Kevin, are you serious?" He said, "Yeah. Look, I know you're disappointed. I know I said he could stay till the end of the season, but I'm telling you as your chairman that he has to speak to Derby County at the end of the game." I put the phone down. Brian could obviously tell by my face. He said, "What is it?" I said, "Deano. Derby are here. He's going to speak to Derby after the game." We were playing Blackburn. There was no score at half-time. We had played with a sweeper in the first half and it hadn't quite worked out, and I was going to change it. On the way up the tunnel, somebody like Mick Moore, the groundsman, said "Hey, Arthur Cox is here in the stand with his tracksuit on." Coxy knew all about Saunders, and to come and actually sit in the stand was so blatantly obvious. Anyway, we drew 1-1, Dean scored, and we were seventh or eighth in the League. I said to the players, "See you Monday," and I said to Dean, "Could you come in the office when you've finished, when you've had a shower." He came in. I said, "Look, Derby County are here to speak to you. Arthur Cox is here, they're going to take you away and speak to you." And he went, "Do I have to go?" I said, "No, you don't have to go, but Derby have been given permission to speak to you." He said, "What do you think?" I said, "Well, you won't know this for a few days but it's a bit of a hornet's nest. It's a long, long story, but I can't really stand in your way, and all that I advise you is that you go in and speak and say exactly what you want from them because I don't think they'll turn you down."

Jim Hunt: Dean Saunders was actually signed in my house. After the game, Arthur Cox said, "Where can we go privately so the press can't see us?" I said, "This office?" He said, "No, they'll know we're here." I said, "The Moat House?" He said, "No, I don't like hotels because they're always there." I said, "The only other place is my house at Kidlington." So Dean Saunders, his wife and baby went over with him. They arrived about ten past six. I actually wrote out all the terms for Dean Saunders. By then it was about 20 past 11 at night.

Mark Lawrenson: My stepfather and my mother had come to the game, and I went home and went out for a meal, and I told them. My stepfather said, "What are you going to do?" I said, "Well, to be quite honest with you, I'll pack it in. Two things. I've been promised him till the end of the season. If that's changed, well, reluctantly, I would have to say, 'Fine.' But the real thing that's got to me is that if I could have had him for two more weeks I could have bought two players, got them in the club and then sold him, because you know yourself that if I've got £1 million from the sale of Dean Saunders and on Monday I ring up Bristol Rovers, they'll say, 'Oh, yeah, you've just sold Saunders, half a million for Penrice.'" I'd tried to buy Penrice in the meantime and I knew he was about 200 grand. I spoke to Kevin on the Sunday morning and said this to him. He said, "Look, I have to be quite honest with you, it's really down to my father. He's coming in from France at 12 or 12.30, why don't you come up with Jim Hunt, the secretary, and have a chat." My stepfather came with me. We picked up Jim Hunt. Jim saw my face, which must have looked like thunder, and he went, "Don't do anything drastic." A lovely man, Jim Hunt. I drove to London, into the Mirror Buildings, went up to the penthouse, had a cup of coffee. Kevin was there. The next thing we hear the helicopter come in from Heathrow with his Dad.

Jim Hunt: I went in and saw Maxwell and he said, "Kevin and I have virtually agreed on £750,000 but your manager believes he's worth £1 million. What do you think?" I said, "I agree with Mark." He said, "Why?" I said, "First of all, he scored 20-odd goals in the First Division last year. Secondly, he's probably the best striker in the Second Division this year. Furthermore, what is the football world going to say about a player going from son-chairman to father-chairman unless it's for a considerably higher figure than what everybody else has offered. Maxwell walked round the table a few times, and then he said, "Alright, I'll offer you £1 million." To which Kevin said, "Thank you very much." I said, "That's not all, Mr Chairman." I still called him Mr Chairman although he wasn't my chairman. Force of habit. He said, "Go on." I said, "Well, when you were chairman of Oxford United, you always told me that we should aim to get 25 per cent of any resale figure. Does that apply in this case?" He said, "Don't be stupid. You've just bumped me up from £750,000 to £1 million. Now you've got the audacity to stand there and ask for 25 per cent of any resale above £1 million." I said, "Yeah, why not?" He went over to the phone and it was one of those where you could hear the other end, and it was Coxy the other end. He said, "What would you say if I say I've just bought Dean Saunders for £1 million?" And Arthur said, "Too much." "What should it have been?" Arthur said, "£750,000." Maxwell said, "I've just told Kevin and Jim Hunt that I'll pay £1 million." Arthur said, "Thank you very much." He said, "But that's not all. Jim Hunt's asked for 25 per cent of any resale figure." Arthur said, "That's stupid. Having bumped you up like that." Maxwell, "Yes, I realised that. Thank you, Arthur." Then he thought for a few minutes and said, "I'll offer you 10 per cent of any resale figure." Kevin said, "Okay." When Dean went from Derby to Liverpool for £2.9 million we then received 10 per cent of £1.9 million.

Mark Lawrenson: The door bursts open and in walks this larger-than-life figure. Obviously I'd spoken to him quite a few times. He came in, and sat on this coffee-table. He wasn't a slim man by any stretch of the imagination, and it literally buckled in the middle. I thought, "This thing's going to give way, and it probably cost a fortune." He sat there and looked at me and he went, "What's your problem?" which really fired me up, because I'd spent nearly 24 hours thinking about this. This stream came out from me. It wasn't a torrent of abuse. It was just, "This is my problem ... we sold him to Derby ... I've been told that he didn't have to go until the end of the season ... if we've really got to sell him, why can't I have an auction for him ... why can't we wait for two more weeks, and that will give me x amount of pounds up front and I can go and get some players ..." And this whole thing came out, I don't know where from. He looked at me and he said, although he actually swore, "It's got absolutely nothing to do with you," and just walked out. I looked at Kevin. I could understand Kevin's predicament. That was his father and he worked for his father. I just kind of shrugged my shoulders, and Kevin said, "Why don't you call me tomorrow." I said, "Yeah, yeah." Anyway, I went back home with my stepfather. He said, "What are you going to do?" I said, "I'm going to resign. It's purely and simply a matter of principle. What am I going to tell the supporters?"

The Monday After the Saunders Transfer

Mark Lawrenson: In the morning I rang Kevin and said, "Can I come and see you?" He said, "Yeah, I think you should. In fact, bring Brian with you." I said, "Okay." I rang Brian: "Look, forget about training, we're off to London." Everything was across the newspapers. They had this story that I was going to resign, and I don't know to this day where it came from. Obviously my family was sworn to secrecy and nobody had mentioned anything. I'd never mentioned this to Brian, until the Monday morning papers, and I said to Brian, "Well, I'm going to." He said, "Well, if you do, I'm going too." I said, "Well, I think you've seriously got to think about that," because he'd just bought his house at Woodstock and had been sacked at Hull. I said, "If they offer you the job, take it." He said, "No, I can't take it. What will everybody think of me?" I said, "It doesn't matter because I know and I've told you to take it." We got to the Mirror Buildings, and I announced that I was here. They said, "Just take a seat." I thought, "Oh, yeah, this is a bit strange." Anyway, two minutes later, Kevin's secretary came out and said, "Brian, Kevin would like to see you," and of course I knew straightaway. Brian looked at me, and I said, "Don't worry about it." About an hour later, I get taken into one of the offices. I'm sat at this big oval board-room table, papers everywhere. Kevin walked in, threw this piece of paper on the desk and it landed near me. I read it and I was being sacked. I gave it back to him. I said, "Well, if you can live with that, fine." Basically, what it was, nobody resigns on the Maxwells. He sacked me. He said it was a breach of contract. I said, "Kevin, I don't have a problem with you at all. You know what's gone on, I know what's gone on. There's other people involved who know what's gone on. As far as I'm concerned, you and I are fine," and shook his hand and walked out. I walked out on to the top floor, and I thought, "Well, I'll wait for Brian." So I waited. About five minutes later, the lift opened, two security guys came out and said, "Mr Lawrenson, you've got to leave the building." We get in the lift, down we go, bottom floor, and as I walked out the double-fronted glass doors, the world's press were there, so they obviously knew. I thought, "Crikey, what am I going to do?" I didn't really want to say anything, because I hadn't said anything and I didn't really know what to say. I thought, "Say nothing. Just say nothing." I got out and saw them all, scrum down. I thought I'd run across the road to a pub: "They're only press men, they'll never catch me, they're not fit." I ran across the road, dodged the traffic, went to open the pub door. It was about five to twelve. Locked. And you know that bit on "News at Ten" at the end, "And finally", when they usually have an amusing item, it was me that night. It was "Have you heard about the football manager who's just lost his job and couldn't get a drink?" and there's me trying the doors of this pub to get in, and of course all the press boys caught up with me. So

I went in a club owned by this Irish guy, and he'd heard the news. He stood by the doorway and he said to all these press boys, "Gentlemen, this is a private, members-only club, you're more than welcome if you're members, but if you're not, I'm sorry, you're not allowed in." I had a cup of coffee, and I rang through to Kevin's secretary and said, "Could you please tell Brian that I'm in Vagabond's and tell him to let me know when he's done and we'll go back." Next thing, about ten minutes later, I heard the blades of the helicopter going, and I thought, "They're taking him back in the helicopter," and they had done. It didn't sour me of management at all. I'd enjoyed it, although it was very, very short. I'd got one or two players to the club who went on to bigger and better things, and I'd left the club fairly healthy, although we still needed players. And Brian had also got the job, which I thought was nice, and it enabled him to appoint David Moss, which again was great. It wasn't all soured by what happened at the end. I just look upon it as experience and obviously tell people the story and smile about it now.

Nick Harris: I was the first person to interview Mark Lawrenson after the problems with the Maxwell family. I remember going to his house, the other side of Church Hanborough, and he was very upfront, very honest about it all. He just felt that he couldn't continue. I think he was doing a very good job when it all happened. It was very unfortunate. I think it was always obvious that Dean Saunders would leave Oxford United but the way it was done turned a lot of United fans against the club. I think perhaps the Dean Saunders affair was the final straw for a lot of people.

Sandy Brewer: I was going up there for 40 years, I suppose. I gave up when Dean Saunders was transferred. With a Maxwell here as chairman, and a Maxwell at Derby County as chairman, it didn't look good to me. I think they gave £1 million for him, and I asked if the club could publish a copy of the cheque. If I could have a copy of it, I could sit on a Saturday afternoon looking at that cheque instead of going to the Manor. That's true. They replied that there was no cheque involved because it was done by bank-transfer.

17 *"He kept the spirit going"*

SURVIVAL, 1988-92

United continued to respond to challenges. Bottom of Division Two in December 1990, Brian Horton's side lost only two of the next 24 League games (and also won an FA Cup game at First Division Chelsea). The following season, 1991-92, when Robert Maxwell died and key players were transferred during the subsequent financial crisis, United avoided relegation with a dramatic last-match win at Tranmere.

Brian Horton's Team

Brian Horton: Generally, when managers take over at a club, they've taken over because the previous manager's been sacked, or they're not doing very well. You don't often get a job when things are going well. There were some problems, obviously, but nothing to do with me. The biggest cause was the sale of Deano. Everybody was adamant that we weren't getting £1 million. They thought that was just a fictitious figure that we could put to the Football League. I think they probably thought he'd gone for 200 grand, but you can't do that. It was £1 million, and that money had to go through the Football League to come here.

Jim Hunt: I know the fanzine doubted whether it was paid, but I can assure you that it was paid. The money went from Derby to the Football League, and the Football League to Oxford, so there was no way that Kevin and his father could have forgotten about the money.

Brian Horton: My job was to get on with the football. At that time, during that first year with Mark, we might have got very close to the play-offs. Then that season [1988-89] dwindled into a nothing season. I did have some money to spend. I bought Paul Simpson, Steve Foster and John Durnin. When I was at Hull City, I'd seen Paul Simpson as a 17-year-old boy in Manchester City Reserves and I'd kept my eyes on him. It was a lot of money, £200,000, but obviously you've got to try to do things to appease the fans and get players in, so I bought Paul and we sold him for £500,000 when things got difficult. He did very well for the club. He scored goals, he was an entertainer, and I think the crowd appreciated Simmo. I bought Steve Foster for his experience. I know supporters will have various opinions about this one, but I felt that Steve Foster helped us to stabilise the club. I think without his experience we'd have been in trouble. He was a very good leader on the field. A lot of it was by talking, but I think he led by example as well. He scored goals from set-pieces where he put his head in where others wouldn't put their feet. That's the way Fozzie was. He wasn't always the best trainer – he was getting on in our day – but when he put the shirt on you always knew what to expect from him. John Durnin came because I'd seen John scoring goals for Liverpool Reserves. That was the level we were looking at. We were always around that £200,000 mark. I don't think John realised his full potential, with his off-the-field activities, if you can call them that, but he did score goals for us.

Winifred Crawford: I always go and welcome a new player. The first game, I go up to him after the match, take my autograph-book, and I welcome him to the Manor. I say, "And I wish you the very best of luck." Do you know, Johnny Durnin caught hold of me, he signed his autograph and he gave me a kiss. He never missed coming over to me. I'd feel a tap on my shoulder: "How are you then?" And he gave me a kiss. Mind you, when he was a naughty boy, in the beginning, I told him off three times. I went up to him and said, "Johnny, you stupid boy, what do you think you're doing? You're putting your football career in jeopardy." Three times he'd got into trouble, with his car and drink and fighting and what. But he's a lovely lad really.

Brian Horton: I knew little Steiny [Mark Stein] as an apprentice at Luton, and he went from there to QPR and he came in the Dave Bardsley deal. Once again, supporters don't know all the situation, because Dave wanted to go back into the First Division, as it was then, so we did a deal with Steiny. For some reason he couldn't score goals while he was at Oxford. Mick Lewis was an unsung hero for me. Mick's enthusiasm and everything. He never missed many games for me. I probably instigated the move to get him here from Derby, because Trevor Hebberd wanted to go, we wanted to do a player-exchange, and I said to Mark about Mickey Lewis. People like that are a valuable part of clubs like Oxford. Dave Penney did well, always the same. Mike Ford, a tremendous competitor. Maurice bought Garry Smart from Wokingham and he did a fantastic job for Oxford United. Les Robinson came from Doncaster. I always felt Les could have done better. When I watched him play for Doncaster he was always their best player. When he came here, at a higher level, I think he thought, "I'm not the best player any more." He always did well, though. You knew what you were going to get out of him. I think that was general with the players that we had. They fought for the club.

Mike Ford: Three occasions stand out in my time at the club – the Tranmere game [1992], the Peterborough game [1996] and when I was in goal against Hull City [November 1989]. I had been in and out of the side and I don't think the supporters had taken to me 100 per cent, and I was substitute against Hull. Alan Judge went up for the ball and came down, and I think he hurt his knee. He had to come off. Brian Horton looked at me, and I looked at him, and we didn't say a word to each other. I just went and put the jersey on. I remember the first cross coming in from the left-hand side – I was down the bottom end – and the ball came to the far post and I dropped it. I think Jimmy Phillips cleared it. I can see the look on the supporters' faces: "Oh, no, what's happening here, Fordy's in goal, we're going to lose three or four." But I didn't have a lot to do. I just remember the incident with Billy Whitehurst [then in his second spell with Hull City] at the top end, second half. He bustled through and lost his balance and fell over. I just picked the ball up. I was in goal for 65 or 70 minutes and kept a clean sheet. 0-0. Supporters were chanting my name and I think that was a turning-point for me personally. I think they took to me after that. I cemented a place when Ceri Evans was injured and I came in alongside Steve Foster. Then Brian Horton sold Jimmy Phillips to Middlesbrough and I played left-back. Success, at that stage, was staying in the Second Division. For a number of seasons we managed that. It was partly down to the management of the club, and it was partly down to having some good players, including a lot of international players – Jim Magilton (Northern Ireland), Andy Melville (Wales), Steve Foster (England) and Ceri Evans (New Zealand).

Brian Horton: Ceri Evans was a dream really. Richard Hill had mentioned Ceri Evans because he'd played with him in New Zealand. We got him up, put him on tuppence ha'penny to play in the Reserves and he went on and played so many League games for us, and he was a tremendous ambassador. He was very good at everything – cricket, karate, chess – and obviously very clever. A magnificent lad. We bought Andy Melville for £275,000 and he eventually left us in a £750,000 deal. I bought Jimmy Magilton from Liverpool for £100,000. When I look back over my career as a manager, I think I must say that Jimmy's been one of my best signings. A good footballer. A bit impatient with himself and with other people at times, but a tremendous footballer. His goal record is first-class. He's a bubbly character, lovely to have in the dressing-room, and he went on to play for Northern Ireland. Paul Kee came for virtually nothing. He had a little bit of criticism off the fans. I think supporters, even for what he did in games like the Tranmere game, should have given him a little bit more support. Richard Hill was a lively lad, good in the dressing-room, but unfortunately he got a horrific injury soon after I'd taken over, as did Peter Rhoades-Brown. We got him a job at the football club as community officer. Tremendous lad, Rosie, in the dressing-room, always singing, making jokes, brilliant. I think that typifies what I had in the club. The spirit within the club carried us a long way. We had some great times at Christmas. Many times we talked about how well we did after Christmas parties. Every time we had a Christmas party we used to go on a run.

The Big Turn-around, 1990-91

Brian Horton: It was a funny season. Just before Christmas we went to Hull City. We conceded a last-minute goal, drew 3-3, and went bottom of the table. A few of the players' contracts were coming up at the end of that season. I rang the chairman, Kevin Maxwell, and said the contracts were coming up, and he said, "Well, get on with them." I said, "Well, the thing is, my contract's coming up, do you want me to be tying players for three or four years?" You have to be sensible about these things. Do you want to be giving them three-year contracts if mine's up and somebody else is going to come? We were bottom of the table. It was a leading question for me. He said, "Well, come and see me and we'll sort it out." I went down. He said, "What are you looking for, two or three years?" He gave me a two-year contract, and I sorted out Paul Simpson's contract and others'. Whether it was the stability that it gave us, I don't know, but we lost two in twenty-four. We won at Blackburn, and went on this unbelievable run. I think at that time we were playing 4-2-4. Phil Heath and Paul Simpson were the two wide players. We were playing some good football. The Chelsea FA Cup win [3-1] was tremendous. We played 4-3-3 there and gave a brilliant display of football. I don't think Chelsea expected us to play that sort of quality football.

Mike Ford: I remember the Chelsea game. I was sub and after ten minutes I was thinking, "We can beat these." There was no reason in the world why we couldn't beat them. I was warming up when one of the goals was scored, and our supporters were all at that end, and it was a brilliant feeling, even if I wasn't playing. The Tottenham game I remember for Gascoigne's goal. Gascoigne's performance was possibly the best individual performance I've ever witnessed. He was magnificent. We actually played quite well on the day and Martin Foyle got two.

Brian Horton: I was a bit disappointed that day, when we lost 4-2 at Tottenham, because I thought, again, we played some really good football, but Gascoigne destroyed us on the day, didn't he? That was one of his better days, notably his first goal, when he got past five or six people. A bit disappointing because I thought we defended quite badly that day. We did very well going forward but I thought we defended badly. But to say we were disappointed because we defended badly is probably being a bit critical because you're talking about playing against world-class players, like Lineker and Gascoigne.

A Youth Policy

Brian Horton: One year we brought seven or eight through, lads like Wallbridge, Tavinor, Druce, Wanless, Mutchell, Robert Ford. They've given me tremendous satisfaction. We played Tottenham Reserves, and I think we drew 1-1. They had Mabbutt and Fenwick and a tremendous side. One of their staff came in after the game and said, "Magnificent, the way your young lads played." Now that's just as satisfying for me as winning a first-team game because that's the way we've taught them. Joey Beauchamp was a very exciting young lad. I saw him when he first came, when he was 16 or 17 years old. Very quiet and introvert, Joey, which we were trying to bring out of him. He always scored goals in the youth team, always in the Reserves. He found it difficult sometimes to be mixing with the first-team players. He can use both feet, good speed, good football brain. Chrissie Allen was another. Very quick. Some managers do not like youth policies because they're not going to be there to see the fruition of it all. I don't go along with that theory. I think if you're a manager then you have to manage the club as it should be managed. Malcolm Elias, and all the people who worked for him, did a fantastic job to produce such players at a very small club. Malcolm knew all the schools and schoolteachers, which is very important. And Maurice Evans played a great part in bringing a lot of the young players through.

The Death of Robert Maxwell, November 1991

Brian Horton: Kevin Maxwell was a wonderful chairman to work for because he never interfered. He could have interfered a couple of times because the crowd were shouting for me to get the sack, but I knew he wouldn't, because that's the kind of man he was. He went against public opinion. I think he thought I was doing a good job because I had bought and sold quite well. When we went into the financial difficulties, when Mr Maxwell died and Kevin had to leave as chairman, that was a hard time, because obviously the bank pulled out, and we had to sell Paul Simpson, Lee Nogan and Mark Stein. You don't like selling players, but we had to to survive. I think it's a part of management that you have to balance the books. You have to sell players when you don't want to. The most important thing for me was that the club survived, and survived at a good level.

Nick Harris: I am in no doubt at all that without Brian Horton not only would United have been relegated but they might also have gone out of existence, because he kept the club together after Robert Maxwell's death. They were within two or three minutes of going out of existence altogether. He kept the players separate from that. He kept the spirit going. Obviously everybody was worried about getting paid the next week. Company cars were being taken back. There were tremendous financial problems, but somehow he and David Moss and Steve McClaren and Maurice Evans kept the players away from all that.

Mike Ford: Brian Horton got a lot of stick here, but during that spell he did a fantastic job – to keep the club in that division in those circumstances. Things went on that we will probably never know about.

We were kept separate from all the financial aspects of the situation. The only time we realised it was when we went in the main office and they all had long faces stuck on the floor!

Brian Horton: We were going to the club every day wondering what might happen. They were talking about liquidation and folding-up and "someone's going to come and take over" and then "they're not". It was horrific. We sold Paul Simpson and Lee Nogan, and Jim Magilton might have gone – we just staved that one off – and it was only the spirit in the club that made us survive that year. You have to keep the spirit in the dressing-room and on the training-pitch. Mickey Lewis, John Durnin, Jim Magilton were the sort of people that kept it going, because they were the jokers, the people who did things to keep it going. But it was tough.

v Tranmere, May 1992

Mike Ford: I'd had a bad injury and I came back with about seven or eight games to go. Dave Penney was playing full-back, and he was playing reasonably well and then he got sent off at Middlesbrough, when I was substitute. Straightaway I thought, "He's not going to be available for the last game at Tranmere." I hadn't played for six months and I'm thinking, "I might be involved." And that was the situation that arose. When it came I wasn't nervous at all. Because it was my first game back I didn't appreciate the whole situation until the game had finished. If we had lost at Tranmere we would have been relegated.

Brian Horton: Leading up to that, we'd gone to Plymouth. Peter Shilton had taken over and Plymouth beat us quite well. I think they probably thought they were safe then but Blackburn had to win at Plymouth on the last Saturday to get in the play-offs, so that worked in our favour. We went to the Tranmere game. We knew we had to win, which I think is a good thing. If you had to go for a draw, you wouldn't know how to play it. We went out to be adventurous. I felt we had nothing to lose. We hadn't got any money that year, but I said to the board, "We must go and stay overnight, we must treat it properly." We stayed at a small place. We found the cheapest place we could. Dinner, bed and breakfast. We took them up on the Friday night. We were quite relaxed about it. We took them out training on the Saturday morning and we trained on the worst pitch you could ever imagine in your life. We had to go over some scrubland and there was this little pitch. It was bumpy. The posts were half-broken. It was on a slope. Both ways, downwards and sideways. In fact we were laughing and joking, saying, "I wonder if we'd be training on this if we were playing at Wembley today." Anyway, we got the balls out and had a warm-up, did the loosener, a bit of ball-work, a bit of pre-match luncheon, and the boys seemed so relaxed. There was no tension. It was amazing. I've been in relegation battles before when you're "white-knuckled", but it wasn't like that on the day. We went out there and in the first half we missed chance after chance. Joey Beauchamp had about six chances. I know he scored but I think he had half-a-dozen chances in that game. We thought, "Goodness, it's going to be one of those days."

Mac: I couldn't go to Tranmere because I was working that night. I heard it on Radio Oxford. I remember hearing the team line-up and Kee was in goal. I thought, "That's it. We're down." But he played brilliantly.

Brian Horton: Late on Keesy [Paul Kee] made a couple of fantastic saves. The game should have been out of sight with the chances we'd had but he pulled off a couple of incredible saves. Looking back, that was probably Keesy's best day in the club. He was magnificent. Anyway, we ended up winning 2-1.

Mac: When the second goal went in, my mate and I virtually pulled the front room apart. Anything that wasn't nailed down we just threw it somewhere. We went nuts. We were running around the garden for about half an hour while neighbours were out sunbathing or having tea.

Mike Ford: I remember Joey tearing their left-back to pieces, especially in the first half. John Durnin was outside-left and he was magnificent. All 11 players were magnificent. The support was magnificent. We finished the game and I think there was a disabled enclosure right by the side of the pitch. There was some fellah in a wheelchair and he was saying something and we couldn't quite make out what he was saying. Somebody else had given us more information, and I said, "Just get in the dressing room, lads, get the results, and if it's gone alright we can come back out and enjoy it."

Nick Harris: We were getting the other scores in. You didn't really know what was going on. It was so complicated, wasn't it? You'd got the Plymouth score, and the start had been delayed. Then there was Port Vale [at home to Grimsby] and Brighton [at Ipswich]. United had won, and we thought it was alright. But we weren't 100 per cent sure. And Brian Horton, even when he came out, wasn't sure himself, and he sent one of the apprentices down to find out. It was only when you really realised that there was no chance of it changing that you felt so good, so excited, so pleased for everybody.

Brian Horton: When it came through we went back out to the supporters. They had been waiting the same as we had.

Mike Ford: I've got it on video at home and you can see the relief in the supporters' faces. Brian Horton had never taken a club down, playing or managing, and that kept that record intact. It was such a traumatic season for everybody involved – players, supporters, staff at the club. It was just sheer relief to get the right result and stay in the First Division. It was like winning the FA Cup. I wouldn't know what winning the FA Cup was like but I assume it was like winning the FA Cup! The champagne was out, the dressing room was packed with people – Jim Rosenthal was in there – and it was a brilliant feeling. Lots of bottles of champagne. That was the best party of my life.

Nick Harris: The players were so, so pleased. It meant so much to them to stay up. I think it meant more to Brian Horton than anything else he'd been involved in. There's no doubt about that. An amazing game. Great support as well. It showed that Oxford United were very much alive and kicking. There is a great community feeling for Oxford. This is what the club is about. It's about Oxford, not just Oxford United. It's far bigger than just a football club.

Winifred Crawford: That was my greatest day, at Tranmere. Staying up. I was up there. That was better than winning the Milk Cup. Who would have expected us, towards the end of the season, to be able to work our way up and stay up? That gave me so much pleasure. I was excited. I didn't know what to do. Everyone around was hugging me.

Brian Horton: The day at Tranmere, when we took all those supporters, that makes it all worthwhile. People might say, "Well, that was a relegation battle." It's amazing what happens when you're either going to get promoted or going to get relegated. It just showed, on that last Saturday at Tranmere, what the true supporters were about. It was fantastic for them as well as me. Then Biomass came in and took over the club the next week. That gave the club a bit of stability for the following season, although there was still no money to buy players.

18 *"The gaffer's ginger wig"*

RELEGATION AND PROMOTION, 1992-96

In 1992, the club was taken over by Biomass, and Keith Cox became managing-director. Brian Horton again steered the team to a safe position in the Endsleigh League First Division (as it had been renamed). The next season, 1993-94, had barely started before Horton moved to Manchester City. When new manager Denis Smith and his assistant Malcolm Crosby took their positions, several weeks later, United were favourites for relegation. A spirited fightback failed to avert the drop. It took United two seasons to return. In 1995-96, under new chairman Robin Herd, automatic promotion was achieved on the last day of the season.

BRIAN HORTON'S LAST SEASON, 1992-93

Mike Ford: I remember the Portsmouth game [November 1992]. There were eight defenders on the pitch – me included – and two goalkeepers and we all had stinkers. If you're a defender and you play well, you don't concede five goals, do you? We were 5-3 down, we got the fourth goal and

I went to the referee and said, "How long?" He said, "Twenty seconds." They kicked off and we scored again – Chrissie Allen's little header. It was incredible. A complete one-off. Five-all. I also remember the time I scored two goals in a game. We were playing away at Cambridge [January 1993]. They'd scored – Steve Claridge opened the scoring – and then the ball was cleared to me all along the floor. Someone was coming from my right-hand side and I was down the middle of the pitch. I don't know why but I thought, "Leave it, I'm hitting this." I was too far out really, but I hit it really well and it went into the bottom corner. Two minutes later they've gone 2-1 up with a penalty. I'm thinking, "I've just scored one from 25 yards and it's all gone to waste." Then about 30 seconds later the ball was headed out, and it bounced up. Normally I would have chested it down and played it wide, but I thought, "Why not?" and hit it and it was the best goal I've ever scored. It flew in the top corner. I ran off towards the halfway-line. Jim Magilton was chasing me and I can see the look on his face now – astonishment. He's thinking, "I can't believe it." Mickey Lewis jumps on my back. Two minutes later we get a free-kick in our half, right by our supporters, and they're all shouting, "Shoot, shoot."

Brian Horton: My last season we finished fourteenth. Now, people might go, "Fourteenth? What's that?" But I thought fourteenth in that division was success when far bigger clubs than Oxford, like West Brom, had been relegated. We'd spent very little money, and we beat the likes of Wolves and Derby, who had spent fortunes. We'd beat those sides but struggle against smaller clubs, and that used to infuriate me at times. Generally, while I was at Oxford, most of the supporters understood what we had to go through. We had the one season where they were pretty horrific towards me, with the "Horton out" campaign, yet I don't think anybody could have done any better.

Nick Harris: Perhaps the time was right for Brian Horton to move on. It was a great move for him. I think he'd done almost as much as he could at Oxford United. I think people do him a disservice. I don't think people realise how a modern-day football club like Oxford United had to be run. His hands were really tied a great deal.

Brian Horton: Clubs are in categories. Oxford came into the smaller category with the size of their crowds. The support is tremendous, but we were getting 5,000, 6,000 or 7,000. I felt that, for the size of the club and what we had, and what we had to spend, to keep the club in the First Division was a tremendous feat. Other managers told me that I did well with limited resources. It's all a vicious circle because the more you pull in through the turnstiles the more you can pay players, the better players you get and the better you do. From my point of view, the last couple of seasons were tough because we had no money. It was wheeling and dealing – free transfers and 70-grand players.

A New Manager, 1993-94

Denis Smith: I knew Brian Horton very well so when the job became available I had a word with him. He told me what the situation was, and I couldn't say it sounded too rosy. He had had to decimate the playing side because of the financial situation. But I thought, "Well, okay, I'll see if I can get an interview." I got an interview and sat down with Keith Cox and Geoff Coppock and Paul Lowe [United directors]. Talking to them was interesting because they were prepared to let me do the job as I saw fit. They were saying, "Yeah, yeah, fine, you can do that, get on with it, but realise that you've got to sell." I said, "Well, as long as I can sell in my own time, when I consider it to be the right time, professionally and everything else, and allow me to use little bits of that money to strengthen, then I'll have a go." I came in, saw Maurice [Evans] and Steve [McClaren] and they said, "They haven't got a prayer really [to avoid relegation]." The squad wasn't good enough. I had been to see them before I took over, and I could see that they had a fair few problems, one of them being that when I walked in the dressing-room I was the biggest lad there!

Mike Ford: We got beat 6-1 at Southend [16 October 1993] and the manager came in afterwards and just said, "See you Monday morning, boys, we'll have a chat about it then." You could have been in there for hours going over what went wrong. It was a difficult period.

Denis Smith: The two centre-backs were David Collins and Anton Rogan. I knew Rogan was better at left-back than as a central defender and I didn't think David Collins was up to it. We had Paul Reece or Kee in goal. For me they were obvious problems that needed rectifying. At the front we were looking at Cusack and Druce, and I didn't think they could do the job at that level. Drucy was young and coming on, and Nick had never been a goalscorer. I couldn't see where goals were going to come from. We'd got two wingers [Beauchamp and Allen] who were out-and-out wingers. They were alright when we were going forward, but we had slight problems when we were trying to defend. And then Mickey Lewis, who was a good lad, and Jim Magilton in midfield. We weren't overstocked with the best of squads. It needed changing. I brought Matt Elliott in, and I think he was a good buy. I took Malcolm Crosby to watch him, the last game before he signed for us, and he had an absolute stinker, and Malcolm thought I was off my rocker! Phil Whitehead was signed as goalkeeper. He has always been a good athlete, and has learned to command his box better, use balls better and talk to defenders. I signed John Byrne, a class player. I first came across John at York when he was a 19-year-old and I went in as manager. He was out of the side and he was the best player they'd got. They said he was allergic to grass or something stupid. Great talent. He played for Ireland twenty-odd times but he could have done more at the highest level. He brought into the dressing-room a standard of fitness that I expected. His time in France had given him a better idea of diet, compared with the English footballer, and that was a good influence. Unfortunately he had to leave. It was for his own benefit really. It wasn't for the benefit of the club.

The FA Cup, 1993-94

Mike Ford: We'd beaten Tranmere at home, 2-0, quite comfortably, and had played very well on the day. We drew Leeds at home [fourth round]. A great draw. Full house. Two up. Playing ever so well. Then they've come down the slope at us and got two goals. It was possibly a fair result but obviously we were disappointed. We went up to Elland Road and I think we just went there to enjoy ourselves. It was Jim Magilton's last game, which we didn't know at the time.

Denis Smith: The game at Leeds gave me great pleasure because Howard Wilkinson was my coach on my FA courses, and I was clashing against him and trying to do something different. We went up there and changed the system. We had one up, two wide and three in the middle, and it took them 20 to 25 minutes to sort it out. That gave me great pleasure, to see them shouting to their box: "What are you doing?" "Shall I push in?" Things like that you remember. And obviously the goal that Chrissie Allen scored. The way he came in and played off Joey was how that system should be played, with the two wide men joining in with the front player. And we had an excellent front player in John Byrne.

Mike Ford: We found ourselves 2-0 up. Two minutes left we think we're at home to Chelsea, because the draw's already been made. Great. Home draw against a Premier League side. Then Strachan whacked one in. Then there was a scramble and David White scored. Two in about a minute and we've gone to two-all.

Denis Smith: I remember how well Strachan played against us. People might think that football managers don't look at the game as supporters do, but I loved watching John Byrne play and got a great deal of pleasure seeing somebody like Gordon Strachan, even though he scored against us. When he got the ball I was frightened to death.

Mike Ford: After 90 minutes, the gaffer is trying to cajole people, and I'm saying, "Come on, lads, we can do it," not necessarily believing it but trying to get it through that we can still win the game. I honestly thought that they would bombard us in extra-time, but for some reason they didn't. We had a throw-in. I took it and it was played back to me. I've clipped it through, Jim Magilton's got on the end of it and stuck it in. And that was another good night. But we paid for it on the Saturday because we got beat 4-0 at home to Charlton.

Denis Smith: The Cup run was something to take the mind off our dire League position. Obviously to go to Leeds and win was a magnificent performance. I think it helped people see that there was light at the end of the tunnel and we were looking to move forward. Then the Jim Magilton sale came at the wrong time for us. The problem was that it was coming up to transfer-deadline day and Jim was out of contract in the summer and was definitely going. He'd outgrown the club to a certain extent. Jim's a super pro, a good player with a great attitude, an intelligent lad, and he knew that he could do better for himself, and I could only agree with him. We'd got to sell somebody to keep the club afloat through the summer and if we'd let it go to tribunal we wouldn't have got the £650,000 that we got. People said, "It was cheap" but Southampton were really the only bidders. It was a decision that I didn't want to make but I realised it was right for the club. It did cost us the next round, against Chelsea, because Jim was the penalty-taker. The Chelsea game was frustrating. In the first 20 minutes we absolutely battered them and I thought, "We're going to walk this." Then both my full-backs were injured, and those injuries were a disaster for us – in the long-term. People will remember the penalty against Chelsea but I think the change in that game was the two full-backs getting injured.

Mike Ford: We went one-up, then Alex Dyer had a great header saved by

Kharine. Then Chelsea led 2-1 and we got the penalty. Jim Magilton had left and he had been the regular penalty-taker. Robbo [Les Robinson] had gone off injured – he took penalties at Doncaster. I'd taken one in a penalty shoot-out at home to Swansea in the FA Cup and I'd scored. It just so happened that when Peacock handled the ball, it fell to me, and I picked it up. Nobody was walking towards me to say, "I'll have it." I looked at John Byrne and he went, "No." He denies this but I think he did! I was captain and when you're captain you're obliged to take them. I put the ball down and I genuinely fancied it. I thought I was going to score. I wasn't nervous. I thought, "Go up and hit it, if the 'keeper goes the right way it'll have too much power and go in anyway." And it hit the crossbar and we went out of the Cup. To say I was disappointed would be an understatement.

Relegation

Denis Smith: I think if we'd signed Paul Moody a little earlier he might have kept us up. He came as part of the Jim Magilton deal. We got him for £60,000 (100 grand if he did well). So he cost us £100,000 which I think is good value. I'd now got a bit of presence in the side. I'd got a centre-half who could head it, besides being able to control and pass the ball. I'd got a goalkeeper who looked as though he could fill his goal and stop things going in. And I'd got somebody up front who could score. That is the basis of any side. You need a backbone. But Peterborough at home was the game where we blew it [12 March 1994]. It was a game where we should have done better. We were always running in quicksand, but we went under in that game against Peterborough. It was a shame really because if we had stayed up we would have gone from strength to strength, and I'd have had a bit more money that next season to strengthen a little bit more.

Top at Christmas, 1994-95

Denis Smith: I brought in David Smith. If you ask in the dressing-room, "Pick the side," then David Smith's the first player that the players pick. They know that he's always there and won't let them down. He's a good professional and he's got a good footballing brain. He doesn't hit spectacular passes or do little tricks but he keeps the game ticking over and you need that type of player.

Mike Ford: I started off the season alongside Mattie Elliott at centre-half and we had a great run. We won the first six games and were really playing well. "Moods" was scoring goals like they were going out of fashion. I got injured – at home to Shrewsbury – when we were second in the division and didn't play again that season. We were still top at Christmas, but then went nine games without a win and the season petered out. We finished seventh.

Denis Smith: Everybody was raving about us during the first half of that season but I said to my wife, "We've got problems." She said. "But you're walking it." I said, "We're not good enough." I knew what the main problem was and I'd got no money to rectify it – we needed another good central defender. Steve Wood had been brought in to do the job but was injured. Anton Rogan was injured. Mike Ford had injuries. All my left-sided central defenders were injured. I had Guy Butters on loan, and he did a great job for me but Portsmouth wouldn't let me buy him for the sort of money I could come up with. I took Dobson from Portsmouth and that did not work out. I was looking to buy or pinch or borrow, whatever I could! Even though we were winning, I knew it was always going to be a problem for us. It was never resolved until too late, when I bought Phil Gilchrist. We were too far behind then and too many doubts had come into people's minds.

FA Cup, Sunday 13 November 1994

Peter Rhoades-Brown: I was working at Oxford United as football community officer, and I was also playing for Marlow in the Diadora Premier League. Because Marlow had a good FA Cup reputation, we went in at the final qualifying round. We beat Sutton United 1-0 and should have lost 9-1. All of a sudden we've drawn Oxford United in the first round proper. I had predicted it, but only as a joke, and when it came out I couldn't believe it. I went to clear it with Denis Smith to see if I could play, because Oxford United were paying my wages. Denis said, in jest, "Rosie, you're 33, you've had seven operations on your left knee and you're a bit of a cripple, son, and you've never been a left-back. We *want* you to play." Well, apparently it's a unique thing. No-one had ever played against their employer before, let alone knocked them out of the Cup.

Mac: The day of the Marlow FA Cup was the greyest, most disgusting day and I was in a recording-studio in Wolverhampton with an eight-piece dance-band called Cornflower Concept. We'd been up all night Friday, had a couple of hours sleep Saturday afternoon and the session was going really badly and I was in an awful mood. The Marlow match was on a Sunday and there was no telephone in the studio. I had to wait until the band's manager turned up with a mobile-phone. I phoned a mate of mine in Oxford just to cheer myself up, asking, "How many did we beat Marlow by?" He said, "Oh, no, it was two-nil to Marlow." I said, "Yeah, yeah, but what was the real score?" Needless to say, the recording session deteriorated rapidly after that.

Peter Rhoades-Brown: There were about seven or eight of us with Oxford United connections. Pete Foley was the manager and Les Phillips was in the team. Before the game we were all talking about it on radio and television. The United boys were top of the Second Division and we were bottom of the Diadora Premier and we were thinking, "If we can keep it respectable, keep it down to single figures, we'll be happy." And we went and won 2-0.

Denis Smith: That was an absolute disaster. There was no way that Marlow should have beaten us, but on the one-off it happens. It was a very low point, and showed our weaknesses. Fortunately at that time the club was doing well in the League. Beating Leeds is fine, but people don't like it the other way round. It hurts. And it will live with me for the rest of my career, whether I like it or not, and I don't like it.

Peter Rhoades-Brown: It was tough for me because I didn't know what to do. I was back in the Boundary House at eight o'clock, having a quiet meal with my wife. I didn't know whether to celebrate or commiserate. I sat in the Boundary with my head between my legs, thinking, "What have I done?" I don't think people realised how hurt I was, or how much it affected me. It cost United a lot of money from future FA Cup games. I went in on the Monday morning and I'd planned it as just another working day. The gaffer [Denis Smith] had got all the boys in because he was so disappointed with the result. When I came in most of them shook me by the hand; a lot of them shook me by the throat. I got boots and everything thrown at me. One of the best moments of my career was when we did the Centre of Excellence display at the Manor. I was over the Osler Road side and Malcolm Elias was on the microphone. There were about 8,000 people there. I was going to walk round the pitch but I thought I'd run across the middle just to get it out of the way. As soon as I started running across some people started clapping, perhaps appreciating how difficult it was for me. Malcolm said, "Put your hands together for Pete – he's been a credit to the club – and well done for last Sunday." Then the Beech Road Stand gave me a standing ovation. I was nearly in tears. I was so emotional. It meant a lot to me. I had been retired for a number of years and there I was in the FA Cup second round. We went on to the third round as a non-League club and that was another dream come true. It just happened that I'd knocked my employer out on the way.

AUTOMATIC PROMOTION, 1995-96

Mac: Christmas-time I felt like all the other supporters: "Oh, dear, the best we can look forward to is a Cup run." Halfway through the season there were supporters chanting "Smith out" but I didn't think we were playing badly. I remember a few conversations where we said, "It's quite obvious what's happening, we're going to have a complete reversal of last season – start badly and then storm it." Well, you live in hope.

Denis Smith: At Christmas, when things were going wrong, I was chatting to the chairman and telling him, "I think we're good enough, I think there's only Swindon anywhere near as good as us." He said, "What's the problem?" I said, "Moods is not scoring the goals I expected him to score. That's the only problem we've got." By this time we were no longer in a *selling* position – I'd got the backing there – but we were not in a very strong *buying* position. So we had to look round very carefully. We came up with Martin Aldridge on a free-transfer, and he did remarkably well for us. He had a lot to learn about his general play but he could score goals. That allowed me to bring Moody off the bench, and he started firing and scoring goals, and that seemed to give him confidence. So when Martin Aldridge got injured, Paul Moody took over and started doing what we thought he would be doing from the beginning of the season. If he had done, he'd have had 40 goals, and we'd have won the league!

Mac: I thought Massey's form changed the whole season. When he gave the penalty away in the Toffee Crisp Reserves Cup, or whatever it was called, everyone was really getting on his back, but I thought he was the best crosser we'd got. Then he scored the goal against Millwall in the Cup and I've never seen him run as fast as when he was celebrating.

Denis Smith: The Cup tie at Nottingham Forest [FA Cup fourth round] didn't do us any harm because nobody gave us a prayer. I didn't see it that way because I knew we were difficult to score against and I knew they had difficulty scoring. I changed the system to play at Forest and then the game at Forest was off.

Mac: We'd made up our Thermos flasks and were about to set off when we heard on Radio Oxford that the game was off, so we phoned every club within a 40-mile radius to find a game. I even phoned my sister, who lives in Nottingham, and told her to get round there with a shovel and get the snow off the pitch. We were desperate for a match but we couldn't find one. We went to the pub and played table-football.

Denis Smith: That postponement got us our first away win because we had the chance to play at Burnley and use the new system. It worked very well and that win did the lads the world of good. They said, "Yeah, okay, we can make the play-offs now."

Mike Ford: Home results were good but our away results were poor until January. There were games we should have won but we were getting beat 1-0. One mistake was costing us. Then we played well at Burnley and it was a psychological boost of winning a game away from home. We went to Rotherham on the Saturday and lost 1-0. Then we played at Nottingham Forest and drew 1-1. Our supporters were magnificent that night – there were so many there – and Stuart Massey's equaliser came late on. He only had to run two yards to our supporters. When he headed it, I was right behind him and that was nice – to equalise late on at a Premier League club right in front of your own supporters.

Denis Smith: When you look at the result here – 3-0 to Forest – I thought it was not a fair reflection of how the game went, but it was a good lesson for us. We were a bit sloppy defensively. It was a good kick up the backside. Defenders had got to the stage where they thought they could just go out there and keep a clean sheet. You can pick up things out of defeat as well as from a win.

Mac: I'm the lead singer for a band called Arthur Turner's Lovechild (ATL) and when Forest came to the Manor we were recording the club song for our compilation album – OXCD. We wanted the song to be from a female point of view, because we'd never heard a football song from the "I'm a girl, I go to football" angle. We were very drunk when we wrote it. We recorded it the next day, put the vocals on it and then recorded the team. It's been critically unacclaimed, which is quite good really because all football songs should be appalling. I'd say it was verging on the

Eurovision. At the Forest game we set up two microphones in front of the London Road end to record the crowd for the end of the song. We sat behind the goal. I did tell Mark Crossley, the Forest goalkeeper, to "get on with it" at one point, and then he told me that United were making a substitution, so I had to apologise.

Mike Ford: Then we played at home to Walsall. We were not very good but Martin Aldridge scored with the last kick of the game and we beat them 3-2. We thought, "We've played poorly and won a game." Then we went to Carlisle and won. Mattie Elliott's strike at Carlisle was probably our best goal of the season. He got a lot of stick after that. I think he was quoted as saying, "I spanked it and it went like an arrow." So every time he did that in training that got a mention. From then on we took off. Our set-pieces began to work – Joey's quality was good from the right, Dave Smith's quality was good from the left, and Mattie's flick-ons were very important. Martin Aldridge got nine goals in 12 games. Moods scored six goals in the last six games. Our momentum carried us up, and Blackpool's momentum carried them down.

Denis Smith: We had a long saga with Joey Beauchamp [who was transferred to West Ham on 21 June 1994 and to Swindon Town on 18 August 1994]. I thought I was doing right for the club – the club needed the money again – and I thought I was doing right by the lad because as a professional footballer if I'd got the chance of playing at Tottenham, Liverpool and Man United or Crewe, Swansea and Rotherham, I know which I'd pick. Joey didn't seem to see it like that. When he went away he was always wanting to come back. People thought I didn't like him, but the move was right for the club and I thought it was right for the lad. But, if the lad decided he wanted to come back, then if I could get the right deal, and raise the money, then I was quite happy to have him back. At £75,000 I think he was a hell of a buy. I thought he was outstanding in the last six weeks of the season.

Mac: We stuffed Swindon at the Manor. Completely played them off the park. I hate Swindon. I don't know why it is like it is with Swindon. It just is. I didn't start it! I just get whipped up in it like everybody else. No surrender, as far as I'm concerned. I suppose it's because they traditionally beat us all the time. How many times have we ever beaten them? Once away.

Mike Ford: I live in Swindon, and all the talk at my local was about those two games. I felt a lot of pressure in those games, especially the home game when we beat them 3-0. We played well that night. We were too strong for them. And Joey got a goal as well – I thought that was nice. Personally that was the best game for me all season. The Swindon games are possibly more important for the supporters but it's almost as important for the players. Swindon only lost four games all season and had the best defensive record in the division, and we beat them at home 3-0 and drew away 1-1. Then there was Joey's goal at home to Blackpool. I think Blackpool came thinking a draw would be a good result for them. It was 0-0 and it was going to take something special to win the game, and that was what Joey had.

Mac: It was an amazing goal, verging on the sexual. After the Blackpool game I went up to Joey Beauchamp in the supporters' club and said, "Joey, that was an absolute screamer, thanks a lot." He giggled.

Denis Smith: Off the field we were saying the right things and starting to put pressure on Blackpool. We kept saying, "Yeah, we can do it." I've had two Championships and two promotions and I know when to put the pressure on and when to keep things going. I always thought we were in with a very good chance of going up automatically. The draw against Notts County knocked us back a bit. The important game came at Crewe, when Walsall were at Blackpool. I told the lads before the game that Walsall would win, and we only had to do our own job. That was possibly the only time I was nervous, when I was sitting in the directors' box at Crewe, and everybody around me was nervous. So I went down on the bench.

Mike Ford: We were 2-1 up against Crewe and Stuart Massey had been sent off. It was a tense time because they were bombarding our goal. Our crowd went silent and I thought Blackpool must be winning, but they were quiet because our game was so tense. It's worse for the people who are watching or listening to the radio. When you're playing you think you can affect the outcome – clear one off the line, a last-ditch tackle, score a goal or whatever. But watching must have been hell, especially when the indirect free-kick went in. Phil Whitehead just let the ball go in and I looked at him and he looked at me, and the referee gave a goal-kick. Phil knew it was indirect. I didn't. Then I said, "I've never seen that before but that was brilliant." As soon as the final whistle went, I went straight to the gaffer: "What's the Blackpool score?" He went, "I think they've lost." Supporters are going, "Yeah, they've lost, they've lost." So we went in the dressing-room, and Simon Marsh has got it confirmed because he's been on the radio: "Yeah, they've got beat." We had a ghetto-blaster in the dressing-room, and I put it on Radio Five and sat there until I'd actually heard the result: "Second Division: Blackpool 1 Walsall 2." And then I said, "We're second." I actually had to hear it from the radio before I could convince myself that Blackpool had been beaten. Then I've gone, "This is it, lads – win Saturday and we're up."

The Last Game

Mike Ford: From the moment we beat Crewe on that Saturday my mind was focussed on the game against Peterborough a week later. I was waking up in the middle of the night and not getting back to sleep. I was thinking about the game. You think about how being a defender you could make a mistake that costs you the game. You think, "Where are we going to get a goal from?" We'd scored enough goals in the season not to worry about it, but you do. Then you think about winning the game and being a First Division player. And you think about the walk round the pitch. For seven days it was just, "The game, the game, the game." That week I went tenpin bowling and I never tenpin-bowl. It was just to do something else. I went to a pub quiz. I had a round of golf, but you stand over a putt and you're thinking about the football. It was a difficult week. It was the longest week of my football career.

Denis Smith: The last game of the season was against Peterborough. I usually make notes throughout the first half, but after ten minutes I hadn't made any notes. I just put my pen and paper away and thought, "That's it, we've won." I looked at our players, looked at the way they were reacting, and I thought, "Yeah, they're on their game." I knew that if our players were on their game Peterborough couldn't live with us. We just needed a break.

Mike Ford: The atmosphere was tremendous. We started off really well, creating chances, and then Rushie missed our best chance. Then Peterborough possibly got on top. You could see some confidence draining from the lads. The ball goes out for a goal-kick and you're walking back to position and your mind's turning. I was thinking, "Play-offs? We've got to pick ourselves up for the play-offs? Or are we going to score?"

Mac: I was getting more and more nervous and people around me were starting to moan. In the first-half we missed about five clear chances.

Rushie dinked that one over the bar with practically an open goal. I thought "Oh, no, we're going to draw nil-nil and Blackpool are going to win, and we'll lose in the play-offs." I was shaking at half-time. I was in a real two-and-eight. I couldn't function as a human being. After being so confident, I really thought that we weren't going to do it. It would have been so like Oxford United to draw nil-nil against Peterborough on the last day of the season. Then I think I had three large whiskies in the space of ten minutes at half-time, and a bottle of Pils as well.

Denis Smith: At half-time, when it was 0-0 and Blackpool were winning [at York], I was never in any doubt that we would go on to win the game. We were so much in control. That's a lovely feeling – sitting there at the last game, knowing that you've got to win and knowing that you're going to win. I went in at half-time and said, "Just go out after half-time and relax, enjoy it, put a smile on your face, you're up." I would have had egg on my face had it not happened, but that's how I felt. You've got to be able to judge the players on the pitch and how things are going. I was very confident.

Mike Ford: The manager said, "Great, you've done well, the chances will keep coming, don't worry about it." It was really quiet in the dressing-room. The lads were just sitting there, thinking. We went out and time was passing. We got a corner, and the Peterborough lad's headed it in for an own-goal. I've been in the game long enough to know that one goal's not enough, but I thought, "It's given us a start." Then we got the second goal soon afterwards and that was the relief. And you think, "We've done it." Then we got the third and the fourth. Twenty minutes to go and you can just enjoy it. We were laughing and joking with the crowd. And it was a great way to finish.

Mac: It was alright in the second half. They were just saving it until they were kicking into the London Road! They must have thought they'd do it in style. I was standing halfway up the London Road, almost directly behind the goal, and every time a goal went in I was over the wall. The surge was enormous. It really took me back to being a little kid again. I felt really young. Rolling around on the floor and getting covered with ketchup and bits of old hamburger and dog ends and empty bottles of pop. Just euphoria really.

Mike Ford: The final whistle's gone, and we're all hugging each other and a few supporters have come on the pitch and we've gone down the tunnel.

I said, "Well done, we're going back out to walk round and sample everything." It's an honour to be captain of the club, especially captain of a side that has finished runners-up in the Second Division. The walk round the pitch was brilliant, taking our time, acknowledging the applause from the supporters and us acknowledging their support throughout the season. We put our hats on and the gaffer's ginger wig. It was brilliant. You could take it all in and think about what we'd achieved. That Saturday was a special occasion. Then we had a party over the road and the chairman came in and we were all singing songs. We went to another pub and had a karaoke, and everyone was together and supporters were there. We all enjoyed it together. That's what it's all about.